Praise for *The Treehouse*

"This book is a buoyant celebration of the human imagination. In sharing her father's writing wisdom, Naomi shows us how the heart is smarter than the head."

—Susan Cheever

"*The Treehouse* works primarily as a how-to book, but it is more literate and more thoughtfully crafted than most such offerings. . . . Exhortations that would otherwise be mere clichés . . . are redeemed by the ballast and authority of Leonard's voice."

—Juliet Wittman, *The Washington Post*

"Personal and inspiring, it'll make anyone wish they had a Leonard in their life."

—*Publishers Weekly*

"In *The Treehouse*, Naomi Wolf beautifully shares with readers the gift of her father's teaching. In a book of candor, wisdom and bountiful love, Wolf reminds us that engaging the creative process is the same as living a meaningful life."

—Sharon Salzberg, author of *Faith: Trusting Your Own Deepest Experience* and *Lovingkindness*

"Unexpectedly warm, intensely inspiring: a work for dreamers—and Leonard would say that means all of us."

—*Kirkus Reviews*

"*The Treehouse* has lofty goals and it achieves them handily . . . even with her softer battle cry, [Wolf] certainly hasn't lost her magnetic ability to rally the troops."

—Elisabeth Egan, *Chicago Sun-Times*

"Wolf's prose surprises with humor, intimacy, and, of all things, tenderness."
—Claire Dederer, *Entertainment Weekly*

"[A] lovely personal memoir . . . Wolf effectively combines a useful, inspirational self-help book with a tender portrait of a passionate soul. . . . A beautiful story told in a unique, engaging manner."

—Mary Frances Wilkens, *Booklist*

"*The Treehouse* is a tender and important book. Its emphasis—that we all have wings and just need help in knowing how to find them—is the best."

—Judy Collins

Naomi Wolf

THE TREEHOUSE

Eccentric Wisdom from My Father on How to Live, Love, and See

SIMON & SCHUSTER PAPERBACKS

New York London Toronto Sydney

SIMON & SCHUSTER PAPERBACKS
Rockefeller Center
1230 Avenue of the Americas
New York, NY 10020

SIMON & SCHUSTER PAPERBACKS and colophon are registered
trademarks of Simon & Schuster, Inc.

For information about special discounts for bulk purchases,
please contact Simon & Schuster Special Sales
at 1-800-456-6798 or business@simonandschuster.com

The names and identifying characteristics of certain
individuals in the book have been changed.

Designed by Dana Sloan

Manufactured in the United States of America

3   5   7   9   10   8   6   4   2

Library of Congress Cataloging-in-Publication Data
Wolf, Naomi.
The treehouse: eccentric wisdom from my father on how to live, love, and see
/ Naomi Wolf.
p.   cm.
1. Wolf, Leonard. 2. Authors, American—20th century—Biography.
3. English teachers—United States—Biography. 4. Fathers and
daughters—United States. 5. Wolf, Naomi—Family. 6. Creative ability.
7. Conduct of life. 8. Authorship. I. Wolf, Leonard. II. Title.
PS3573.O488 Z96 2005
813'.54—dc22   2005041261
ISBN-13: 978-0-7432-4978-2
ISBN-13: 978-0-7432-4977-5 (hc)

The author gratefully acknowledges permission from the following sources
to reprint material in their control:

New Directions Publishing Corp. for lines from "In My Craft or Sullen Art," from
The Poems of Dylan Thomas by Dylan Thomas, copyright © 1946 by New Directions
Publishing Corp.

Alfred A. Knopf, a division of Random House, Inc., for "Anecdote of the Jar,"
from *The Collected Poems of Wallace Stevens* by Wallace Stevens, copyright © 1954 by
Wallace Stevens and renewed 1982 by Holly Stevens.

For teachers,
who help us climb

Contents

Introduction

LEONARD WOLF, my father, is a wild old visionary poet. He believes that the heart's creative wisdom has a more important message than anything else, and that our task in life is to realize that message.

Leonard has spent a lifetime identifying his own heart's desires, and it shows in the things that surround him. He has twenty ancient typewriters. He has a kukri knife, used to behead bullocks in a single stroke. He has an elaborate filigreed toiletry set used to remove the earwax of a Persian caliph. He has driftwood in piles, and heaps of seaworn glass in bushel baskets lying around the house. He has a box of horseshoe nails "because horseshoe nails are intrinsically beautiful." Those are all part of his heart's desires because they are symbols of a life of adventure and discovery.

Among the things he does not have: current maps for a given destination. Like most men, he does not wish to ask directions, so my mom, my brother, and I often find ourselves patiently biting our tongues in the backseat while he navigates by memories of foliage and lyrical years-old impressions of passing landmarks. ("Can the Golden Gate Bridge be on the *right*? When did that happen?") However, he happily brought home from one trip a collection of silk paratroopers' maps dating from World War II, which show roads and boundaries of countries that no longer exist. He gave them out as useful gifts. The idea is that you keep the silk map handy in your breast pocket as you are parachuting into, say, Greater Poland, so you can find your way around once you hit the ground.

My father does not have a cell phone or a personal organizer. He is the only person in America who kept the impossible-to-remember generic e-mail address that AOL assigned him. I have been trying to explain to him the principle of compound interest for my entire adult life. He overlooks these details because they have nothing to do with what he thinks really matters.

One of his greatest treasures, one that sat proudly displayed on the bookshelf in San Francisco when we were children, is a set of medieval Arabian astrolabes. They are crusted over with what looks like recent antiquing, and are probably mass-produced. He needs them because Chaucer used an astrolabe. Most of these were bought in North African bazaars for exorbitant prices that my father, who is far from wealthy, was always glad to pay.

It makes him happier to pay more for something he can believe *is* a medieval astrolabe than it does to pay less for what he must then acknowledge is probably *not* a medieval astrolabe. The very words "medieval astrolabe," and the way they flow off the tongue, add to the objects' value. North African souk dealers see him coming from miles away, and when they part, they do so, after many glasses of sweetened mint tea, as the dearest of friends.

("How do you *know* they are not real?" he wrote in a testy hand upon reading this.)

Why did Leonard accumulate a series of astrolabes? After all, he does not live on a ship: "You live in Manhattan," someone might say.

"It's surrounded by water," he will point out. Why, he feels, should you accept that your life will never call upon you to navigate by the stars? How sad would that be?

My dad is still a very handsome man: six feet two and distinguished-looking. He has an aquiline nose, fierce white eyebrows that seem to have lives of their own, gray-white hair that, depending on how it is brushed, makes him look either like an elderly Lord Byron seated at a formal dinner or like a homeless man having an alarming vision, and smiling hazel-brown eyes.

He is a teacher, and has taught in every kind of setting, for almost sixty years. He changes people's lives because he believes that everyone is here on earth as an artist; to tell his particular story or sing her irreplaceable song; to leave behind a unique creative signature. He believes that your passion for this, your feelings about this, must take priority over every other reasoned demand: status, benefits, sensible practices. This book is about why he believes this, and what this belief does to the people around him. Most of all, it is about the power of the imagination.

Leonard feels that your medium may be words or music or paint; it could also be the guiding of an organization, the baking of a certain kind of cake, the edging of a garden, the envisioning of a new kind of computer network, or the gesture that brushes the hair away from the forehead of a hurt child. What matters to my father is not whether the creative work is valued in the marketplace; what matters to him is whether or not it is *yours*.

He wants to know you have put your emotion into it, driven your artist's discipline into it, seen it through to completion and signed your name to it, if only in your own mind. If you do, he believes, your work comes alive and gives life to those around you. And it gives life, he is sure, to you.

My dad makes Xerox copies at Kinko's of the phrase *Verba volant / Scripta manent*—"Spoken words fly away, but writing remains"—meaning, get it down, do your creative work, whatever it is. He passes out the Xeroxes to everyone he thinks needs reminding: his grandchildren, his acquaintances, the guy at the cleaners.

He believes that each of us arrived here with this unique creative DNA inside us. If we are not doing that thing which is our innate mission, then, he feels, no matter how much money or status we might have, our lives will feel drained of their true color. He believes that no amount of money or recognition can compensate you if you are not doing your life's passionate creative work; and if you are not doing it, you had better draw everything to a complete stop until you can listen deeply to your soul, identify your true heart's desire, and change direction. It's that urgent.

Leonard believes if that particular story of yours is not told—if storytelling is your medium—or if that certain song is not sung—if you are meant to sing—and even if there is almost no one to hear it at the end, then it is not just the artist who has sustained a quiet tragedy; the world has, too.

Leonard believes that you can learn how to live from literature, from art, and that the key to leading a happy, meaningful life is to be found not primarily from the self-help section of a bookstore or from a therapist's couch, but from paying careful attention to poetry, to whatever constitutes poetry for you.

All my life, I have seen how his faith in this possibility—that an artist inheres in everyone—actually does change people's lives: the students he has taught over the course of four decades are changed, but so are the lives of people who are simply passing through. His faith in ordinary people's innate artistry gives him a kind of magic touch. I have seen how his belief has led people with whom he has come into casual contact—friends of mine, friends of his, strangers he meets on trains, the staff in his building—to suddenly drop whatever is holding them back from their real creative destiny and shift course; to become happier.

When people spend time around my dad, they are always quitting their sensible jobs with good benefits to become schoolteachers, or agitators, or lutenists. I have seen students of his leave high-paying jobs that were making them miserable, or high-status social positions that had been scripted by their families, and follow their hearts in the face of every kind of opposition to become, say, dirt-poor teachers of children in the mountain villages of the Andes. I've seen the snapshots they send back to him, of themselves with their tattered, clowning kids, their faces suffused with joy. They have found their poetry.

My father believes in passionate love, in placing passionate love at the very top of your list of priorities, and in making room for passion at the center of your romantic life, no matter how domestic it is. He believes no one should settle for less. His students are always leaving safe but not essential relationships and finding something truer—whether it is a fierce attachment to someone they would have overlooked before as being "unsuitable," or whether it is taking the risk of solitude in a renewed search for their soul's real mate.

My dad routinely addresses the artist in them, and his students respond accordingly: as artists. This is not calculated on his part; it is truly what he sees. Other teachers have used similar unself-conscious tricks; I think often of Martin Luther King Jr., who always addressed the innate peacemaker in everyone to whom he spoke—even those people who were trying to wipe him from the face of the earth. I think the great teachers always speak to the potential they see in their students as if through an X ray, and not to the actual student as he or she appears at that moment to the less intuitive eye.

My father is never surprised at the treasures that come back his way. The superintendent of my father's building, John Maudsley—a man who is very good at his job—talked to my father one day and disclosed his secret passion: in his off hours, he painted: he was "a sign painter and frustrated artist," as he put it. Leonard did whatever magical thing he does—which is as simple as saying a matter-of-fact "Yes, of course, this is your calling"—that ignites the power of imagination in otherwise "ordinary" people.

Now, in buildings throughout the neighborhood, you can see the masterpieces that emerged from Mr. Maudsley's basement: a rocking horse painted a gleaming sky blue, with velvet-black reins festooned with crimson roses, as if it has escaped from a merry-go-round; a persimmon desk-and-bench set scaled to the size of a toddler, with gold and violet edging—all are influenced by the brilliant palette of his mind's eye.

He is still a super, and still a good one. But over time, the super's office seems to me to have changed, showing the artist, too: there is a mock-Tiffany lamp illuminating the steel-gray file cabinets with particolored light, and a line of toy antique trucks, orange, black, and yellow, is parked across from the Formica desk and the standard-issue office chair. The sensibility changes the room, the job, the life, though it is the same room and job and life. In addition, something unique to him that derives from his upbringing, as well as from his own individual eye, is blooming in the living rooms of Manhattan. Mr. Maudsley seems to me a happy man.

This outcome doesn't surprise Leonard. He believes that the creative act is the secret of joy, and in spite of his occasional fits of pro forma testiness, Leonard is the happiest man I have ever known. My father's sense of optimism—that the world would always be full of surprises—was helped by the fact that he thought of his own persona, from day to day, as a surprise.

Leonard owns some unusual clothing. He has a cowboy's jacket, cut long to protect the rider's legs when rounding up cattle on the range; a Stetson—original, now a bit battered; a Basque shepherd's shirt with ruffles down the chest, made of red flannel for those cold nights in the hills of northern Spain; a white linen sharpshooter's shirt complete with epaulets for extra cartridges, if you happen to find yourself in a duel; a Persian goatskin coat ("made by the Kashgai tribes that wander across the Iranian desert," said Leonard), with tribal embroidery and primitive bone buttons, that was heavily worn in the winter after the Summer of Love: it still smells of tanning pits. He has a professional bush photographer's vest, with netting over the pockets so the veld flies don't get tangled in one's equipment. Its many small compartments for film and cameras flap when he walks down city streets in the insectless breeze.

Leonard has some unusual possessions, too. A saddle— English equestrian, naturally, made of fine old leather— perched on his computer, though it has been years since the horse passed away. He likes having the saddle handy. You never know.

His belief goes something like this: Why stick to one identity? Why limit your limitless self every day to the costume of a suburban housewife, if once in a while you can be Salome? Why dress in the costume of a stockbroker—or a retired college teacher—all the time if you can sometimes be a Zouave horseman?

I BELIEVE my father's insistence on creative freedom may be the secret to happiness. I wanted to gather his central ideas about writing and about life, which to him are the same, to frame a portrait of a moment and a man. And I wanted to trace the little worlds, off the mainstream of midcentury America, that formed my father. This book will tell how Leonard came to believe the things he does, about how your heart's creative desire—in his case, poetry—can change your life, and can, in certain ways, set you free.

My father came often, over the course of six months, to a house my husband and I own in the woods in upstate New York, to help us build a treehouse for his granddaughter, our daughter, Rosa. During the time Leonard and I worked, we talked in a way that I had been too busy—or rather, resistant—to do since I was a girl. As we hammered and sanded, Leonard talked about his favorite poems, what they meant to him, the lessons they held. After each conversation, I found that I wanted to share the insights with close friends or students whose problems were pressing on me—and his insights also called me, uncomfortably but unmistakably, to reevaluate my own life.

Finally, I decided I did not want to get just the glimmers of insight scattered here and there; I wanted him to teach me, too, formally, what he had taught his students for the decades during which he gave a famous class in poetry and creative writing—and, many of his students felt, in how to live a life—at the school he eventually settled into, San Francisco State University. He obliged me by finding his yellowed lecture notes.

The notes came down to twelve basic lessons. I learned their titles with a tremendous sense of recognition, though I had never heard them before; they were the background music of my childhood. "Be still and listen"; "Use your imagination"; "Destroy the box"; "Speak in your own voice"; "Identify your heart's desire"; "Do nothing without passion"; "Be disciplined with your gift"; "Pay attention to the details"; "Your only wage will be joy"; "Mistakes are part of the draft"; "Frame your work"; "Sign it and let it go" . . . these themes struck me again like a bell I carried within that had stopped resonating so long ago I had forgotten the sound. I realized—slowly and painfully, because I did not want to at first—that everything sensible that had ever guided me rightly was there in them, not just about writing but about life; and that when I had gone astray, it was because I had deliberately ignored, or insisted on forgetting, as daughters do who are trying to forge their own identity in the world, one of those twelve lessons about literature—lessons that are really, or equally, about life.

While he was there, teaching me, a multitude of friends and family came to stay, or passed through. Some friends of mine, whom I will call Sophia, Teresa, and Clara; Leonard's son, my half brother, Julius; David Christian, a landscape worker; a then-three-year-old grandson, Joey; a then-seven-year-old granddaughter, Rosa; and several young women from the Woodhull Institute, a leadership organization with which I am involved: I will call them Madeleine and Eva and Alison. I saw him teach them, too, directly or indirectly, because he is a teacher and that is what he does naturally. He can't help it. I watched yet again, as I have all my life, how people—turned in an instant into students, artist-apprentices—would talk to him, or hear his suggestions, and think about what he had said, and slowly or abruptly shift direction.

I too let myself be a student to him, letting go of the daughter's resistance, and I shifted direction a bit, too. I let his lifelong advice and example sink in, and started to give the heart, including my own, the respect I had for many years reserved only for the head.

Leonard has taught poetry all his life, in a thousand contexts. "Gladly wolde he lerne and gladly teche," he chortles about his adventures, quoting from Chaucer's description of the Clerke in *The Canterbury Tales* (the man will quote Chaucer at the drop of a hat). He taught at twelve universities; he taught orthodox Jewish Yemenite immigrants at the University of Be'er Sheva, and Catholic men at a single-sex college in a tiny California town, and Muslim students at the Shiraz University in Iran.

Leonard says, "Teachers are the people who are the living signposts of your life. They see you coming, and, prescient, they know in which direction you ought to go, and they point to it. They see into the heart of your matter."

He is a teacher who is a humanist, because he has found that great poetry crosses all boundaries; that all human imaginations tune to love, music, death, and loss in similar ways. In the shah's Iran, he taught Matthew Arnold's "Dover Beach" to students who had never seen an ocean. ("I said, 'Go out and find a pond. Make it bigger, and make it bigger. And make it bigger. Just keep making it bigger, and add salt and waves, and you've got the sea.'")

Just keep making it bigger, and add salt and waves; I am

afraid that if I don't get it down, I will forget how to do that in my life when I cannot see the ocean, and my father is no longer here to remind me that I can always see the ocean.

I wanted to tell the story of what I discovered from my eight-decades-old father for myself, and for others who will never get a chance to know him. I have met so many people who are artists in some way but do not realize it; or who, even if they are struggling to do creative work, feel erased *as* artists by a culture that picks losers and winners on a commercial basis and gives the rest the message that their creative vision does not count. All these people—who may not be professional painters or writers or musicians but whose heart's desire is to live a creative life—deserve to know why at least one man believes they are the real world-changers. I wanted, too, to write about his kind of teaching, because in the course of that summer, I accepted my own role as a teacher; and I came to notice that whenever I said something that changed a young person's outlook, it had come straight from my years of having been around my father. Finally, I wanted to capture some of what he taught me about love, happiness, loss, and, above all, about the power of the imagination, as I learned from him how to build a treehouse in the woods.

LESSON ONE

Be Still and Listen

You have to understand that you are a recipient as well as an actor in the world. Silence is a healer. In silence, it's as if your nerves get a chance to reposition themselves to attend; to pay attention, which is what a poet must do from the very beginning. You can start clean, with your sensibility refreshed, ready to receive whatever is coming—whatever messages the universe is sending. It can be just the noise of a bird. Or it can be the message the universe needs to send you about a complete change of direction. But you can't hear either till you sit still and do nothing.

DURING A YEAR of chaos, right after I turned forty, I bought a nearly derelict house in the midst of a desolate meadow that was dense with thorns.

I had seen this house when the field in which it was sited was covered with snow. It was surrounded by barren trees and edged by a narrow, fast-moving stream. The house had looked lost, nestled at the base of a massive gray-brown mountain. Something inchoate had drawn me into that silent structure, which had been for sale forever. No one had wanted it, including its elderly owner, and it was easy to see why. It was a wreck.

The house, a small homesteader's cottage, was almost unchanged since it had first been thrown together around 1910. But it was a wreck surrounded by peace, and I had been for too long living in clamor.

I come from the West Coast, where mountains break through into clouds. On the East Coast, where I now live, the landscape often seems tame to me. But the flank of the Taconic Range behind the house was a real mountain, massive and stern. The mountain rose at just the point where Massachusetts, New York State, and Connecticut meet, and it looked like a resting giantess.

There was a wildness to the area that reminded me of where I had come from; even the thunderstorms, which routinely crashed the electrical systems of homes at this corner of the valley and plunged us into a state of darkness, with no running water, were fiercer in Boston Corners, the no-man's-land at the base of the mountain, than they were in the rest of the Hudson Valley basin to the west.

Dutch settlers had left their poor farms in the 1700s to come here. Then Scottish settlers had arrived, having fled the famines and massacres in the highlands. The immigrants had settled in the region, raised their children, and eked out their living. Their descendants live there still. In the early nineteenth century, Hudson, the nearest city, was a whaling center, and the area had a brief industrial boom. The names of towns and rivers were Dutch and Scottish: the nearest town was named for the Scottish town of Ancram, and Campbell Hall lay across the Hudson. To the west and southwest lay the Dutch place-names: Val Kill, Beaverkill, Kaaterskill. The Roeliff Jansen Kill ran turbulently along the valley floor parallel to the mountain.

But the area directly around the house, in the shadow of

the mountain, had not Scottish or Dutch place-names, but rather criminal place-names and place-names of despair—Sinpatch Road and Sodom Lane; Drowned Lands Swamp. According to local historians, in the early 1800s, men and women on the margins of the law—gamblers and highwaymen and prostitutes—had settled in Boston Corners. The difficult journey west across the mountain from Massachusetts meant that, for a time, there was little rule of law in the hamlet. Even the state to which the area belonged was in question—none of the three states whose borders met there had clear jurisdiction over the land—so renegades built their homes in a motley community together, far from respectable society. I was intrigued by the fact that the little house was just above a marshland; there was no good land for farming, or for dairy pasturing. How had its first owners made their living?

By the mid–nineteenth century, iron ore was being mined just up the road by Irish immigrants who had fled the anti-Irish sentiment of New York City. Some Irish immigrants also worked on the railroad that once stretched up to Copake Falls. Since boxing matches were forbidden closer to Manhattan, famous boxers of the era would face off in local fields, drawing thousands of riotous day-trippers from the city; the fights are now commemorated, here and there, by rusting placards.

The house's hastily-put-together nature reminded me of the home in which I had grown up—and which had been suddenly rendered uninhabitable, one day when I was seventeen, by a burst city water main. I had never had a chance to say goodbye to it, and had missed that lost house all my adult life. The floorboards of this house swerved, just as the floors in my childhood home had done.

The house's gray-brown exterior was ugly. The heavy front

door, made of a solid slab, as doors used to be made long ago, was painted a drab wine-stain brown. The yard was overgrown with frowzy plantings and was surrounded by a wall of black-berry brambles. The two acres of land that came with the little house were impenetrable. They had been ignored so long that a particularly nasty kind of brush, made up of fast-growing canes of thorn, had taken over. It was so thick that you could see only the crowns of the trees, and it warded anyone away from the banks of the small river that ran along the base of the mountain.

The house had been built to the standard cottage plan, but in miniature. A steep wooden staircase was flanked by two tiny parlors to the left, with a small dining room and a lean-to-like kitchen to the right; the kitchen was an afterthought that had been slapped on in the 1930s. Up the rickety stairs were four bedrooms, two to the left and two to the right, each just large enough for one double bed and a bureau pressed close beside it. The bedrooms, dark and musty smelling, with wet streaks disfiguring the haphazard white paint, looked out onto a forest that was like something out of a Grimm fairy tale. Above the forest, you could see the flank of the mountain. By the stream, birches shivered.

The twelve-by-twelve-foot dining room also had streaks of damp ravaging its walls, and the two small parlors, awkwardly placed one against the other, were murky with the dust that blew out of an antiquated furnace vent. The kitchen had raw plywood flooring with vinyl tiles peeling off sadly. The water heater yielded enough hot water for a bath only halfway to your knees. The paint throughout was peeling away in long strips: layers of white revealed a layer of hospital green left from what looked like the 1950s. The house had no attic, just a crawl space; no basement, just a cellar in the wet, rocky ground; no closets, no insulation; no dishwasher, no air-conditioning; and wiring that blew out at whim. The drawers of the house were stuffed with flashlights and the ends of candles.

I was desperate just to sit there.

Eventually, I asked to negotiate a purchase. The owner was delighted to get rid of it for a damaged-goods fire-sale price.

After we closed, I got what I had been so longing for: silence. I had been besieged by e-mail, CNN headlines, phone calls; by my weighty, warm, engulfing responsibilities as wife, mother, teacher. I sat in the desolate house for a whole afternoon, alone, on the wooden floor, missing no one—no context, no family, no computer, no byline, no phone—soaking in the silence.

Night fell. My family knew I was gone overnight; our babysitter was with the children until David could get home. I did not know any of the neighbors in the rural area. There was no alarm in the house. Wildlife of all kinds lived in the forest around the little house—I had heard from a guy at the gas station down the road that there was one last, lonely mountain lion in the woods—but I felt unafraid. I slept alone on the floor upstairs. I woke up in the morning to see red-gold autumn light against the mountain.

When I looked out, the narrow rippled-glass windows in the bedrooms seemed like the windows of the imagination, looking right onto a forest in a dream. I was looking at a place that I had forsaken for a long time.

My father came up to visit. He went out of the house on a cold morning to find an outlet for the electric drill. "There was a rabbit waiting for me," he said when he came back inside. "He looked at me and turned and ran away. Have you heard the geese out there? There are thousands of them somewhere. They are going crazy."

Leonard was helping Rosa and me build a treehouse. Rosa, who was then seven, had decided she needed one. She had a baby brother who did not understand how to stay out of a big sister's room, and we lived in such a noisy, crowded small apartment in the city; I understood her longing for a place in the trees that no one could get to. My best friend, Sophia, would often come up to the house to get away from a difficult marriage and to have time to think. She helped me with the sweeping, the painting, and, finally, the carpentry. She, too, loved my dad and was happy to learn whatever he wanted to teach us about woodworking, and to talk with him about love.

Before we began in earnest, Leonard wanted us to spend some time learning about wood. He wanted us to understand wood before we learned the basics of carpentry, the same way he wanted his poetry students not only to understand grammatical structures, but etymology as well. Leonard wanted us to have a feel for the wood of the old furniture we had brought into the house; not all wood is the same. He explained the differences between the lesser woods—plywood, of course; cheap knotty pine; pine without knots—and the better woods: oak, with its Midwest feel and honest tabby-cat grain; cherry, with its amber shine; creamy maple; and the most noble of woods, in his view, the old mahogany that was black, with red tones underneath.

There is a hand-painted rocking chair, which Leonard had reclaimed from a coat of black paint, that I must have heard about a thousand times in the course of my childhood; he was as proud of that as he was of any of the books he wrote. I remembered how, when I was a child, he had spent a year or so chiseling a salad bowl out of a block of solid olive wood, the fragrant shavings falling on the floor around his feet in our living room, giving it the feeling of a Bethlehem carpenter's stall. He had shown me that the olive wood produced its own thin sheen of oil, like magic. I don't recall ever eating out of that salad bowl—I think the chiseling of it was its own reward. Even now he orders pieces of especially beautiful wood from a catalog. Though he has made gifts for our children—a crib and a wagon and a truck—mostly he enjoys showing visitors just how gorgeous the grain is in the unworked pieces.

After he had explained something about wood, he taught us to sand, prime, paint, repaint, and varnish a piece of furniture, if we felt we had to; or, better, he felt, to strip it and stain it; or, best of all, to strip and then wax the wood so that the hidden grain could glow. He thought that it was really important to reveal to the light good wood grain that had been crusted over with paint or grime. Watching him show us a stretch of magnificent grain emerging from underneath layers of ill-judged or dingy paint made me think about his way with his students—which was not yet my way. He was always sure the beautiful grain was there to be gently, patiently revealed; he was often telling us how important it was not to go against the direction of the wood grain in our work. With his students, he "went with the grain." I was, I feared, sometimes too impatient to do that; I feared I sometimes yielded to my temptation to paint over in my own colors their utterly unique, utterly beautiful natural patterning.

Leonard taught Sophia and me the difference between Butcher's wax, the pasty yellow fudge that you rub into unvarnished wood to make a mellow glow, and Johnson's liquid wax, an oil meant to produce a glossier surface. Leonard can barely keep from swearing when it comes to Pledge. He disdains it because it is chemical-based, not natural. He feels just as contemptuous about varnish: "Varnish *embalms* wood!" he scoffs. Once, when he saw that I had painted, rather than stripped and waxed, the trim of a cheap oak dresser, he grew apoplectic: "How can you *do* that to this beautiful grain?" he demanded, before calming down and apologizing.

Sophia and I began to hang out in Herrington's hardware store in Hillsdale, or, if we needed detailed advice, at the less crowded Herrington's in Millerton, down Route 22. We had a lot to learn. The men who worked there and their clients—the painters and contractors and carpenters—were sometimes amused by our inexperience. Once Sophia said to the store clerk who was helping her, "I think I used this spackle for the wrong purpose." An entire row of men in overalls and leather tool belts, waiting to pay for their purchases, fell silent and turned around to enjoy the moment.

But we showed up often enough, and struggled sincerely enough to understand what we were doing, that eventually we found mentors at the Millerton Herrington's. Chris, a dad our age, who has freckles, a short-cropped red beard, and a merry expression, was willing to take time to explain thoroughly to us the point of everything we were undertaking. He explained the value of using Goo Gone to remove the adhesive grime left over on the stairs from ripped-off carpeting. He showed us how to twist U-bolts to tighten a rope for a swing for the treehouse. He explained the aisle that held brackets and demonstrated that, of course, we would want to drive the screw into the bracket for a treehouse base from below.

"'Of course' to *you*," I said.

Chris smiled. "If you are making a treehouse, you need a cordless drill," he said.

"I'm scared to learn how to do it," I confessed. It was true; for some reason, the way the drill bit fit into the chuck—that is, only through tightening, without any bolts—unnerved me. What would keep the spinning drill bit from flying out and piercing someone's eyeball?

"You will love your drill; trust me. You have to learn to do this," he said. Patiently, he put a yellow plastic-cased twelve-volt DeWalt cordless drill—not the fourteen-volt version that Chris had at home, which, he explained, I could not easily manage—into my hand. It felt heavy and awkward and full of potential. "You will love this," he repeated. "You will never stop using it. I use mine all the time." He slipped the battery into the base, shifted the key from left to right, and showed me how to pop a drill bit into the chuck; interior teeth rotated and gripped the bit. Then he showed me how to rotate the barrel in the opposite direction, and the drill bit popped out into his hand. He put the drill into my hand, and on the second try, I inserted the bit; I whizzed the drill in the air and felt an exhilarating buzz. On the third try, I released the bit into my hand. "This is great!" I couldn't help exclaiming. Adrenaline rushed through my body, as when I drove a car by myself for the first time.

Chris smiled again. "The best part of building a treehouse is this stage—picturing it," he said. "The adults have more fun than the kids." It turned out that Chris himself had built a three-story treehouse for his kids.

I bought the drill, screws, brackets, U-bolts, additional drill bits, plastic safety goggles, and a charger for the drill's battery. "Good luck," said Chris. It was the first day someone working at Herrington's had spoken to us with no apparent, if subtle, irony.

I felt strong discomfort as we piled into the car with our possessions. In Herrington's, I was undefended; I had no résumé, no accomplishments. Just as it was awkward for me to hold the weighty DeWalt drill steady, it was also awkward, after fifteen years of expressing my own opinions for a living, to be once again an unskilled learner. It was humbling. But there was no way to get to what I wanted to do but through being willing to become a beginner again, listening to someone more expert, who was willing to teach me—how to polish wood, how to build a treehouse. I would need to drop a well-guarded part of my own defenses in order to be a decent learner again; it was like opening a portcullis or letting down a drawbridge. The hinges were rusted and they creaked, and it hurt.

A week later, it was time for a visit to a lumberyard. We all drove back to Herrington's lumberyard on a chilly, gray day. We came back with two-by-fours sticking out of an open window and cold air blowing in. We brought home two boxes of nails— "Twopenny and fourpenny!" Leonard explained the Dickensian names for them with relish—a half-dozen steel brackets, and a good saw.

WE BEGAN by laying out some plywood that had been left in the garage, and measuring it. We knew we would have to buy more lumber, but this way, we could get a sense of the dimensions first. As my father worked—holding out the measuring tape, marking the lines in thick pink chalk borrowed from his three-year-old grandson, Joey—he would burst abruptly into fragments of verse that seemed to be provoked by a thought sequence known only to him. This is not unusual behavior for Leonard.

He stood up, dusted off his hands, wiped his forehead, and caught sight of a turkey hawk flying in circles overhead. He tilted his head back farther. "'I caught this morning morning's minion,'" he said. "'Kingdom of daylight's dauphin, dapple-dawn-drawn Falcon, in his riding / Of the rolling level underneath him steady air, and striding / High there, how he rung upon the rein of a wimpling wing . . .' Isn't it amazing, honey, how you can have these lines that may at first seem incomprehensible to your logical ear but make a kind of perfect sense to your heart? You feel without understanding that this is about the magic of flight—emotional flight as well as literal. The sounds enforce the words' meaning for you, they build up and up . . . Hopkins is talking about the windhover—a kestrel, but also a metaphor for God's son." Leonard knelt back down just as abruptly and began to prise staples out of the plywood with his screwdriver.

I felt my eyes sting. My father had talked to me like that all my life; his explanations of poems were the intermittent commentary underlying our ordinary lives. As a child, I had adored listening to him; of course, he knew everything. As a teenager, I had taken on board what he had to say about poetry and the well-lived life, and had taken seriously a kind of apprenticeship with him. In my young adulthood—of course, of course—he knew nothing, or nothing of use. His views were old-fashioned, I had learned in my twenties; to learn from him was, among other things difficult for me, to subjugate myself. I had needed to topple the statue, find the fault, see the feet of clay. I had separated my sense of myself as a writer from his teaching, his worldview.

But he was eighty; and I was now forty; and for many reasons, I knew I had taken a wrong turn.

Dante's *Inferno* begins with the narrator lost: "In the middle of the journey of our life I came / To myself in a dark wood

where the straight / Way was lost . . ." In the middle of my own
life, I was lost, in some ways. I realized, while we stood over the
sheets of plywood and the turkey hawk swung overhead, that it
was high time my rebellion was over. I needed to move on to
the next stage of my life. I had to be willing to learn again,
from him and from others. I had to be willing to learn to listen,
and to listen in order to teach. I had to grow up, essentially.
Neither of us had forever. I saw the shadows lengthening where
we stood; suddenly, I realized I wanted to formally learn the
course he had taught, which had changed so many of his students' lives.

"Dad . . ." I said, almost shyly. "Would you be willing to go
through your lectures with me? And actually teach them?"

And so our work began.

My father was back in the dining room a week later. He was
going through a faded manila file and had a pile of books at his
side. He was drinking hot water, honey, and vinegar. (Periodi-
cally, Leonard comes up with strange new beverages so that he
can banter with pretty waitresses about them.) Postum, the
grain beverage promoted during the coffee shortages of World
War II, had preoccupied him for some years in the 1980s. Oval-
tine had followed. The honey-and-vinegar combination—a
Russian medicinal beverage, he noted—was making a come-
back; I remembered it embarrassing me in restaurants in the
mid-1970s. I was drinking ordinary Lipton tea.

Lesson One, he said, was about how you have to start with a
healthy respect for silence.

"First, just be still; listen," he said. "Matthew Arnold speaks
of the leisure to grow wise. I would extrapolate from that 'the
silence to be attentive.' It is a disaster that we are losing the option of silence—with all these televisions, all these channels,

these devices you carry that constantly interrupt you. Rabbi Akiba, in *Ethics of the Fathers*, says that "a fence to wisdom is silence"—meaning that silence defends wisdom.

"Thoreau, in *Walden*, describes how important it is to sit quietly by the pond: 'Time is but the stream I go a-fishing in,' he writes. Wordsworth writes about the tumult and noise in our lives: ' . . . late and soon, / Getting and spending, we lay waste our powers: / Little we see in Nature that is ours; / We have given our hearts away, a sordid boon!'

"The very first lesson to a young poet, or anyone starting in on creative work, is this: go somewhere quiet and listen inwardly. What you hear internally might completely surprise you; and it won't be true *unless* you hear it first internally."

I felt ashamed as I took my notes. I had to face the fact that for a long time, I had not been still, and I had not been listening. Okay, for years. I could not swear that I had been doing what I knew was true by the guidance of that inner whispering.

WITH EVERY weekend that I spent wrapped up, sitting in a rattan chair in the corner of the old sunporch, listening to nothing but the wind toss the trees, I realized I had lost contact with part of myself.

My father had raised me to honor the power of the imagination above all. Once, when I was about eight, my dad had called me over to look at something. He held up a polished slice of whitish-cream agate, the kind you could buy for fifty cents in tourist shops down on Fisherman's Wharf. The outside of the circle of agate was rough, and the interior layers were swirling, alternately translucent and opaque. Leonard held it up against the incandescent bulb of a table lamp, and a world lit up within it.

"What do you see?" he asked.

"I see a . . . an ocean," I said.

"I see a cityscape, with a set of towers," he said. "Van Gogh painted like this." Then he showed me a reproduction of *Starry Night* and some prints of van Gogh's provincial cityscapes. I could see the swirls that nature had crafted in the slice of agate echoed in the technique of the artist's paintbrush. Leonard put the agate down on the heap of treasures that we had assembled in the corner of the living room—twigs, sand dollars, baskets of blue, green, and bronze seaworn glass that we had found on the beach. He was not surprised that we saw different things in the slice of agate. He would have been surprised only if I had seen nothing.

When I was a junior in college, I dated a Marxist, whom I will call James. At that time, I still fully embraced poetry. I was reading and writing it and, like so many undergraduates, deeply believed in its magic. James, a graduate student, was the first person I met who rejected all of that in favor of historical materialism—the belief that nothing was real but politics; the rest was bourgeois affectation. God, verse, romance, beauty: all seduced one away from the hard work of analyzing who has material power and who suffers. James's approach fascinated me, but its starkness also horrified me, and I wrote a love poem, as undergraduates will, arguing with him about it, in which that agate surfaced again:

> *Let me hold the stone up to the light:*
> *You see how, in the midst of a sea of milk*
> *Rises a whiter city, of white onyx,*

Translucent, barely visible? . . . This is it:
The glass seed in the milk-heart of each word.

"But here *is where we live," you say. "And thought*
Should be a laser cocked against the stars . . .
. . . Consider jails and satellites, in terms
That slide home like a bolt . . ."

By the time I was a graduate student, I, too, had lost my way
to the silent city in the slice of agate. I had become more like
James, who was, by the way, a most unhappy person. I, too, had
begun to believe that only words that slid home like a bolt, that
did something in the "real world," were valuable. In the eternal
daughter's resistance, I could not be loyal to my father's alle-
giance to the heart over facts, numbers, and laws, simply because it was my father who saw things this way. I needed to push
against that worldview to feel my path was really my own.

Then, in graduate school at Oxford, I became further "rad-
icalized." This meant that I was supposed to scorn the canon—
those poems my father so loved. I had become persuaded, for
various reasons, that poetry was owned by the power structure.
Those words came from the heart? They were the hearts, I
learned, only of white men steeped in privilege. Feminist theory compounded personal experience: the words that had
seemed to express my own soul's longings could never truly do
so, I was taught, because the writers did not know what it meant
to be female.

Not surprisingly, during these years—they were years of bad
hair and bad fashion, of bad food, being bundled up against
the icy wind whipping down Merton Street, wearing the same
straight-leg black jeans and black boots that every other young

Marxist at that time in Europe was wearing; years of reading *The Guardian* while eating milk-chocolate cookies and thinking about "structures of oppression," hunched against the electric fire in my room—I hardened myself somewhat in my relationship, transatlantic though it was, with my father. I stopped asking him for advice or telling him what I was reading. I would get a tense feeling at the thought of trying to explain to him—though he was always interested in what I was working on—what Hélène Cixous was so mad about; of course it was hopeless even to try, since you could never say a phrase like "phallocentric patriarchy" to your father, even over the phone. I was being taught to be angry at the patriarchy, embodied in Milton and Shakespeare, Auden and Frost, those voices I had so loved. And it was hard to deconstruct "the patriarchy" without deconstructing—and demoting the wisdom of—your own personal earliest patriarch, your real dad at home. Our conversations became somewhat strained; he was eager to talk about what I was thinking, but I felt an impatience surge when we chatted: the impatience of someone who needed to break away.

On a personal level, I did not feel that I could become authoritative without getting out of the shade of his authority. He had been a teacher, my teacher, for so long that I felt if I was to have a voice of my own, I had to forget the sound of his.

I had absorbed the then-current feminist theory that the tradition was oppressive. Adrienne Rich wrote that it was change in the real world that mattered most. Young and foolish, I decided to believe her wholesale. But at what cost to myself, to my heart's desire? Since my "radicalization," I had not written a poem. I had scarcely read one. It had been twenty years.

"'Poetry makes nothing happen,'" my father used to quote

Auden, admiringly, meaning: the change is within. But we young Marxists and post-Marxists saw such quotes dismissively, because we took them literally. Poetry makes nothing happen! Look, Dad: oppression, injustice, exploitation in the real world are the only things that count, I wanted to say, and when I came home for breaks, we sometimes argued about it.

I was busy casting out my father's worldview as something I did not want to modify, because I was reluctant even to engage with it. I knew it was a challenge to everything I was learning and the new identity I was forming as a baby activist and polemicist. But, as rebellions like that so often do, I was shouting to my dad by withdrawing from his wisdom: "Look, Dad! I reject what you stand for! I need to make things *happen* with my words."

When my friend Peter would ask, "When are you going to write a poem again?" I would feel something snap, for many reasons, across my heart—like a band sealing off a room in which a crime had been committed. But I would try to shut that feeling down. I told Peter not to ask me anymore.

Finally, when I was twenty-six, another turn of events divided us. There was an early commercial success with my first book, and I found myself in a different world from my father's—the world of greenrooms and TV sound bites, of overnight deadlines and public controversies. This, I imagined in my young woman's arrogance, was a field of experience that my father's wisdom could not help with; it was a long way from "The Windhover." It was not till that field of experience left me spiritually depleted at forty, looking for the windhover again, that I realized how very much his wisdom could have helped me through.

I had forgotten that there could be a world in which people did not have to argue a point, and win or lose, in order to justify a perception. I had forgotten that a perception can be for nothing but itself; Madame Bovary's simple human loneliness; Turner's light on the water; a city or a tower or a world, depending on what you are looking at, in a slice of agate.

I REMEMBER a conversation I had with Leonard as we drove to visit my grandmother Fay Goleman in Stockton, California. It was the year 2000. On either side of our rented Honda, the glades of what was called Eden Valley—deep green hollows and stands of California Valley oak—fell away from the sides of Highway 580. Every time I drove through that part of the highway, my heart hurt; subdivisions were marching ever closer to the once untrammeled paradise between Altamont and Pleasanton.

I had just told my parents that I had agreed to be an adviser to Al Gore's presidential campaign. I was advising on women's issues, passing on what I understood to be many women's feelings about things like equal pay, Social Security, health care, gun violence, and education. These were all issues that I cared about. This political world was real, all right: Adrienne Rich's real world, with no equivocation. But I was appalled by the cynicism, the bullying, the cut and thrust of politics played out at that level.

To Leonard, the old lyricist, my working on such a thing seemed like a kind of prostitution of whatever gifts I had. I saw exactly what he meant. But children always need to overthrow their fathers, especially when the fathers are right. The pull to act in the real world was just as strong in me for a long time— no, stronger. But it had brought me little peace.

My father liked nothing about my new arrangement. He

did not like it that I was using my abilities to help a politician, even one he supported. He certainly did not like the dishonesty at play as, week by week, I pushed for disclosure of my involvement, and the campaign, for fear of the controversy that would (and did) follow, refused. My father was offended on many levels. Of course I knew he was right.

"But Dad," I argued unhappily, "for ten years I have listened to women say that they are struggling—for decent wages, for safety from domestic violence, and so forth. How can I live with myself if I don't do what I can, given the chance?"

"Honey," he said sternly, "there are a hundred apparatchiks in Washington who can help him do that. Even if your guy does win, that is beside the point. He and his influence will come and go. But no one else has your particular voice. Someone speaking in his or her own voice—even if hardly anyone ever hears it—changes the world much more profoundly than someone just getting elected president."

"Helping a political leader you believe in is a *shande*, a shame?" I asked, defensive and annoyed, especially because the nerve he had struck was already sensitive.

"It's not at all a *shande* for someone whose mission in life it is," he said. "It's a *shande* for *you*. It's a waste. You're a writer. You have more important things to do."

There was a long, angry silence on my part, then we both tacitly agreed to disagree and changed the subject.

I HAD PUSHED that advice away. Not just with my ill-fated role in the campaign but in all the years, before and after that, of living as an activist and ignoring the—what? The soul?

I had turned my face away from the grace of the imagination.

As I knelt on the steep pine treads of the staircase in the upstate house, scrubbing with steel wool and Goo Gone, I felt some powerful drive inside me that was more than a wish for a house that was decently clean. I was scraping away layers of film obscuring the true wood grain of the steps as if scraping something from inside of me. It was only after days of steady work, when my clothes and my nails were filthy, and I sat in silence on the screened porch and looked at the waving of the trees, that I began to see a glimmer of what I had come out there to find. Of what I had misplaced—no, actively scorned—and needed back.

I WAS NOT ALONE in my longing to escape to somewhere quiet to think. Sophia, still struggling in her marriage, would join me sometimes upstate, to get away so she could consider what to do, and to help me work on the house.

Sophia and I tried to paint the downstairs yellow. We could not avoid streaks and brushstrokes overlapping the molding. Finally, I gave up and asked a professional painter to paint the upstairs bedrooms: pale blue, pale rose, and yellow. They were colors that were long out of style, but they were right for the old-fashioned place.

Sophia, my father, David when he could come up, other family members, the kids, and I often went to junk stores. The adults spent a lot of time hauling things up the stairs. Slowly, the upstairs filled with ordinary pieces of Edwardian furniture: low tables, used pine bedsteads that we painted, and dusty oak dressers that Sophia and I wiped down and polished with furniture wax.

Sophia and I went to Kmart for cotton floral-print curtains.

As I chose them, I recalled a description of similarly printed cotton that Laura Ingalls's mother had used to make Laura a new dress in the *Little House* books. (Images from the first books you read are indelible; I have looked all my life for the buttons, in one of Ingalls's descriptions, that were like blackberries.) I found a soft red couch and easy chair on sale. Sophia and I dragged it from the side porch, where it had been delivered, and through the grass, the legs leaving lines into the mud, so we could hoist it into the front parlor. With all the reds and yellows downstairs, the rooms began to feel warmer, and the desolate feeling diminished.

Sophia, a director of a high-profile nonprofit organization devoted to public schools, had been racing in her life for as long as I had. She had been married for eight years to a man who, it was apparent to me, would never begin to understand her. She lived with him and his moods in a seven-room apartment on the Upper East Side; she had a closet full of designer clothes that he approved of; and she was desperately unhappy.

This was especially hard for me to watch, because Sophia's true metier is happiness. There really is such an art. Sophia was made to be happy herself, and to be the cause of happiness in others. In a discount store, she will instinctively start chatting with the elderly saleswoman; the two of them, together, take pleasure in finding Sophia a necklace to match her sweater, or in locating a good watercolor set for her three-year-old niece.

When Sophia goes out for a meal in a diner, she will, for instance, thank the Greek waiter not only with her words but with a smile in her eyes. Suddenly, he is not just an undocumented worker in a diner on Sixth Avenue; he'll recall that he is handsome and strong—or has been, not so long ago—and will smile back at Sophia and lay down the omelette on the oval platter in front of her with flair. Like a perfume, happiness is the atmosphere she carries with her.

The trouble was that Malcolm was a dark personality. That would not have been fatal; there are a lot of dark personalities who are profitably attracted to brighter spouses. The trouble was that he seemed to like his darkness, to embrace it. I felt that he absorbed her capacity for warmth and joy, then, after absorbing it, he seemed annoyed that her happiness had diminished. He didn't understand what an artist she was, and that she could not do her work entirely alone.

In the city, I listened as Sophia talked through with me how to get her marriage into a better place; she was trying to figure out how to stay with Malcolm. I reassured her as well as I could: "Keep working on it, honey," I said. "It has to be worth it."

I supported her in doing everything possible to make it work. Counseling? Malcolm wouldn't go—didn't believe in it. Could she challenge him to take steps to come out of his rotten moods? She had tried. Adapting to them the best she could? She was doing that now, and it was killing something essential about her.

I spent time with Sophia, doing what we, as women friends, do to make sense of the emotional world: I listened to her carefully tell her story. But as she talked about her dilemma, weighing whether she should stay or go, something struck me: talking was the last thing she needed to do. Maybe she should stop racing around—physically, but also inside her head. Maybe Sophia also had to be still, to listen to what her own silence was going to reveal to her.

Or maybe she was talking so desperately, and walking so fast, because part of her already knew what her silence would reveal.

*   *   *

WHEN I HAD first met Malcolm, I could not understand what Sophia was complaining about. He was a charming, well-spoken British economist, the son of a cultivated Scots family that now lived in London. Though a progressive, his father, also an economist, had advised the Thatcher government, and his mother was well regarded in their socially conscious Hampstead neighborhood for her work with troubled young people.

Malcolm was tall and even-featured, with that languorous frame you sometimes see in old Scottish families. He wore his hair in a dashing brush cut, like something out of *Brideshead Revisited*. His white oxford-cloth shirts, worn open at the neck, and his well-washed chinos hung pleasingly on a build strengthened by years of athletics. He was handsome, evidently, pleasant, and smart. And he adored her. What more did she want? I wondered.

Not only was he attractive, he sparkled in conversation. On that first meeting, he seemed entranced with Sophia, who had then been his wife for seven years. Between bursts of conversation, Malcolm gazed at her possessively. When we all got up, he held her coat out for her so she could shrug her shoulders into the sleeves, and he encircled her waist as we all left. He gestured that she should stay on the dry pavement so he could wade into the splashing traffic to signal for a cab. Who did that anymore?

They had met in graduate school. I could see the attraction Sophia held for him. She is an embodiment of feminine warmth. Malcolm had been sent off to boarding school at seven. Sophia—who grew up in a noisy, happy household in New Jersey—was gentle, yielding, and kind. That could, I saw, be irresistible to Malcolm.

But as time went on, I began to see what haunted Sophia. As

I got to know him better, I saw that it was as if a light switched off in Malcolm once he had established the pleasantries. One evening we had all met, Sophia with Malcolm and I with David, in a Village café. Malcolm had been civil enough, but I felt chilled sitting near him. Sophia looked to be policing herself and holding her natural ebullience in check.

I had made some silly joke, and Sophia had started laughing. Her cheeks turned a delicious shade of pink.

"Darling, can't you laugh without turning it into a scene?" Malcolm had snapped. Then he turned back to the general conversation as if he had said nothing unforgivable.

She was under so much stress; something had to yield.

Sophia came up to the house, ostensibly to help me paint, but often really, to talk to my father. She had met him several times when he was at our apartment in the city, visiting the children, and she had fallen then, as people do, into conversation with him about love. He had become, in a casual way, a grandfatherly romantic adviser to her, and he was happy to listen to her up in the country as well. He believes that it is extremely important never to hurry women when they are talking about matters of the heart. Sometimes, as my dad and I worked, Sophia would sit on the red couch in the living room, looking at the river, tears occasionally streaming out of her eyes; she would unself-consciously wipe them away. My father, with his long experience with love, would not intervene; he respected her grief and he would let her cry.

Sometimes he would bring her a cup of tea, then come with me into the red dining room and let me get on with the discussion about poetry; she knew we were there if she needed us.

"Listen, honey, to Dylan Thomas," said Leonard one afternoon, loud enough for both Sophia and me to hear him:

In my craft or sullen art
Exercised in the still night
When only the moon rages
And the lovers lie abed
With all their griefs in their arms,
I labour by singing light
Not for ambition or bread
Or the strut and trade of charms
On the ivory stages
But for the common wages
Of their most secret heart.

"Listen: the 'art' is 'sullen' because it is not forthcoming unless you go into silence and listen. The night is 'still.' But one quatrain later, the 'light' is 'singing'; the only difference is that the poet has described how his listening to the stillness has called the music into being."

Leonard cleared his throat and diplomatically looked away from the stricken Sophia in the next room. Leonard understood that she had all her griefs in her arms.

BE STILL AND LISTEN. Leonard believes that there is always guidance from an inward voice and illumination from an inward light. Some people understand this spiritually; Leonard, who claims to be an atheist, is convinced that there is an internal spirit—an anima of creativity—within you that will address you directly, personally, if you let it; if you listen.

Everyone is an artist if he or she is living the right way, my father often explained. Was I living the right way?

The screened back porch, with its cracked concrete floor,

where I could sit and look at the forest, became my oasis as I began to ask myself this question. I had made a lot of judgments about what was happening to Sophia's creativity. But what about me?

I had rejected what my father had always taught me. In doing so, I had harmed only myself.

Poetry was a metaphor for something I needed to listen to. What had I lost? Was it peace? Was it the need to get closer to a sense of God? Was it the longing to quit work in the public dog pit—where one must strive, compete, and produce the way men have traditionally produced—and to do more of the traditionally "female" work of planting seeds and watching children? Was it a wish to have a sense of place—this mountain, this valley—rather than an address with a numbered avenue on a numbered cross street? To have neighbors, not a row of anonymous doors down a hallway? To be in a setting so quiet I could remember my dreams when I woke up, and hear no sirens? I wanted to listen to a child, not a meeting. I wanted peace, not war. God, not Mammon. Family, not itineraries.

Poetry, not polemic.

So, I thought, considering my dad's first lesson from his class notes, everyone needs at crucial times—especially in times of flatness or of crisis—to stop; to be silent. To go to a treehouse.

But this is hard, I argued with my inner voice, which I was reluctantly beginning to acknowledge. Where can anyone go to be quiet these days? I can't stay on my back porch for long. We can't all have a tower like the one Yeats built for his writing. Even if we are lucky enough to have a quiet place somewhere, we—especially those of us who are mothers—can't leave jobs, children, computers every time we need to be still.

But maybe this porch could, for a little while, be my treehouse. Maybe one's treehouse can be a garage workshop or an attic. Perhaps any place can be a treehouse.

Maybe it is a seat on a train when someone is going to work and can dream before her day begins, when no one from home can find her and she has not yet arrived where her fellow workers are waiting for her. Maybe it is someone's seat on the train going home, where he can look at the lit windows of the houses going past, and the sky, and become someone else altogether— or no one, because he has not yet arrived at the place where he is expected to be on top of the kids' homework and taking out the trash. Maybe it is in your bathroom, when you have drawn a bath and closed the door. Maybe it is someplace you have found that no one knows about: a café where no one bothers you, or a park bench where you can sit looking at a pond in which ducks are diving.

Perhaps even a stolen hour can be enough: maybe one has to build a treehouse internally, I thought. Perhaps it is a time: five A.M., when you wake up to make a cup of coffee and think—or not think, your only quiet time before the children wake up and the lunch has to be made and the school bus met and the car filled with gas.

Maybe, under duress, it is neither a place nor a time but only a possibility: a place in one's mind where no one can reach you, but where you pull back a kind of awning to look up at a kind of sky.

But I saw what my dad saw—that this search for a treehouse was not trivial but urgent. We need to find that place, or appreciate those moments, right away. Because if everyone is an artist, then everyone needs a treehouse.

*   *   *

I HAD TAKEN Rosa up to the country the first week of September. David and Joey were inside, watching a show about monster trucks. Rosa and I went into the woods.

Up on a rise, on the small, overgrown meadow that lay at the base of the mountain, I showed her an old tree that I thought she might like. It was a maple, about forty feet high and probably a half-century old. Its bark came off in curious patterns that fit together like a puzzle: white on the outside, and brown and then green underneath. We dragged an aluminum ladder from the side of the house where someone had left it after painting some upper window frames. I clumsily extended the ladder and placed its feet in the tangle of poison ivy that grew at the tree's base. I hoisted Rosa over the poison ivy and helped her get her footing on the ladder. She scrambled up at once to its first level of branches, which were perfect, heavy and thick, almost two feet around. Two such round branches formed a strong horizontal Y, and where they met created a perfect seat, a living wooden cubby big enough for a child, or even two.

"Come up!" she said. "It's great."

I made my way, tottering a bit, up the ladder. I sat with her in the joining of the branches, in the maternal lap of the tree. We leaned back and looked up: green, flat, fanlike, waving leaves made a living latticework, bending and fluttering for miles, it seemed, over our heads.

Rosa went quiet.

Eventually, I asked, "Want to get down?"

"I'll stay a while," she said.

I left her to listen to the silence, in the tree, and dream.

LESSON TWO

Use Your Imagination

Coleridge says the secondary imagination "dissolves, diffuses and dissipates" what it sees in order to re-create it in some more universal context. When any creative person looks at an event, the event is more than itself.

MONTHS HAD passed. The snow was still deep in the valley but beginning to melt on the mountain. The river was louder than ever as the snowpack from the Berkshires ran down into the valley at the base of the Taconic Range.

Before we could begin to work that day, Leonard caught a glimpse of something that he could not resist: a red fireplug standing in a last drift of snow. I was in midsentence, asking him if he would like some tea, but he rushed out of the house hatless, his camera in hand.

"I took a picture of your fireplug," he announced as he came back in the front door, drifts of snow falling from his hair like a cake disintegrating off the head of a Dadaist performance artist. The snow melted in rivulets and soaked his wild gray-white hair. Leonard took off his green rubber boots and left them in the hall; he was wearing a yellow rain slicker, exactly like Paddington Bear's, which he didn't notice he still had on. He prepared his hot beverage and sat down to work.

Today Leonard was drinking yerba maté, an Argentine tea that you have to press with a flattened silver spoon and sip through a complicated fired-clay utensil. It was a foul-smelling brew rumored to support longevity, with bits of dried herb floating on top like straw on silage. I gasped at the clouds of steam and cracked open the window. "You should try it!" he exclaimed, as he always did. He settled further into his favorite chair, a wooden captain's chair in the red dining room, and consulted his yellowing notes.

"In Lesson Two," he said, "I ask my students to notice 'the secondary imagination.' I have them look closely first at, say, a tree, and then ask themselves: What besides what they are looking at might they be looking at? A tree is a tree, but it is also a life cycle. Think of Shakespeare's Sonnet 73: 'That time of year thou mayst in me behold / When yellow leaves, or none, or few, do hang . . .' A tree is old age, is approaching death."

"Or, say, look at a button: a button is a button, you would think. But when holding the dead Cordelia in his arms, Lear says, 'Pray you, undo this button,' and the button is a symbol of his hope that in the face of all evidence against it, Cordelia is still alive. The imagination can see the whole anguish of a daughter's death in a button, just as Blake saw the universe in a grain of sand."

Cradling his mug, Leonard showed me a quote from the poet Hart Crane: "I admit that the freedom of my imagination is the most precious thing life holds for me." To Leonard, it does not ultimately matter that Hart Crane committed suicide young; his was a successful life because of the freedom he gave to his imagination.

That evening Rosa was excited by the thought of building a place for herself in the trees. She described the treehouse she had seen in her imagination. The more she focused on the vision of it in her mind's eye, the more energized she became.

"There are pulleys," she tried to explain to me and her grandfather, "that you can put on ropes—and the ropes go from tree to tree . . . and you can hang from them and sort of go flying. Have you ever seen one like that?"

"No," I said. "But go on."

"Let me draw it." She took a sheet of paper and, with a blue marker, drew a rough map:

The treehouse she had sketched out had two stories. It had a chute that you could use to send messages from the upper level to the lower one; a basket on a rope that you could raise and lower for snacks; and a miniature refrigerator for cold drinks. It had room for a little bed; a porch where she could hang out with her friends; and a hammock in the branches, where she could lie around and read. It had jungle webbing you could climb for quick escapes—from adults or little brothers or animals. The webbing came up after you so that no one could follow. There was a swing, and a cup to hold birdseed, and an area where a round pillow was to be placed, for Rosa's wished-for dog. The treehouse had a kibble dispenser and flags flying from battlements. It had an outdoor chair and table on the deck so you could drink Cokes—generally forbidden in real life—through curly straws. The reading area had a bookcase for all of one's favorite books. The treehouse had a swimming pool.

"Can I build a treehouse like that, Mom?"

"Yes," I said. "Sure."

By now, purple and lavender crocuses were emerging from the melting drifts of snow. We were sawing two-by-fours to the length of the base and trying to arrange them on the grass to get the dimensions of the floor of the treehouse. Rosa had drawn the picture, and my father had created a simple sketch for a wooden floor with an A-frame roof. His idea was to build it in the yard and then somehow hoist it up into the tree. I think we all understood that the notion of building it within the tree itself was now beyond any of us, or even all of us together.

We had to start with our frame, and for that we needed more wood and nails, as well as our DeWalt drill. Leonard, Rosa, and I went outdoors together. We stood in front of the garage, where we had arranged the lumber. I watched my father plug the larger electric drill into the exterior electrical outlet, then find the place at the edge of the two-by-four where the drill would drive a hole to fasten a steel bracket. He had given me a fluorescent plastic measuring tape as a gift, and now he showed us how to drive the electric drill bit into the wood; a small spray of pine dust flew up alongside the bit as it drove into the two-by-four. When he was finished with four holes for the first set of steel brackets, and our fingers had started to get numb from the cold, we went inside. We were starting slowly because we had so much to learn.

The next day Leonard and I began work in earnest. I watched his hand take the bit and fix it into the chuck of the electric drill and tighten it. "This is a chuck key," he explained, showing me how it held or released the bit. Some vestigial daughterly courtesy told me that I should let Leonard show me again what I had learned at Herrington's. The drill bit whizzed. His right hand trembled. I said nothing. But as he drove the bit into the wood, the hand that had steadied me when I was walking as a small child, steadied itself.

We sawed the two-by-fours into four-foot lengths, and aligned the corners of the boards. I did not try my cordless drill yet; I was still nervous. We were trying to make a frame for the treehouse floor.

After we had created a corner, we tried to hammer the boards parallel along the edge of the frame, but hammering was a lot harder than it looked. I would try to drive the nail in straight, and would make it halfway, but then one blow amiss would bend the nail. I would wrench the nail out with the hammer's claw and try to drive another in, straighter. After many bent and wasted nails, I began to feel what it was like when my aim was true and the hammer's peen struck the nail head straight on and drove it into the pine wood in three or four good clean strokes. It was a feeling of almost indescribable assurance when the nail went home. It had a rhythm.

As time went on, I held the hammer higher in the air, with more confidence, so that its weight would swing down harder. My first row of nail heads to go in flush to the surface of the wood pleased me immensely.

"Good job, Mom," said Rosa dryly.

Rosa eventually went upstairs to play. My father and I left the frame only a quarter finished—a pine-board L on the lawn—and settled down in the dining room. We could see, through the window, the two-by-fours that we had already sawed to the proper lengths propped against the garage. The L was finished, but the other three corners of the treehouse floor were drilled and ready for the steel brackets that would fasten them; "coward's carpentry," my dad had called it, because we were not bothering to use the more difficult wooden dowels to hold the boards together.

The flank of the Taconic Range soared above the lumber and the garage, overlooking the wintry trees. The mountain was turning plum-colored behind us, and navy-gray clouds were piling and scudding. The shadows from the trees were growing long. I could swear I heard an owl call from the forest. In the gathering dusk, the single L of the frame of the treehouse was gleaming. The pale yellow of the pine boards shone in the dusk.

"Grandpa, that is great," Rosa said, looking out of the window. She came out and leaned against him, admiring the work.

My dad believes that the making of a beautiful thing cracks open the painful or ugly ordinary world, and then something amazing shines through, which you have forever; which can make you blind with tears.

LEONARD's discussion of the primacy of the imagination brought back memories of how it felt to be a child: as if my brother Aaron and I were cocreators of a surprising story, in which everything was itself and something else at the same time.

The little house in Boston Corners made me feel the way I felt when we were growing up—that I had entered a kingdom of pure imagination; that the "real" world outside had rules and limitations and laws of nature, but inside where we lived, anything at all could happen.

Our house in San Francisco had been built in 1890, in the style of a hunting lodge. Its foundation, we were always being reassured, was on bedrock. It had survived the 1906 earthquake.

Nonetheless, maybe because of the quake, it leaned visibly out of level. You could put a marble on the floor, or a rubber ball, and it would roll until it hit a wall. I did not live in a room with level floors in it until I was old enough to vote. It was easy, in a house like this, to believe that the imagination was a world that was as normal to inhabit as any other.

The front door was indeed set on the bedrock, but the house was built so that the entire back end was pitched straight over a cliff. That half perched on two big timbers, with a sheer drop fifty feet down. The cliff-side balconies sagged markedly. Every time you went out on one, you were taking your life in your hands. The front half of the house was buried in wild growth: tangles of nasturtium and ivy covering a steep forest floor, overshadowed by eucalyptus and Monterey pines. When you stood on the roof of the house—which my parents insanely allowed me to do—you could see all the way to the Golden Gate Bridge in one direction, and all the way to the Bay Bridge in the other: a silver necklace and a golden chain binding the city at both harbors.

Leonard had found the house in 1960, before his marriage to his second wife, my laughing and dark-eyed mother, Deborah Goleman, who is fifteen years his junior. He had known a troubled young woman named Constance, who was married to a career officer in the navy. My father had been kind to her. When the military husband was transferred to Germany, Constance passed their rented house on to Leonard.

Constance had been even more desperately unhappy in Munich; she wanted to come home to San Francisco. She was also obsessed with her passing youth. She did not want to turn thirty. When she was twenty-nine, she got everyone out of her car—including her daughter, who was twelve at the time—

raced it as fast as she could on the autobahn, and killed herself in the crash.

Our house surely had ghosts. I never wanted to be on the landing at the top of the stairs, where eaves on either side sat filled with darkness. I never even wanted to be upstairs alone. But when my family was home, the ghosts seemed to retreat to the eaves or the attic, and a lively chaos reigned. Then—as I spent time reading and dreaming, or fighting with my brother, in the house's strange, green-lit children's bedroom, where leaves pressed against the windows; or as I curled up with a book in a niche by the ash-laden fireplace, looking out at the evergreens that surrounded the house, continually painted and erased by the fog, like the trees in a Chinese wall hanging—I experienced the house day-to-day as a crucible of magic.

My mother, a child bride in the 1960s turned anthropologist in the 1970s and therapist in the 1980s, was always on hand for the wild ride of the imagination. Was she reacting to her own rigid upbringing? To my eyes, she was a distracted, gorgeous gypsy accomplice, always ready to defend our right to be filthy where other children had to stay clean—as long as we were having fun. (It helped that she had turned against housework early on.) She was the Dulcinea to my dad's Quixote.

For a long time, I thought that everyone's house was like that.

It was a place in which, if it came to the imagination, you knew the grown-ups would always say yes.

"Can I be in the circus?"

"Yes, probably, let's look into it."

"Can I paint my face with your lipsticks and eye shadow, Mom?"

"Yes. Put the caps back on when you are done."

"Can I sleep on the heater in the hallway in your chiffon peignoir?"

"Yes, if we make you a cozy bed."

"Can I draw on my body with pens?"

"Sure, what color?"

"Can I move out all the packed boxes stored in the eaves so that Aaron and I can fight a battle with his soldiers and castle with the crenellations and the real drawbridge?"

"Yes."

"Our miniature world is so great now, we have these two armies set up, and there are knights coming on horseback, reinforcements for the ground troops, and the castle is totally surrounded and we are laying siege to it, but the siege is not going to be over before dinner. Can we leave our stuff out?"

"Yes."

"For a week?"

"Yes. Yes."

"Can we boil some oil?"

"No. Too dangerous. But you can boil some tea to pour on your army and pretend it's oil. Look, if you let it steep, it looks almost the same. Just put some newspaper down."

In that house in the woods, the adults were supposed to provide whatever was reasonably needed for the children's miniature world. The rule was that an adult was never supposed to disrupt a miniature world if he or she could reasonably avoid it. The miniature world was one of the most important things you could have.

When I was in the house in Boston Corners, I felt the same way I had felt kneeling in the eaves with my brother, calling down to our mother as the knights arranged themselves in a semicircle, and you could just about see them moving, shifting their crossbows, and you could just about feel the reinforcements coming on horseback from the valley behind the stacks of boxes, but they could not get through—and you could *almost* see the three princesses, daughters of the king, looking down from their towers in resolution and terror.

"Mom, Mom, we need more room. Can we move out *all* the boxes?" It's so important, see, because everything up here is finally coming to life.

"Yes," came the distracted shout from below, always: "Go ahead, yes."

So the magical realism of childhood—the way the shadows of the house at night were like crouching animals, and the fog rolled under it like a white ocean, and the sizzling embers in the fireplace burned purple and red when we fed it with the sand-laced wood we had gathered at the beach—was not tempered by our parents' practicality. More normal families seemed to manage or channel their kids' erratic imaginations and ease them into adulthood; but in our house, the adults did not dampen, but rather, they fed that childhood sense of slightly out-of-control adventure. When I read, as an adult, that Edna St. Vincent Millay's mother had poured water on the kitchen floor when they were too poor to heat the house in winter, and, when it froze, let her daughters ice-skate on it, I smiled and thought of my parents. They, too, were yes-sayers.

The yeses were built into every task of ours that might tap into a creative act. One chore we had, as we grew up, was cooking. The deal was we had to plan meals once a week as kids, cook the food, and clean up. (Aaron always made tacos on his day to cook. But since our parents' rule was that each kid was entirely responsible for his or her creation, there was no interference if things were gross or repetitive or just plain turned out weird. We had Aaron's tacos weekly for seven years.)

Aaron was the normal one, with normal friends and interests. I was a weird kid, bookish and often alone. Reading was my social life; characters in books made more sense to me as companions than did the noisy, garrulous, socially adept kids my own age. My parents did not try to make their younger child, the loner bookworm, any more popular or gregarious. They figured books were as good a place to grow up in as the playground at Grattan Elementary School. If I was going to be weird, they figured, I was going to be weird.

My mother claims that I made food that came out of books I was reading. One week it was a feast from Chaucer, which my dad had been declaiming to us. The monk in *The Canterbury Tales* eats a fat roast swan; well, we couldn't manage that, but I put out hunks of black bread, gobbets of cheese, and something that was supposed to be mead. My dad looked in the encyclopedia to explain that it consisted of water and honey fermented with malt and yeast. I had wanted "head cheese" and was sorry to find that it looked like mottled, glutinous bologna in a flat Oscar Mayer wrapper, rather than what I had imagined: a fine boar's head carved out of cheese. Impressed with details of how medieval diners spat their scraps onto scented rushes on the floor, where greyhounds lay waiting, I went out and ripped up some heather fronds from the hillside. I strewed them on the cork floor of the dining room—and my parents let me. I used the Sabbath cups as goblets, and some wooden cutting boards as trenchers.

Aaron rolled his eyes at what was on the table and went to the pantry to get his usual Cheerios. The adults sat there, braced themselves, and ate.

Another time, they let me try the eighteenth century. I insisted we had to make jugged hare. I asked Barbara, the babysitter who benignly neglected us every afternoon while my mom was in graduate school, to buy me a rabbit. She put the thing on the counter with a look of hostility. I, too, was horrified at the way the thing looked, wrapped in plastic. "It was slick and pink," recalled my mother, "and looked like an aborted chicken." In the book I had been reading—something British— the rabbit had sounded tangy and delicious. Again, we prepared it and my parents somehow got it down. Aaron unwrapped another frozen pizza.

When adults protest the inconvenience and messy outcome of going where imagination is driving their children, the adults are right—in their world without magic. And children, feeling that imaginative drive as more than an appetite—as an aggressive instinct, really—are also right to resist their parents. The question is just what kind of world you are training children to perceive.

If the adults do not eat the magical thing that the children have concocted, no matter how disgusting it is—or if the adults only pretend to, humoring the child, but slipping the leftovers into the trash and arranging for one parent to make a quiet drive for takeout—it is like telling the child they do not believe in what he or she sees.

Leonard's class notes reminded me of how he had bought a manual tortilla maker when we were kids, so that we could mold Mexican corn flour—*harina*—and water into balls, then smash them in the iron machine, one by one. The corn flour was not easy to find. He had trekked out into the Mission District to bring home a cotton sack of it, and it had a dancing Spanish girl with red skirts and a black mantilla on it. It was exotic to have that nineteenth-century ten-pound cloth sack in the pantry, waiting, instead of just Skippy and Cheerios.

Molding and then smashing those little balls of cornmeal was satisfying. We rarely had tortillas because it was such hard work, but it was a party when we did so. A guest, watching how labor-intensive this process was, once remarked that you could buy packages of tortillas, frozen and ready, in any Spanish-neighborhood supermarket. But the tortillas were themselves and something else at the same time. I remember all of us in the family trying hard to be polite and not explain why that would be completely beside the point.

The needs of the imagination always trumped more banal, practical matters—often to my delight, but also to my exasperation.

When I was eleven and Aaron was thirteen, and we still did not have a washing machine, Dad actually got a horse. It was a twenty-one-year-old retired jumper—a blue roan. He was still dignified, if elderly. My father had bought the horse for a song, and he brushed and curried Blue Boy devotedly. I recently asked him about the horse, mentioning my vague sense that he had been sent off somewhere not long after my dad had purchased him. To the knacker's yard?

"I had him for a year!" Leonard objected. "The knacker's yard! How could you think that?"

"Well, what happened to him?" I asked.

"When he got too old to ride, I shipped him off to Virginia to be put out to pasture. So much for the knacker's yard! Blue Boy loved to stand in the water of the incoming tide of Ocean Beach, and he loved to run and jump," Leonard recalled dreamily.

"How did you know when he was too old to ride?" I asked gently.

"He began to . . . slow down," my father recounted with hesitation. "We used to run furiously on the beach. He began to show that he was tired. But not elderly," he insisted. "He was a fine jumper to the end."

In Leonard's imagination, even before Blue Boy entered his life, he had always had a horse. Because, in his imagination, he is not a bespectacled Jewish kid from a poor family; he is a poet in the British tradition who loves to ride, and if you are a poet in the British tradition, you need the damn horse. "I rode an English saddle," he recalled of that persona he had tried on. "I wore English boots, jodhpurs, and carried a riding crop. I wore a velvet riding cap—the whole pretentious regalia. And as I mounted my horse, I muttered to myself, 'And I speak Yiddish.'"

It was wonderful, when I was eleven, to have a four-wheel-drive vehicle appear overnight because my father decided—seemingly overnight—that we were all going to pull up stakes for a year and embark on a family journey through the Amazon jungle. ("It was 'jungle' then, not 'rain forest,'" he said.) But it was a problem not to be able to afford a washing machine, and to lug laundry up six blocks of San Francisco hillside.

The wild ride of highs and lows did not bother my mother much: she seemed to understand that it was a tradeoff—that you couldn't have both the washing machine and the man who would drive you overland to the jungle, who would make your married life in the early 1960s, with you the mother of two small children, into a crazy adventure. She seemed to accept that it was a choice, and that the astrolabes and the twenty ancient typewriters and the saddle and the elderly horse we could not afford and the cowboy hats and the equestrian boots were of a parcel with the sonnets to her and the trips to see rainbows and jewels in the seaworn glass on the beach, and that some discomfort was a small price to pay for all of that excitement.

THAT HOUSE in San Francisco was a fitting home for someone who had become a self-invented magician, and who had started out in a wooden house in the rolling hills of Rumania, planted with corn and ragged gardens. Leonard's mother had used her imagination to survive poverty and seven years of isolation from her husband, who was among the emigrants whose imaginative vision of streets paved with gold led them to abandon Eastern Europe and all that they knew.

My grandfather, Joseph Wolf, had been born in the hamlet of Kolochava; his wife, Rose-Ita Engel, had been born nearby, in the agricultural village of Venihova, which at that time was part of Czechoslovakia. At nineteen, Joseph Wolf was conscripted into the military. An orthodox Jew, he served as an infantryman in the German army, on the western front, during World War I. After he was discharged in 1918, he returned to his hometown and let it be known that he wanted to be married.

Marriages then, in that part of the world, were made by families; no one courted. A matchmaker would go back and forth between families, looking for a good match of money, character, temperament; looks were last on the list. Rich fathers of daughters looked for a brilliant Talmud scholar. Rose-Ita Engel was neither rich nor beautiful; she was a modest twenty-year-old girl with clear skin and hazel-brown eyes. Her only vanity was her chestnut hair, which fell down, when loosened, to her knees; by day she wore it wrapped around her head in braids so long they circled her head three times. (She flouted tradition after she was married by refusing to cut it, as orthodox women were expected to do.) Joseph Wolf, though tall and handsome, was no scholar. The *shadchan* made a match for him with the shy Rose-Ita.

When Joseph came to Rose-Ita's village, the matchmaker contrived to have her stand at the window and catch a glimpse of her intended. The girl liked what she saw. She was lucky. Her own mother, Golda, hadn't been so lucky. She had been affianced, at fifteen, to a young man who had died. According to biblical custom, Golda had to marry his surviving brother, Isaac. She was so appalled by the prospect of having to marry her beloved's brother that she tried to run away, fleeing to an aunt's house in a village nearby. Her parents dragged her back by force and made her marry Isaac. Rose-Ita and Joseph were eventually married in Venihova.

Rose-Ita's parents were small farmers who grew barley and corn. Joseph's father, Mordecai, was wealthier, a farmer-merchant who grew prosperous buying discarded army tires after the war and turning them into *posteles*—sandals for peasants. He had a huge warehouse on his property that was full of tires; there was a sawmill, too. It was a hilly parcel, covered with scrub wood, but there were streams running throughout, rich with fish. My father remembers, as a five-year-old, watching a local soldier lie down beside one particular stream with a fork in hand. When a fish would dart by, the soldier would reach in and spear it and hold it up high on the fork. My father recalls the fish glistening in the sun, squirming, beautiful and scary.

Joseph and Rose-Ita's was the palimpsest generation; the lost are layered in shadow over the survivors. On Joseph's side, of twelve brothers and sisters, five would die in the Holocaust. On Rose's side, both her sister Hendl and her brother-in-law Shmuel would be murdered by Nazis in Czechoslovakia. Czech collaborators with the Nazi regime would take the property, the warehouse, and the streams full of fish.

In the 1920s, though, Venihova was a profoundly isolated village of Jewish and gentile farmers. The roads were made of mud and gravel, and the traffic was horse-drawn wagons and people on foot driving cattle. When the rare automobile drove by, the children of the village would run out to stare. There was a river nearby, and huge rafts of logs lashed together were floated down the river to lumberyards, with three or four men seated on each raft, atop a clay platform on which they built fires, sat, and cooked; the rafts were called, in Yiddish, *die bokkeres*. They were manned by lusty, hearty men—tough Jews—outdoorsmen, one step away from lumberjacks.

The couple's first son, Maxim, was born in Rumania within the first year of their marriage; the second son, my father, then named Ludovic, was born a year and a half later. Six months after my father was born, my grandfather left for America.

Joseph entered the United States through Ellis Island and took a train to where Rose-Ita's relatives lived: Cleveland, Ohio. He had thought he could get himself established in a few months, then send for his family, but a wave of anti-Soviet hysteria passed over the country, which resulted in a change in immigration law. Suddenly, no immigrant could send for his loved ones until he had become a citizen himself. Joseph did not see his family again for six years, though he sent back money.

"My father wasn't poor to start with. He became poor in America," Leonard said, chuckling. Joseph Wolf, he said, was a one-man corrective to the notion of a universally prosperous American Jewish immigrant experience. "My dad," Leonard said, "was just about the only Jew in America who managed *not* to become better off here than he had been in the Old Country."

Rose-Ita, in Rumania, did her best with two small boys. They lived in a one-room wooden house with a woodstove but no electricity or indoor plumbing. It was lit by kerosene lamps, and there was a shared outhouse in the courtyard. Their house was built, as such homes were, in a line of similar houses arranged around a courtyard. They were built on wooden blocks, not stone foundations, so the wood warped and sagged. There were holes in the floor of Rose-Ita's house; when a piece of wood rotted out, there was no man around, so it could not be replaced. When rats came into the home, they entered through the holes in the floor. Occasionally, at night, Rose-Ita would hear a scuttling and throw a shoe in that direction. This was not poverty; for that time and place, it was a respectable home.

Rose-Ita cooked, over the flames, *tokkan mit brinze*—cornmeal mush with cheese—and ordinary polenta for daily meals. On special occasions, she made *kishke*: cow intestines stuffed with rice and ground cow lung, with lots of *schmaltz*—rendered chicken fat—mixed in, tied off like sausage links, and baked. When the boys were sick, Rose-Ita would feed them chicken broth into which she had stirred a raw egg.

Rose-Ita made stuffed cabbage; she rolled out the dough for noodles on the one table and chopped it into ribbons; and she cooked chicken gizzards, boiled and flavored with garlic. A treat would be *gumbotzes,* a Hungarian dish of potato-flour dough, with sweet cherry or plum jam in the middle, boiled and rolled in bread crumbs. Yet another of the boys' favorites was potato-flour dough rolled out into long cylinders, cut into lengths, and sautéed; everyone, even the ladies of the village, called the dish *tzigayner shmeklekh,* or "gypsies' penises."

Rose-Ita tried to decorate the bare wood of the walls by cutting cloth into shapes and sewing them into wall hangings. In one, a woman's figure is surrounded by a half-dozen chickens, and the Hungarian legend reads, "A busy woman makes a happy life." She made lacework and draped it on the simple wooden furniture ("There was no upholstery until we got to America"). "She was an artist, though that concept would never have occurred to her," recalls Leonard. Rose-Ita's lacemaking, her cooking, and her arranging of bright scraps into wall hangings also eased the sting of bare wood and the six years of loneliness a bit.

When the family was on a visit to relatives in Venihova, Ludovic, then eight months old, caught what must have been an intestinal flu, with diarrhea and fever. He was burning up, in bad shape, growing more and more feeble. There were no doctors.

At her sister Hendl's suggestion Rose-Ita sent for the local wise woman—a gentile. The wise woman looked at the baby and said that he had to be dipped in the belly of a freshly slaughtered ox. The village belief was that being plunged into the macerated grass in the ox's belly would draw out the poisons that were in the baby's system.

Villagers brought the live ox to the door of the house and killed it on the doorstep. An ox has two stomachs; the butcher slit open one of them, and the wise woman immersed the crying baby boy into the steaming mass of intestinal matter for three or four minutes. She had prepared warm salt water, and she washed the baby off in it, then wiped him with oil, wrapped him in cloth, and put him to bed. The butcher cut up the ox and took the meat back to his shop, and the baby slept deeply. When he woke up, he was fine. My father was never seriously ill again.

(Leonard's friend, the poet Robert Duncan, thought this story was a presage for the rest of my father's life: "Dipped in shit and comes out singing.")

The boys grew. My father remembers his family visiting Hendl and her husband in their big wooden house in Venihova. It too was heated by woodstoves and lit by kerosene lamps. There were no toys as we now know them: "We played with pebbles, corks, spools from thread. We built cities out of mud and twigs. I haven't the slightest memory of a single toy in my childhood. But there was plenty to do. There was a grain warehouse owned by a Jew—ten- or twelve-feet-high bins filled with wheat, corn, and oats. He would let us play in the bins: we would climb to the top of the mounds of grain, slide down it, roll in it. It was marvelous."

In the back of the house was a barn that the children turned into a castle. "Three or four of us little kids would climb a ladder to assault the castle; we were climbing into the hayloft. I was carrying hay to the hayloft. I was greedy—carrying two buckets of hay while trying to climb the ladder," my father recalls. He fell ten feet and was unconscious for two or three days. The blow to his head would resurface in his fifties as epilepsy.

At home, Rose-Ita inadvertently tortured Maxim by showing more affection for Ludovic—nicknamed Lotsie—than for the older boy. One fiercely cold winter afternoon, fed up with how spoiled little Lotsie was, Maxim loaded his brother onto a sled and tried to sell him to the gypsies camped at the edge of town, who were often accused of stealing children. The gypsies finally decided the transaction was not worth the bother and gave Lotsie back. When the boys returned home, Lotsie was so chilled that he could hardly move. His mother ill-advisedly thawed him out by the fire, instead of rubbing him with snow, which was the better remedy to restore circulation. Lotsie was in agony.

Finally, the letter from Joseph arrived: come to America. In 1930, Lotsie and his family took trains from Vulcan to Paris, then set sail from Le Havre on the Cunard ship the *Berengaria*. After a seven-day voyage, the ship docked in Ellis Island. There was a long line of immigrant adults and children filing past a doctor. The doctor checked mouths, throats, and eyes, and every so often he would identify an immigrant with a serious illness, such as tuberculosis, draw the person out of the line, and send him or her back. "At intervals," my father said, "while you were waiting on the line, you would hear this unholy shriek."

The young mother and her sons were lucky; they were detained only because the boys had lice. Officials deloused them and shaved the boys' heads. For three days, the family stayed in a barracks, on cots stacked in three high rows. Once released, they found their way to the train that would take them to Cleveland.

The reunion was traumatic. The children were not used to having a father, the father was unused to having a family, and Rose-Ita had grown unaccustomed to having a husband. When the six-year-old Ludovic, who had always slept next to his mother, protested at being sent to sleep in a cold bedroom across the hall, his father beat the child with a strap. That was my father's introduction to his own father, and to the United States.

The upstairs neighbor, a housewife who had been in America for a little while, sniffed at the names Ludovic and Maxim. "These are American boys now, and those are no fit names for Americans," she told my intimidated grandmother. "This one is Leonard, and that one over there is Melvin. Rose-Ita? No, no, *maidele*. You are now Rose." And so it was.

Rose had refused to cover her head in the old country; in the new country, she even refused the American fashion of cutting and bobbing her lovely long hair, though she left off her buttoned black boots and wore modern black patent-leather shoes. There had been nobody to dress up for in the Old Country. She now put away her ankle-length dresses, acquired a girdle, and took to wearing floral cotton housedresses that fell just below the knees, as "real" American women did in 1930. The boys—who had been photographed in Rumania, standing proudly in white curled-lamb fur coats like little Russian princelings, their black hair combed with oil that shone in the photographer's light—quickly learned to wear newsboy caps and knickers, and to play in dirty vacant lots, or else face the consequences.

Joseph had found a five-room apartment on 118th Street, a working-class neighborhood of two-story, two-family houses. There was a living room that no one entered, with a set of Grand Rapids furniture made of mahogany veneer—a plush dark green sofa and an easy chair in the same fabric. On the floor was a cheap machine-made imitation Oriental rug in blue-green shades. An arched wooden Philco radio sat on a wooden end table, and a hearth with imitation logs lit by gas jets created a fireplace. Above it was a mantel on which two cast-iron panthers faced each other; to my father's eyes, they looked fierce. On the wall was a framed color print of a rabbi teaching two Talmud scholars in side curls, seated together at a table—the only picture.

In the dining room was another suite of veneered Grand Rapids furniture. Lotsie—now Lennie—defended his favored-child status by dusting the claw feet of the table for his mother. On the table was a crystal bowl, and in the bowl was a toy poodle with bright red glass eyes that Rose had knitted. The Crash took place four months after the family arrived. Joseph lost his glazier's job, and the family moved frequently, each time into surroundings that were more meager. Finally, they lived in a flat in which the children's bedroom was taken by a blind boarder, and the two boys were put to sleep on the floor in the hall. For the next eight years, Joseph was either unemployed "or so poorly employed that it broke his heart," said my father.

Rose went to work in her brother's delicatessen and became the family breadwinner. This was necessary for the family but humiliating to Joseph and enraged him even further.

Leonard's stories of his childhood are filled with violence: as a European father, Joseph believed in corporal punishment and was often severe. He would beat the boys with his leather belt at the slightest infraction. Rose, too terrified to intervene, would cower until the rages had played themselves out.

By 1938 a baby daughter, Shirley, was born. She alone, the apple of her father's eye, was never beaten. Joseph brought her little presents from the dime store and listened to her attentively. By then he had become a different father. "He had become an American father," my dad recalled, "full of indulgences."

The stories are also filled with poverty. When Leonard was young, he had to stand in an outdoor line at the welfare office for the weekly ration of surplus food; sometimes his hands and feet would grow numb with the cold.

But in the midst of violence and hardship, there was also the strangeness and wonder of ordinary life: when Leonard saw fuzz on a peach for the first time and tried to rub it off so he could eat the fruit; or when, in synagogue, after the bar mitzvah boy gave his speech, the women upstairs would throw hard candies down among the benches, and the little boys would scramble for them.

And, Leonard said, no matter how poor they were, there was always something good to read. His father and mother were illiterate in English, but his mother made sure there were books in the house: serious books on inexpensive paper, having to do with the Torah and Talmud, as well as light reading. Rose would read aloud from the *Jewish Daily Forward*'s "Bintel Brief," the column of letters from immigrants seeking advice, which was "as good as a Dickens novel," my dad remembers.

Reading saved my father. Stories and poems made reality bearable and were palliatives against beatings and poverty.

When he was eleven, Leonard got some pocket money from selling newspapers. He used it to buy his first book, a collection of poems in English, bound in green hardcover, that cost a dime at Woolworth's: Walter de la Mare, Joyce Kilmer, and A. E. Housman. "It was published by Whitman Publishing Company in Racine, Wisconsin," said Leonard. "I remember that to this day. It was called *One Hundred Best Poems for Children*."

"Why did you buy it?"

"I wanted to read one hundred best poems, and I was a child," he said. He added, "And I had a dime."

On a winter afternoon, alone in the cabbage-smelling sixth-grade lunchroom of Alexander Hamilton Junior High School in Cleveland, Leonard was marking time so he wouldn't have to go home too early. He read, in his second language, about another young man's easy walk through a grove of blooming cherry trees in rural England:

> *Loveliest of trees, the cherry now*
> *Is hung with bloom along the bough,*

And stands about the woodland ride
Wearing white for Eastertide.

Now, of my threescore years and ten,
Twenty will not come again . . .

And since to look at things in bloom
Fifty springs are little room,
About the woodlands I will go
To see the cherry hung with snow.

When he read that poem, it was as if a door swung open, in
the very center of his daily life, onto a lovelier world.

AT JOHN ADAMS High School, Lennie discovered the imaginative world that robber-baron philanthropists had left for him
and other poor children: the public library. He would finish
his classes by one o'clock, gobble his lunch, then take a street-
car and a bus to the library at 130th and Kinsman, where he
worked until nine o'clock at night. He worked a full eight-
hour day after school, but he was earning thirty cents an
hour—more than his father had earned when he had work.

"How did your dad feel about that?" I asked.

"Not good."

"What did he do about it?"

"He hated me. *Qu'est-ce qu'on peut faire?* I was my mother's
favorite—which meant that he was out of the loop with his
wife."

"I thought she liked him."

"She did. But she doted on me." He laughed.

Joseph was a skilled craftsman who couldn't keep a job. He could fix anything: windows, plumbing, electrical appliances. If he saw a screwdriver in Leonard's hand, he would not just take it out of his hand but snatch it out. He would say to the teenager, "Give that to me, you're too stupid to do that." "As you may have noticed," said Leonard, "now I adore tools. Obviously, I am telling my father that I can too use tools. At the time, though, I retreated into my book. That is the standard sensitive young person's way of dealing with terrible things. He reads."

In spite of his mechanical skills, Joseph's lack of steady employment lasted for ten years. Rose would complain bitterly that her husband would not get a proper job. "I *can't* get a job!" he would protest. "I'm trying!"

"Look at Kessler! He is selling scrap iron! You go sell scrap iron!" she would wail.

Joseph couldn't bring himself to do those things steadily. He felt demeaned by them. Finally, he could not feed his family. Though Leonard's wages helped—and Melvin's too, since he had begun working as a printer—the family was still at the poverty level; they were all being fed by charity from the Jewish Social Service Bureau and the Cuyahoga County Relief Fund. Joseph was in despair.

He did the jobs that were, as my father remembers, without dignity. He drove a coal truck; he was a laborer; he tried peddling for a while. He tried to sell mismatched socks, and school jackets on which the school name was misprinted, from a horse-drawn wagon. He tried to sell live chickens. "He had to chop the heads off," Leonard recounted, "for *goyische* customers who wanted the bird slaughtered right there in the back of the wagon. Jews don't have chickens killed that way; Jewish chickens are killed by a *shokhet*—a religious slaughterer. That is ritual and related to God; this was just crude bloodletting. He hated it. Chickens, when you put their heads down, just give up; they lie there. Sometimes he would miss! It was ugly. For a man who should have been a scholar, his sensibility could not tolerate that kind of work. In a forgiving mood, I tell myself this; it helps explain my father's harshness to both his sons."

Throughout high school, Leonard and his family were still receiving donated food. The social services agencies would give them powdered milk that had caked and was unusable. Leonard would grind it laboriously into something like powder. To make a little money, he sold packets of ground-up powdered milk to the upper-middle-class gentile kids in a school nature club to bring on their hikes.

"That was *infra dig*," he said. "It must have confirmed their worst image of Jews—the money-grubbing entrepreneur . . . They let me come on their hikes," he said. "But finally, one of them took me aside and said, 'Leonard, I like you. You should know that you can come on our hikes, but no one will ever let you into the club.'

"'Why not?' I asked.

"'Come on man, you're a Jew.'

"But by then," my father twinkled, "I had sold them twelve packs of powdered milk!"

MY FATHER and his friends were the Jewish kids in the Young Communist League. They saw their parents, bright, frustrated people, do the heavy, repetitive work of laborers and shopkeepers. The kids, educated by the public school system and the public libraries, were given the chance to glimpse another

path, where culture lit the way. In *Wasn't That a Time?*, Robert
Schrank's memoir of being a teenage Communist during the
Depression, he recalls how the labor and Communist movements, for children of working-class immigrants, were filled with
cultural and social activities: amateur theatricals and discussion
groups, where young people who were machinists and garment
workers by day talked Hegel and Schiller by night; impromptu
dances at someone's apartment, where swing bands played on
the Victrola, to fete volunteers going off to Spain and the
Lincoln Brigade; free classical concerts in Central Park
attended by idealistic youths who would talk revolution and cri-
tique the performances afterward at a nearby diner. In the
1930s, for many children of immigrants, Marxism and the labor
movement offered an overt invitation to a better world, and
music, philosophy, theater, fiction, and poetry reached out to
them at the same time.

By the late 1930s, these teenagers, the bright children of
the working class, were looking around at America and wondering, What else can I find? What else can I be?

In the depths of the Depression, across America, the unrelated consciousness of the next generation of poets and artists
was being shaped by common events. Poet Diane di Prima, a
child in Brooklyn, escaped into reading poetry to avoid her
Italian family's strict rules about girls' behavior and her
mother's emotional instability. Poet Delmore Schwartz was a
beautiful, pretentious young man studying at NYU, trying fran-
tically to escape his manipulative mother Rose's tiny apartment
in Washington Heights. Allen Ginsberg was a child in a fairly
poor neighborhood in Paterson, New Jersey, where he and his
father, a high school English teacher, tried to grapple with his
mother Naomi's severe mental illness. The young Ted

Solotaroff, who would become an influential editor, had been hemmed in by his glassmaker father's abusiveness toward his fragile mother; "the dump by the railroad tracks" housed his father's rages. Jack Kerouac, as a child, was watching the Depression cast his father into poverty amid the hard-hit textile factories of Lowell, Massachusetts.

These children and adolescents, who would be the bringers of a new kind of Romanticism after the war and into the early 1950s, were living lives far removed from those of the more stable, if often shabby-genteel, childhoods of their older peers whose parents were native-born. John Cheever was a young man who had left Thayer Academy for New York City; in 1931, he was on a walking tour of Germany and Great Britain. His mother was forced to run a gift shop, but it was an elegant gift shop that gave her a kind of social status and a steady income. Poet May Sarton had been supported in comfort in Manhattan and Europe by her upper-middle-class father; in the midst of the Depression she was producing plays with her father's money. "O Daddy it is wonderful to have such a *large* allowance thank you!" she wrote him. Robert Lowell had grown up in the Boston area, a descendant of two great families.

For the immigrants' children, in contrast, reading and music and painting—culture—were not simply part of a solid Andover and Princeton or Smith education; rather, they were lifelines for psychological and emotional survival. It makes sense, given their reality, that they would come to believe that art can change you and even save your life; the worlds they glimpsed through books were so much more alluring than the lives they lived as children and teenagers in the depressed industrial cities—Leonard's Cleveland, Allen Ginsberg's Paterson, and Alfred Kazin's Brooklyn—where their parents did blue-collar work.

In Cleveland, in 1939, my father was sixteen. He sat with his buddy Phillip Perloff, above Phillip's parents' candy store. The parents—"gray people, beaten down," my father recalled—"were working twelve-hour days, like everyone's parents who were lucky enough to have jobs. The store always smelled like mayonnaise and pickles; it was dusty and greasy, a stale smell. You went upstairs, and the colors were dark: everything was green or brown in our families' apartments during the Depression."

In Phillip's family's apartment, the floor was brown linoleum, with no rugs. A brown fuzzy settee with matching chairs, like the Wolfs' green plush set, was arranged in the living room. There were no books or pictures.

"But what they had, this family, was a Victrola," my father said in a hushed voice. "And all these black records, not vinyl—it had not yet been invented—in paper sleeves, that Phillip was allowed to scatter on the floor as he wound that thing up. Phillip said, 'Do you want to hear some music?'

"I said, 'Sure.'

"He put on an opera—*La Bohème*. I had never heard anything like it. I had heard nothing, practically, but *nigunim* in the shul. And I could tell something extraordinary was happening.

"Something extraordinary was happening in the music," he said, "but something extraordinary was also happening in me."

LESSON THREE

Destroy the Box

Because we are all human, there is really only one set of sto-
ries that we all, no matter our superficial differences, can
understand: the quest, the love triangle, the tragedy, and so
on. The Bontoc Igorot will understand Lear.

A FTER I HAD cleared away some of the weeds, a thicket of
yellow daffodils had cropped up along the foundations of
the house. "'A crowd, a host, of golden daffodils!'" my father
exclaimed, quoting Wordsworth, glancing out of the window.
He leaned back comfortably in the wooden captain's chair,
stretching out his long, thin legs to start our note-taking session
for his third lecture.

On this cool late-spring afternoon, Leonard was drinking
black coffee. "Coffee should never be anything but black," he
remarked. "Especially if you are a writer." This confused me; his
array of marginal beverages was usually explained as substitut-
ing for coffee, which he went long periods eschewing.

"I thought you stopped drinking coffee . . ." I ventured.
"Um, last week."

"Did I? Oh well—coffee is just too good to give up. As

Emerson put it, 'A foolish consistency is the hobgoblin of little minds.'"

Today Leonard was evidently a shepherd from some Latin country; he had arrived wearing his red flannel Basque shepherd's shirt, a black leather Argentine gaucho hat, and a three-quarter-length shearling coat. His gray-white beard had not been trimmed for a while, and it looked as if birds could nest in it. Indeed, his eyebrows, which had lives of their own, looked as if they could serve as perches.

Leonard usually came with gifts. He knew that Joey was fix-ated on the inner workings of clocks, so he had scoured thrift shops until he found a rare nondigital clock. He had brought the clock up to the house, along with a hammer. The hammer was for Joey to use to destroy the clock, so he could see what it looked like inside.

Joey was beside himself. He put the clock on the concrete floor of the sunporch and began smashing it open with rapt concentration. You could say that it doesn't make sense to give a child a present just so he can destroy it. But if destroying the present *is* the present, that is another way to see.

My father truly believes that creative vision can emerge only when you are willing to challenge and, if you have to—no matter how scary this may be—to reject every outside expecta-tion about how you should behave. "Before you can even think about finding your true voice, you have to reject boxes," my fa-ther said, deciphering his crabbed writing as the wind rustled outside the window of the dining room. "Smash them apart." In other words, he explained, look at what box you may be in and be willing to destroy it. Clichés are, among other things, boxes. Whenever you are saying or doing something that is too familiar to you, that does not let you surprise yourself, you should rethink your situation. "Boxes in life are clichés about how people should behave: your father was a lawyer, you have to go to law school. Whenever I am asked to fit into someone else's rigid structure, I get uncomfortable," Leonard explained. "And I have always hoped that my students would learn to be equally uncomfortable. People are more alive when they stop thinking in terms of boxes. I have my students buy themselves a Hallmark card, then I ask them to say what it says—but outside the language of the Hallmark card."

I thought of a friend I had in college, Harry. Harry's father was a famous judge, but Harry longed to be a cartoonist. He was very gifted: his drawings were original, dense, hilarious, and weirdly compelling. But he was terrified by the idea of telling his serious father that he wanted to entertain people as his life's highest calling. He spent three miserable, soul-killing years in law school, and three inhibiting years as a successful, sought-after law clerk. His father's ideas about what success meant were the box for him. When he finally left his box—it took him years—and became a writer on a show that did nothing but make people laugh, it was a liberation for him. But I always felt sorry about his wasted years.

I thought, too, about Dan, my friend who is now a broker. When he was younger, he wrote one perfect short story. It won a major competition and was published in a respected literary journal and included in a year's best stories anthology. The diffident young man was so startled by the big, noisy life that his story had immediately taken on—a life that was not comfortable for him—that, in spite of his gifts, he had never written another. He confessed that he had parts of a novel in a drawer, and he still works on it after his day with contracts is over, "but of course I am no longer a writer."

I thought also of a woman I met once, Terry, who has an ebullient singing voice that makes everyone who hears her want to get up and dance. She sings only when begged, at weddings or at family reunions. By day she sells ad space. "I'm not, of course, a singer! I'm not a professional," she protests. But her soul is in her singing, as Dan's soul is in his writing. In Leonard's ideal world, Dan would write and share his work—with friends, with colleagues, with his own knowledge of himself, ignoring the question of his writing's marketability. Terry would sing with no reluctance, at home, after dinner, with friends, with family, everywhere, and never belittle herself by comparing herself to the professionals with their managers and producers and slick CDs. To Leonard, Dan practices brokering but *is* a writer; Terry sells ad space but *is* a singer. Leonard wishes they would break the boxes that insist that what they do for a living is who they are—the boxes that occlude, to themselves and to the world, the artist that is central in each of them.

A box can be a personal enclosure of an individual soul, or a box can enclose a whole nation, a whole era. The twentieth century was the great century of boxes—of "isms"—and Leonard rejected them all. Leonard was born into a rigid Orthodox Judaism, and as soon as he was a teenager, he rejected it, "because it was a box," he says, laughing. Leonard was drawn to Marxism, but he found, as a poet, that it was ultimately another box. Drawn to fight for his country in World War II by patriotism, he fit poorly into the rigidity of military life. As a Jew during the Holocaust, his hatred for Nazism yielded to simple human compassion for a teenage German prisoner of war whose wounds he tended. In ism after ism, his *humanism*—his conviction that we are more than our labels—emerged paramount. I had been a vocal feminist for a decade. Humanism seemed to add the next, vital dimension to my understanding of the world.

After the war, Leonard married and turned away from the box of that era—the commercialization and conformity of late 1940s–early 1950s American mass culture—to seek a higher meaning in poetry.

In this way, he was only one of a large graduating class. Postwar America, in the small centers of experimentation where poets and writers gathered, was a place where bright young people, many of them immigrants' children, read and wrote and loved and drank recklessly, wantonly. They had faith that no matter what the marketplace had to say about your work, art could save you and change you—faith that young writers and poets no longer have so absolutely.

Leonard's is not the well-known story of a group of Middle American men and women, the Greatest Generation, who came of age in the Depression and war, learned about sacrifice, and came home believing in the goodness of the status quo and longing for order. Leonard is part of another lineage altogether, with different values.

Leonard's world was filled with people who were also outsiders. Ten thousand of his peers followed the same path my father did, out of the poorer areas of the cities, into the public universities on the GI Bill, and then into the marginal neighborhoods of defiant individualism in certain college towns and in certain neighborhoods on the East and West Coasts: Greenwich Village in New York; North Beach in San Francisco; Wellfleet; Berkeley. Historians have called these areas Bohemia, for lack of a better term, but as my father points out, "Bohemianism is just another ism; Candide was not a Bohemian. I prefer to say I belong, rather, to the genre of people who don't belong."

The members of that generation lived through the Depression and the war along with their more mainstream peers, though they came out of those experiences wanting not the suburbs and the corporate ladder but the magical power of art. They wanted to demonstrate how in America anyone can live a creative, individuated life. These young men and women longed to find a transcendence implicit in everyday experience.

They are old now: old poets, old publishers, old rogues, old renegades, who, when young, were writing at dawn in cold-water flats. The various kinds of freedom—creative, material, romantic, psychological—that they claimed for themselves all helped to shape Leonard's Romantic, individualistic conviction, now out of fashion, about the artist's way.

Listening to Leonard's next lesson, I realized that I wanted my dad's help not in building the treehouse but in figuring out how to take a more meaningful direction in my own life. I wanted to teach better, to listen better, and he knew how to; I sensed that my father's faith in humanism—in the transcendent possibilities of each of us becoming the artist we are meant to be in our lives—had the power to change his students. I felt an ache to get it down, like an archivist listening to an old English ballad on a porch in Appalachia, sung by one of the last people who can remember the words. I wanted his words down on paper; I wanted them to remind me what to believe when I could no longer simply call him on the phone. Like any writer, I was trying to make a miracle with words; to use them to hold him a little bit, for something to stay behind with me always, even in the face of death. My father had turned eighty in March of that year, and though he looked years younger—we often joked that he had an aged portrait hidden away somewhere in an attic, like Dorian Gray—I could no longer pretend to myself that Leonard would live forever.

Sophia's grandfather, a beloved rabbi, had recently died. She said there had been so many things she had wanted to ask him. I had told her that I wanted to interview my father, but I had been resisting doing it, too—it was painful when I let myself think about why, now especially, I would want to gather up what he knew. She had looked at me with a deeply compassionate expression and said gently, "Don't put it off."

But as I listened to Leonard that summer, I became something other than an archivist; slowly and reluctantly, I became one of my father's students at last.

As I INTERVIEWED my father, I was forced to examine the box I had created for myself. I was now the activist who thrived at the expense of the mother; I was the prose writer who disdained poetry.

All my adult life, I had tried to use words to make change in the real world; I had believed in "us" and "them": "the patriarchy," "corporate collusion," "the right." I had gotten caught up in seeing my work, my words, primarily as a way to fight for certain outcomes.

Those outcomes were still so important to me, but was fighting my only reason for being? Was there a way to integrate politics and poetry, mind and soul—feminism and humanism—to make something larger than the sum of each principle?

Since I had begun teaching at Woodhull, I had started to wonder how I would bring that "something larger" to my students. I was in over my head. I was unsure about this new force that was calling to me in my own life, and resistant to taking on the role of teacher.

Ego was another reason for my resistance. Accepting that I was a teacher meant that it would not be all about me; it would be all about my students. After my years of working to a byline, this would take grace I did not yet have.

My resistance had layers to it. I had reached a broad arena when I was young, and I had become attached to an idea of youthfulness. Now I had turned forty; shifting from talker and professional insurgent to listener and teacher meant accepting a more mature role. It meant facing my own aging.

Finally, there was the wrenching aspect of how this process would rip up my identity if I moved ahead with it: I felt competent, by now, at what I did every day. I was better at going on *Crossfire*, or writing an argumentative op-ed, than, say, my father was. I had "won" that Oedipal struggle. But my father was a better teacher than I was. Maybe, in some ways, a better person.

If I was going to take the path that was beckoning me, I would have to be willing to be bad at something again. All these aspects of what lay ahead if I listened to my heart filled me with dread.

My conversations with my father were starting to make me look at something I did not want to confront: I had stopped listening. I had stopped learning. At least one loved one had said to me, in the middle of what should have been a heartfelt argument, "You're not on *Meet the Press* right now." There had been more than a few moments when either Rosa or Joey had said in exasperation, "Mom, you're not listening!" And, to my astonishment, Wende, my mentor and the head of our organization, had said gently to me, when I asked her if I had really been too hard on a colleague in a critical e-mail, "Look, you're a social critic for your living. That posture can become a habit. I thought you knew how judgmental you were being. I thought it was a choice you were making."

I was starting to feel a little sick at my own mind-set of certainties. By giving so much energy to argument, I had neglected the development of my own heart.

Anyone can write a political slogan or take a position, but I was beginning to look at my writing responsibilities with weariness. For a long time, I had taken positions, and I had spent a lot of creative energy arguing my points, but my students, my kids, did not get what they needed from me when I took a position; on the contrary. I thought of times when I had been teaching my section on public speaking at the Woodhull Institute and the psychologists who are always on hand had to talk to me afterward because, while my challenging style worked well with most of the young women, there were some who felt diminished by it. I thought of my reaction—it was the same kind of impatient "should" feeling that I had when I was holding a line in some TV debate ("Women *should* get paid family leave!"): it *shouldn't* be too hard for a bright young woman to stand up and present a speech to an audience, I had countered. She *shouldn't* have to dissolve in tears. It's not torture—they aren't in a gulag. Yet here they were: in every class of twenty-one, though eighteen thrived at my approach, three became teary when they made their presentations and I coached them. Those three were as much my students as the other eighteen.

I was in my head at those "should" moments, I realized—not in my heart; it was an emotional withdrawal from those students who were not producing the outcome I wanted. It took my friend Robin, the psychologist who had created the program with me, many conversations to try to get me to understand empathically that all students are different, and that for some of them, public speaking *is* torture; that my "shoulds" just got in the way. I hated to listen to her, and I had tried not to take in what she was saying.

But as I talked to my father, who kept insisting on the wisdom of the heart, I began to realize how poorly I had been teaching at those moments. The students who did fit my expectations at those times got what they needed from me, and the others did not. I began painfully—it was a physical pain, like blood rushing uncomfortably into my heart—to feel that all my students would get what they needed from me as a teacher only when I was utterly open to each of them as individuals, having dropped my "shoulds" about whom they had to be. I was going to be a decent teacher only if I could be truly willing to learn from my students and accept that I wasn't necessarily right all the time. I realized that there was something in me that was no longer growing the way it was meant to.

My children did not need my reasoning at all; they needed me to drop any sense of how I thought they had to be. They needed me to be curious about them and to love them; they needed me to help them imagine themselves. My students did not need me to give them analytical tools alone. They may have applied to the program to learn those skills, but once they were there, as they stood before me in their flesh-and-blood vulnerability, their hopefulness, "with all their griefs in their arms," what they really needed was a teacher's wisdom and faith. What they needed most from me as a teacher was, in essence, my love.

They needed my intuition about their potential, and my imagination in service of what they could become. They were knocking at my door, and really, I had to admit, at my heart. And—I had resisted this for twenty years!—I needed my dad to teach me how to teach them.

Ouch, I thought, looking up from my father's notes to the clumsy beginning of the treehouse floor outside.

I FIRST REALIZED it was time to shift priorities, to "think outside the box," when the new century opened before me. After September 11, the world had drawn lines in the sand: emerging patriotism at home countered militant Islamicism abroad. We were being encouraged to see the world in terms of us against them, the good guys versus the bad guys. The story the Bush administration was spinning was that we were right and they were wrong; we were civilized, they were animals. God was our lead character, in our narrative. On the other side of the world, militant Islamicists were drafting their own stories in similar ways.

Death was still all around us at home. A year before, the Twin Towers had fallen. All that winter, the city had been stunned and gentle. Slowly, horns began honking again in the traffic, and people began to shout at one another over contested taxicabs. I had listened with relief to those very first honks and shouts, coming after the stricken silence and unfamiliar courtesy of a city of strangers who had all come together in mourning. It seemed to me that they were signs of a more normal appetite returning to a body that had been in shock.

At bedtime, in the city, we always heard sirens. The fire station across from our living room, Ladder 18, sent its truck—a brand-new truck to replace the one that had been lost on September 11—out at all hours. By winter we had watched as, day by day, piles of flowers were left outside the firehouse door for the seven firefighters who had died. Flickering votive candles had taken the place of the flowers, and finally, a plaque was installed to commemorate the seven, whom we remembered, too. We remembered Manny Mojica, the dark-haired bear of a man who had let Joey try on his huge rubber boots, and Dave Halderman, the ruddy man with a sparkling grin who had let Rosa climb into the cab of the fire truck and honk the enormous horn loud enough, to her delight, to startle the entire street.

Now there were no flowers or candles left, only a poem composed by a firefighter. It was sheathed in plastic and remained posted outside the entrance where the fire truck backed out and returned, night after night.

But the world after that had seemed to grow ever more coarse and brutal. Manhattan lived on a thin wire of tension. The United States was bombing the mountains in Afghanistan. The language scared me: the Bush administration declared that the enemy was "holed up" like "rats." Months later, we were bombing Baghdad, taking arms against "evil."

Individual human stories on all sides were being swept away under the weight and agenda of rhetoric. Civilians died in the attacks on Baghdad, but their stories were lost; records were not being kept. Young men and women in the U.S. military were flying to their deaths, a few every day, but the ends of their stories—the individual coffins—were coming home in secrecy. What would happen, I wondered, to the Muslim prisoners who were arrested, their human stories vanishing into secrecy in Guantanamo? "They will be dealt with," explained members of the administration. Of course, history makes clear that terrible things can happen when governments deny individuals their identities, their stories. There is a reason that after the Holocaust—a massacre in which names became numbers and numbers became tattoos, human bodies were stacked like cordwood, and Jewish teeth and buttons were sorted like industrial slag—Jews ultimately mourned their dead not with calls for retaliation but with calls for remembering, for storytelling about each lost individual. There is a reason that African-American historians of the slave trade—which renamed Africans and wiped out their religion and their family lines so that they could be sold as products—reacted to that Holocaust by unearthing the faces, the journals, and the stories of their ancestors. Storytelling is the humanist political response.

How different this administration's rhetoric was as it revived the Cold War discourse of "us and them." Even those who were against the war were falling into the same trap: they were talking about different tactics, not about a common challenge, a terrible conflict cleaving a common humanity.

But my father saw a bigger picture. To him, it was all nonsense, such language; racism, Stalinism, fascism, all war propaganda, were all simply disastrous failures of the imagination. I turned to him with renewed questions. I wanted now to ask him about his belief that all stories participate in the one human story, and that the life of the individual imagination can stand against the isms that divide us and make us into caricatures to one another.

The real world was not listening, it seemed, to the story of the imagination, which can make all empathy, and all connections, possible. Commentators and political leaders insisted that we could never understand our enemies, and they, in turn, could never understand us. Meanwhile, what I kept seeing was the one human story, and it was a tragedy. I was starting to see as my father saw, not in terms of geopolitical realities ("a million brown hands under a black sky") but as the inward universal stories of the heart ("the glass seed in the milk-heart of each word"). An Eskimo, he always insisted ("Not 'Eskimos,' these days, Dad," I would say, laughing; "the term they prefer is 'Inuit'"), would understand Hamlet. A right-wing homemaker in Omaha would understand the Rubaiyat of Omar Khayyam.

Which is stronger, the politician or the artist? I thought I knew, but I was learning that I was wrong. I had scoffed at my father's conviction that one poet telling the truth, even if almost no one heard him, was more powerful than a president. But I was looking again.

My father pointed out that the politicians and warriors of history who burned the libraries are now mostly forgotten, but the poets and artists themselves have often survived. Caesar's armies are charged with having burnt the library in Alexandria, but a few papyrus fragments of Sappho survived; today teenagers in Prague and Vancouver and Beijing, lovesick, read, "As I look at you, I convulse, greener than grass." In the thirteenth century, Christian armies burned the libraries in Muslim Spain; then a century later, rescued manuscripts of the Turkish doctor Galen's work were teaching monks how to save the plague-ravaged Christians groping at their doors.

As terror alerts in the city continued to escalate, I found that the children turned to David and me to see how frightened they should be; since I was frightened, too, I found myself turning to storytelling to comfort and reassure us all. I had invented two turtles for the kids, Fala and Lala, who lived with their animal friends in the river in the forest; they were joined by a new character, a big friendly dog named Rascal. Then, as the news got worse every day, two more animals emerged in the story: flying horses, one black and one white, Grimaldi and Al-abaster. The winged horses would tap on the children's windows with their hooves—"Tap-tap! Tap-tap! And guess who was at the window?" The horses would lift the children up on their mighty shoulders and spread their huge feathered wings. They would fly the children above the vulnerable city, over the exposed train tracks, up the river, over the forest, and down through the trees, and gently ease them off their backs to put them down on the banks of the river where all the animal friends were waiting. The adventures of the children and animals always ended with a big party, with lots of food, beside the deep pool where the turtles lived. The adventures were narratives of safety.

On a primitive level, I wanted the children out of the city. I felt we were living where hunters had been. I kept fantasizing about what I knew from other times when children had been taken out of dangerous cities, sent away from buzzing planes, to farmhouses in Surrey or Devon.

Before I took the children up to the Boston Corners house on the weekends, I would first have the kinds of discussions people were having in New York then: Was it more dangerous to take a train or to drive a car on the highway? This was the time when rumors about forty missing yellow Ryder trucks—to be filled, presumably, with explosives—were rife. People were balking about getting on airplanes at all. Rational or not, it was only when we were letting ourselves into that house, behind the screen of the thorns, in a place of no geopolitical interest to anybody, that I felt fully at rest.

As winter began turning to spring, the snow outside was deep enough to make angels in. You could see the man-made berm, a low straight hillock you could walk upon, through the bare trees. We went hunting for the footprints of deer, which looked like stitching on the white counterpane of the snow. The patterns ran lightly down to the bend in the little river where the deer must have been coming to drink when we weren't here. We saw the mounds of droppings that the brown rabbits had left, and the places where their long back feet had pushed against the snow. Once Rosa and I saw the heavier, flatter prints of what must have been beavers. We found the impressive woven-twig wall of their dam, which forced the river to pour itself into a deep, drinkable stone cup. Trout, we knew, lived in that stream.

When we had to go back into the city, I would tuck Joey into bed, and, as squad eighteen pulled out of its garage, sirens blaring, I would tell him stories about the turtles safe in their limpid pool.

In our imaginations, things made sense; in the real world, psychotic fantasy seemed to have broken out. Day by day, horror had unfolded. First it had been the *Star*, with the deadly anthrax powder on its premises; then a *New York Post* reporter showed her own skin lesions to the camera. The skin of a seven-month-old baby—the son of an ABC producer—erupted in lesions: skin anthrax, said his pediatrician.

I needed those stories about the animals in the woods perhaps as much as the children did. There was the day when I had been traveling on business in Toronto, and I sat, watching the news in the foyer of an office building, as my husband's office at *The New York Times* was evacuated. Someone had sent an envelope filled with white powder to the reporter who covered bioterrorism. She had opened it, and the dust had flown into the air in the newsroom.

I bathed the children's soft bodies and wondered if we were doing the right thing by staying in the city at all.

An elderly lady in Connecticut died. Postal workers died. A boy told Rosa that her father's office at the *Times* had been infected with anthrax. Rosa came home crying. We stopped letting that child play with our daughter. But every day, when David went to work, I felt a bit more numb with fear inside. He couldn't come up with us on many weekends because he had to stay within an hour and a half of the city in case he and his colleagues were called upon to cover another attack.

Everyone held his or her breath a bit at the end of Ramadan, at New Year's. Rumors circled that the Brooklyn Bridge was next, that you should stay away from Macy's during Thanksgiving weekend.

Everyone, it seemed, was on antidepressants or antianxiety medication. Rumors spread that the air was bad downtown, and the government was covering up information about just how bad. Our little boy had trouble breathing. Was it ordinary childhood asthma, or a symptom of the cloud of toxins from the incinerated towers?

Was it war or peace? It looked like peace, felt like war.

By now, it was mostly new faces in the firehouse. But the world they tended remained surreal. A big mustachioed firefighter, one of the leaders of the special units trained to handle hazardous materials—the haz-mat guys—had chatted with me as I paused to look at the fire truck while pushing our son's stroller. "I'll tell you this, ma'am," he said, "if there's a dirty bomb down here—well, they don't want this to get around, but our instructions are to just put black tags on the bodies and leave them there." A newspaper quoted a U.S. military leader noting, without attribution, that women soldiers would deliberately be used to humiliate Muslim prisoners at Guantanamo. It seemed that dehumanization had become normal to people on both sides of the conflict. Was the human imagination the antidote to this spreading toxin?

My students at Woodhull have been taught—if they went to colleges influenced by political correctness, and especially if they are white and middle-class—that they have no right to try to imagine someone else's life. "How can I understand," my students ask rhetorically, repeating what they have been instructed by their right-on professors, "what it is like to be black, to be gay, to be working-class?"

I found their reluctance to trust their own imaginations a huge hurdle when it came to teaching them. I brought their arguments against imagining someone else's situation to my father, to get his advice. "Ridiculous," he said when I summarized the politically correct arguments. "In spite of everything, people have been saying for the last fifty years about cultural relativism—and you should remind these professors that the reaction against the universal truths began in the twenties, it's very old—there *are* universals. Father-son, father-daughter, mother-son, mother-daughter relationships; somebody climbing a mountain against odds, somebody falling into a pit. These are universal moments. A great work of art will speak with universal emotional value. It will have a universal fictive structure."

"That's humanism," I said sadly.

Humanism—the view that the human perspective and human emotions were universal and that the human creative imagination was the most precious quality of the species—was vanishing rapidly from world ideologies; it had been vanishing, too, for a while, as my students' reactions demonstrated, from left-of-center classrooms. I described what my friend Vivian—a literature professor, just as my father had been—had told me. She said that you can lose your job in the academy for teaching about universal human feelings these days. "But it is the only way of teaching," she said, "that makes my students' eyes shine. I close the door and sneak it in. They light up."

"I believe it," said my father. He adjusted his reading glasses—he buys them from dime stores by the dozen, so he can safely lose and refind them—and smoothed the every-which-way-ness of his hair, to no effect.

Today my father's humanism is an old-fashioned, even discredited, point of view; a faded idea, like a jacket cut to the body and altered by hand. But it is one that should not be lost.

I thought about my father and this kind of humanism later, when I found myself sitting in a living room at VCCA, a writer's colony in Virginia. The Blue Ridge Mountains outside the plate-glass windows were darkened by a thundering electrical storm. Crevasses of white lightning streaked from time to time from the earth to the sky, something I had seen only in photographs. Every few minutes the air lit up with purple-white neon.

The artists, writers, and composers were done with work for the day, and we had all gathered in the common room for a little human contact and comfort. We were, I think, a bit intimidated by the vastness of the forces outside. Far away, there was a war on. But it was warm and bright in the living room. The room was ringed with generations of books left behind by other visitors.

The younger writers were asking Ann Birstein, a writer in her seventies, about the writers of the 1940s and '50s. Despite the lines on her forehead and her pewter-gray hair, the blue-eyed beauty and caustic wit that had attracted Alfred Kazin and Bernard Malamud were still apparent.

There was longing and envy and something like disbelief in the eyes of the younger writers as we all sat listening to her report of a world in which young, crazily confident children of immigrants plunged into words as if into an ocean, in a mid-century America in which ordinary people waited for the next great short story the way we wait now for a summer blockbuster movie. We listened, trying to get a little wisdom to find a way to live a life something like the one that generation had lived. Birstein was not optimistic.

"It's gone, that life," she said ruthlessly, as sheets of rain slashed down. "Even the concept that you learned about life from the novel does not exist anymore. Think of Tolstoy, of Faulkner—they wrote from an omniscient point of view be-cause they *were* omniscient. They were these huge people. You don't get that anymore.

"No one," she said abruptly, as if refusing to be elegiac, "stands at the dock anymore waiting to find out what happened to Little Nell."

My father and his generation of poets and visionaries were the ones who would have stood at the dock. In Leonard's youth, truth had not yet been deconstructed. Since the trend of poststructuralism entered the universities in the 1980s, young writers have been taught that it is naive and even politi-cally suspect to believe in universal values or stories that can touch anyone's heart; nothing, they are taught, is inherently true. Humanism has been demonized as "secular humanism" by the religious right—as if faith in art and in people's creative potential rules out faith in God—and it has been derided as passé and irrelevant by the Marxist and feminist academic left, who dismiss it as playing down difference of race, class, and gender in its commitment to a human point of view that can transcend all such divisions.

There have always been two different views of literature in

the American mind, the arguments of the head versus the insights of the heart. One argues that literature is for enlightenment or social engineering. That is the viewpoint that prevails in academia now. Something is wrong with society, and we need to "fix it." In universities today, you "fix it" by opening up the canon to writers who were not included in the past—women, people of color—and, more questionably, you also "fix it" by seeing literature not as a bridge between human beings but as a map of oppressive power relations.

The other view, that of my father's generation, is the heart-centered one. They were reacting against a similar time—the 1930s, when Marxist intellectuals argued that poetry and novels should stick to social realism with the main goal of addressing the workers' plight. The humanist view was and is that art—literature—is a key to unlock the universal soul; that in the end, we are stuck with fallen human nature; that to be human is to be in Plato's cave, in limitless shadow, and we have to look at ourselves for illumination; that imagination is the flame, and art the match.

My father was arguing against Vivian having to teach a humanist view of literature behind closed doors. "Take *Pilgrim's Progress*," he said. "It's a Christian document, but no one reads it for that anymore. They read it still because it is a profoundly wonderful adventure story.

"My understanding of the historical context in which Pope was writing adds not one iota to the luster of his creative accomplishment or the reader's engagement with it. It does add academic insight—what I call gossip. Which is different. Shakespeare's Sonnet 73 is one of the most beautiful love poems ever written. It makes not the slightest bit of difference that it was a love poem written by a man to a man. Scholarship is useful for telling you about the life of the artist, but not about the life of the work of art. These are two different lives. And the work of art is its own living, breathing reality.

"The guys in my reading group resist this idea very much. They read the book reviews, and they want context. There is no distinction today between the creative work and the gossip about its manufacture, no distinction between the sacred and the profane—or the mundane.

"I make a distinction between the author's intention and the work's intention, which are not always the same thing. You might say in that sense that I am thinking mystically because I strongly believe that the work has a life of its own, is a living entity.

"If it works at all, then it always works."

I thought of my students; I wished they could hear my father just then. I wanted that confidence for them. I, too, wanted to learn to teach in a way that made young people's eyes shine.

WAR WAS in the air when, at eighteen, Leonard went away to college. He was the first member of his family to do so, and his departure took place much against the wishes of his father. Before Leonard left Cleveland, the Jewish Social Service Bureau insisted on testing him and Melvin. A man named Goldhammer—"may he live in infamy and roast in hell forever"—had Leonard come see him. He was sitting at his desk smoking his pipe.

"Leonard," my father remembered that the man had said, "I see that you are planning to go to college. I've looked your test scores over. I'm sorry to tell you this. You can't . . . cut . . . the mustard."

Leonard recalls, "It was one of those moments when you have to make a decision—who is right? I must have made some kind of internal decision, because the next moment I was at Ohio State University. My family did not want me to go—the defense factories were gearing up, and people were making money. I had given them money from my own work." Leonard had worked at a welding rod factory—a pure nightmare, he said, because he couldn't keep up with the conveyor belt. "I came to work one day, and a note on the time card said, 'Wolf, if you can't keep up with the machine, go home.' So I went home. But first, my mother, may she live forever in heaven, had put every penny away in the bank for college. My father knew and did not like it."

At the end of that summer, my father was a freshman in Columbus, Ohio. Word was that Eleanor Roosevelt had once gone to a football game there and remarked on how much space was wasted under the stadium seats, so a spartan dorm had been built for the scholarship students—underneath the seats. At game time, the students would climb up into their rafters and peek at the action through the holes in the roof; when the crowd cheered, the fans' stamping feet vibrated the ceiling.

"I was reading; I read Chaucer to Thomas Hardy for freshman curriculum, which in those days stopped at Hardy. I was reading Shakespeare and Milton. I was also reading *The New Masses* every week, and *The Daily Worker.*

"We scholarship students were all living on bologna sandwiches on white bread. I earned eight dollars a month cleaning mice droppings out of cages at the genetics lab.

"I was in love all the time. A young woman from my Young Communist League cell, Caryl, was in my classes. She had chestnut hair; she wore saddle shoes and lovely cashmere sweaters.

We would go together to sell *The Sunday Worker* to poor black people for a nickel.

"Over Christmas break, before I left, the YCL organizer of our cell—Boris Axelrod, who was tasked with getting and maintaining new recruits—drove me from Cleveland to Columbus, back to school, in a driving snowstorm.

"We were in this snug bubble of air, with snow coming down so you could hardly see the road. The headlights were on. The heater was on. The windshield wiper was going back and forth, back and forth, creating little crusts of snow with each stroke."

"Windshield *wiper*?" I asked.

"At that time they didn't have two. And he twisted my arm. He made a heavy pitch for me to enlist at once to serve the Communists' aims, so that I could be taught to use weapons.

"The Party believed that the revolution was in sight and that this was the beginning. The Marxists thought at the beginning of the war that this was going to be a battle between capitalist states and that they would destroy each other, and that then world revolution could take over. The Soviet Union was not yet in the war, but you could feel it; it was in the air; they would be. From his point of view, if I joined the army now, I could prepare to be a soldier in Boris's revolutionary battalions of the future.

"Through my head went the thought that he was counting on. I thought, I am a good Communist, I have a responsibility to the revolution. I want the revolution to succeed. But there was a momentary struggle, and what came out of me was 'no.'

"I said, 'No.'

"He said, 'Why not?'

"I said, 'Because I am a poet.'

"He said, with the weariness of a man profoundly disappointed in the man to whom he was talking, 'Len, when the revolution comes, nobody is going to ask whether you are a poet. They are going to ask if you can shoot.'"

My father was inducted into the army when he was twenty. He was shipped from Cleveland, Ohio, to Camp Roberts, California, for basic training, where he was assigned to an artillery unit and trained in the use of the 105-millimeter cannon. But he was continually being given tests for aptitude. As a consequence, he was sent to the Army Specialized Training Program in foreign languages, at Stanford University, to become a translator on the front lines with German prisoners of war. At Stanford, since the army had concluded they now had enough translators, there were more tests. Leonard qualified for the army engineering program at Berkeley.

He was sent to live in Bowles Hall, a student residence hall then housing soldiers on one end and sailors on the other. The young men, though students on a campus, were military men above all and remained in uniform every minute; in summer, they wore their "suntans," and in winter, their uniforms of olive drab wool with brass buttons. They awoke at reveille and were counted at roll call in front of the building, where they shouted, "Here sir, here sir." They were forbidden to mix with the other students except after hours.

One fall day in 1943, Leonard saw a beautiful young woman standing in a twenty-by-thirty-foot hole in the street, interviewing the construction workers. She was tall and slender, with long light-brown hair and hazel eyes: "If Whitman had been straight he would have described her in glowing terms," Leonard said, laughing. Her name was Patricia. "That she was a shiksa was part of the attraction, beyond any doubt."

Patricia, a fledgling writer, was doing an article for the humor magazine *The Pelican*, about construction holes in Berkeley; that was why she herself was standing in a hole. She looked up and saw a soldier grinning; she said something witty to my father, my father replied, and then he climbed down into the hole. They started dating and were soon deeply in love.

Not long after the affair began, my father's relationship with the army deteriorated. He was dating Patricia, but was also involved with half a dozen other young women and was caught up in the emotional turmoil of those relationships; he was also entering into a tremendously productive time as a poet, and the words were pouring out of him, but he had no time to write and no leisure to think. He began to behave erratically as a soldier—though his behavior was normal for a poet—and his superior officers began to notice.

He was not a good soldier: he would be in a physics class, assigned to perform an experiment, and he would write twelve poems instead. It got worse from there. "I was writing an enormous amount of poetry—it spewed out of me.

"I had a hard time in the army specialized training program, though I tried my best to be a good soldier. There was a moment when I was walking across campus and I encountered my commanding officer. Of course I saw him. I started to walk by him."

"He shouted 'Soldier! Why didn't you salute?' I explained that I had not saluted because I was out of uniform; I was not wearing my peaked cap. That drove him wild. *I* was right, I was not supposed to salute if I was out of uniform; but *he* was right, I was not supposed to be out of uniform! It went down in my file as disobedience on my part.

"Even before this, when I was inducted, the army psychiatrist had stamped my file 'neuropsychiatric.'"

"Why?"

"I was twitchy!"

"Why were you twitchy?"

"I was a young poet, and I was not the sort of person who should be in the army! I don't want to say there are some kinds of good people who are not well suited to the army, but creative people have a hard time fitting into these little units. I will never forget: I went through induction, they were poking and prodding me, and for five minutes I talked to someone they called a psychiatrist. At the end, I was getting dressed, and the man picked up this stamp and went, boom, on my file, and there were these big red letters: 'Neuropsychiatric.'"

My father was becoming more and more depressed, though unaware that that was the problem. He went to an army psychiatrist with the complaint that he was sleeping too much. The psychiatrist saw that Leonard was very troubled. My father did not reveal to him that he had begun hoarding sleeping pills.

In 1944 his mental illness became so severe that he was hospitalized for a month at the Oakland-area naval hospital. He had his twenty-first birthday in the mental institution. Patricia came to see him, and they celebrated with coffee and cookies in the visiting room. Leonard shared a room with a sweet southern kid whose name was Toy Justice; Justice mostly sat on his bed and stared in front of him, mute.

The psychiatrist at the institution asked Leonard if he was shirking. No, he replied, he was perfectly happy to go back to duty. So he was sent back to his residence hall at Berkeley.

When he walked into the dorm, the rooms were empty. The unit had been sent overseas; it was the time of the Battle of the Bulge.

"I had packed my barracks bag again, with my orders in

hand, and was walking out the door to ship out to join them when the sergeant, finishing up paperwork in the empty dorm, said, 'Hey! Are you Wolf?'

"'Yes, sir.'

"'Wolf! Wait a minute!' He went through his file and pulled out this little card and said, 'You ain't going noplace. You've qualified for the med program.'" Leonard's buddies, unspared by the bureaucratic selection process, were shipped to the battlefields of France. He never saw anyone from his unit again.

Leonard was posted to the medical program at a hospital in New Orleans. In December 1944, Patricia and Leonard married, and Patricia followed my father to his new posting. They found a one-bedroom apartment on top of a garage.

My grandmother Rose-Ita took to her bed at the news of the wedding, and the relatives called Leonard to say he had killed his mother by marrying a shiksa. Upon getting no reaction, Rose-Ita eventually got out of bed. But it took many years, and the birth of a granddaughter, before my grandparents would speak to their daughter-in-law.

"The army had scheduled me to go to the medical school at Tulane later that year. Meanwhile, I worked at LaGarde General Hospital in New Orleans. I was a wardman: we worked twelve hours a day, six and a half days a week; we emptied bedpans, changed bedding, swept, washed the patients, and moved wheelchairs.

"By that time, we knew that in Germany, they were killing Jews. I had a fantasy that I would kill the first German POW who came my way. I vowed I would cut the throat of the first one I had to deal with."

"Well, the first German who came my way had fallen wounded on the battlefield, and the medics had wrapped him from neck to toe in plaster of Paris to immobilize him. It was my job to cut the plaster of Paris off his body. He was twenty, a kid, the same age I was.

"When I cut off the plaster carapace, all of the skin on his body looked wrinkled. I rubbed it with cotton and alcohol. By the time I had cleaned him up, all the rancor in me had disappeared. He was a human being, completely helpless.

"I could speak Yiddish, I knew some German; we chatted over the days; we talked about the German poets. We had fascinating conversations in which he denied that the poet Heinrich Heine was Jewish. He had the whole line about Jews, that they were a subhuman race who had contributed to the destruction of German power. He was horrified to discover that I was Jewish.

"He was having the same experience I had: shock that I was just another human being. It couldn't be true, what he had been told about the monstrous Jews; after all, I had been tending him, looking after his needs, feeding him, cleaning him, taking him to the bathroom. *He* said, 'Oh, my God'; *I* said something like 'Oh my God.' I had to change my mind, too. I had been expecting a Nazi."

"He *was* a Nazi," I said.

"I had a Nazi . . . who was a person," said Leonard.

"When you discover that somebody is a living human being, it shreds your prejudices. Literature is endlessly shredding our prejudices; revealing the expressions of one's humanity."

In January 1945, yet another senior commander saw that my father was not stable.

"A Major Rosenthal observed me at work and saw there was something wrong with me: I was distractable and still not a good follower of orders. Instead of deciding I was bad, he thought I might be sick. He called me in: 'What's troubling you?'

"'I'm not troubled,' I said.

"'You're troubled,' he said.

"We talked about the poet Muriel Rukeyser. The next thing I knew, he said, 'You don't belong here.' The army concluded that this depressed poet was 'thirty percent disabled' and gave me an honorable discharge.

"I went to work for Higgins Industries, which was then making landing craft for the war. My research unit was trying to develop a flotation device that would give downed airmen the ability to make seawater into drinking water. We used early plastics, and the earliest microwave ovens to anneal the plastic.

"As the war was ending, in 1945, Patricia and I went back to California. We moved out to Big Sur, to live together with a bunch of poets and writers in some huts on the side of a cliff."

To live in a hut on the side of a cliff. Well, I thought as I washed and stacked the dishes that evening, that would solve a lot of problems for a lot of people in the short term; it wasn't an option people of my generation thought we had. I thought of Sophia, who had called in a low moment, and I wished, irresponsibly, that she could escape in a similar way. But then I thought of her frequent refrain: "I am thirty-three; I want to have a child; if I leave this marriage, I will have to start all over, and I might not make a new relationship in time to have a family of my own; and truthfully, there is the security . . ." Then I thought: perhaps boxes come in many shapes and guises, some of them very alluring; and maybe escape from the box is a step you take first in the imagination.

LESSON FOUR

Speak in Your Own Voice

It's your story.

M Y FATHER sat down again in the dining room, dressed in his best intellectual-in-the-1970s outfit. It was archival; I remembered it from about 1974. It involved a burnt-orange shirt with a silk necktie that featured a repeating pattern with stylized naked women. He wore wide-wale dark green corduroy trousers and suede lace-up shoes. When we were children, he had occasionally smoked a pipe to complete this particular tableau. I recall an actual meerschaum pipe, the style of pipe that had originated with the Dutch intelligentsia, and which you can sometimes see in seventeenth-century Dutch still lifes; it had a bearded face carved in it. ("I smoked that damn pipe until I was carrying a big box home one day, and the box kept banging the pipe against my teeth. This is stupid, I thought, and snapped it in two, and threw it away.")

Through the windows of the dining room, we could see, scattered throughout the lower reaches of the riverbanks, the beginnings of violet and lavender loosestrife. The green stalks of the daylilies had begun to reach their full height but had not yet blossomed. The leaves in the trees were tender.

Mr. Christian, a landscaper and excavator who had a yellow bulldozer that infatuated Joey, had come a few weeks before and cleared the entire area around the base of the tree in the forest where my father and Rosa and I thought the treehouse should be built. The raw earth had now begun to grow grassy again.

Rosa and I had gone out with some yellow plastic rope to the designated tree, carrying with us a thick twenty-four-inch bough that we had discovered on the ground. We wrapped the rope around both ends of the sturdy bough—I still did not feel completely comfortable using the drill, and I did not trust my father's tremor on a piece of wood this uneven—and we tied square knots on either end of it. Then we looped the two ends of the rope around the heaviest branch of the tree and knotted them once again, making a swing. Finally, I threaded both ends through two U-bolts that Chris at Herrington's had recommended we get for just this purpose. I doubled the ends through again, then tightened the bolts as my father had shown me to do back in the house. Rosa held the body of each U-bolt steady as I did the tightening.

When we were done, we had a swing that Rosa could use beneath the as-yet-unbuilt treehouse. It hung a little crookedly. We found out the hard way that after six or seven swings, Rosa had to readjust her weight to avoid banging into a protruding knot on the side of the trunk. But she sat and swung with an unusually peaceful expression, looking out at the tangle of growth on the banks of the river below. Soon she was automatically shifting her weight at the right moment, almost as if in tune with the rhythm of the oddball swing. Awkward as it was, it was better than any other swing, because we had thought of it and made it.

Back inside, I sat down in the dining room with my father. "Lesson four," said my father, who was off coffee again and now drinking Swiss Miss instant cocoa ("Remarkable! You don't need to add milk!"). "It's your story. No one else can construct your narrative for you. I tell my students they can choose any format they want—fairy tale, fable, memoir, bare dialogue—at this point in their lessons, but it has to be authentic. I don't want a polished imitation of some fashionable writer or trendy genre. I would rather have something raw but genuine.

"One of the assignments here," my father forged on, "is to write a two-page piece told from the point of view of a child. I am constantly wanting to give them an opportunity to experience things they haven't experienced."

"But haven't they all been children?"

"They haven't *written* from the point of view of a child. Their writing set is adult. I want to move them from where they stand."

"Then why not ask them to imagine being an alien? Why something so mundane?" I asked.

"There is nothing 'mundane' about a child, if you are paying attention. You will get twelve different takes on writing from the viewpoint of a child. You don't need to become another species to explore deeply; it is all there in the human imagination. I want them to notice that even the most 'mundane' event is capable of being transformed by who *they* are.

"Emily Dickinson's famous poem goes: 'I heard a fly buzz when I died.'

I heard a Fly buzz—when I died—
The Stillness in the Room

Was like the Stillness in the Air—
Between the Heaves of Storm—

The Eyes around—had wrung them dry—
And Breaths were gathering firm
For that last Onset—when the King
Be witnessed—in the Room—

I willed my Keepsakes—Signed away
What portion of me be
Assignable—and then it was
There interposed a Fly—

With Blue—uncertain stumbling Buzz—
Between the light—and me—
And then the Windows failed—and then
I could not see to see—

"That's it! Just a fly buzzing at a window, the most mundane thing in the world. But look at what Emily Dickinson did with it: the contrast between the dying self and the furious buzzing of the living creature—those are the things experienced by the reader. Dickinson impressed that moment with Dickinsonian tone, voice, and imagery, and this created the drama of the event. She used the moment of death to italicize the power of a living creature; and no one but Dickinson could have made the reader think of a buzzing fly in this way. It does not essentially matter that she was not known in her lifetime. She knew, in her own lifetime, that her own voice was absolutely unique."

It is hard to imagine a young Emily Dickinson—remaining

unknown and unpublished but taking her own gift so absolutely seriously—today. Indeed, not only is it difficult for the young people I teach to respect their own creative work if they are not paid for it, it is hard for them to trust the authority of the inner voice at all.

Many of my students have come from an education that is preprofessional. They are trained to see what they have to say not in its own light—the old liberal arts ideal—but in terms of various marketable categories. As a result, they tend to be intimidated into using corporate-speak, PC-speak, nonprofit-speak, screenplay-speak, literary-speak. The notion of one's own unique voice and vision—as understood outside the context of the marketplace—is as arcane an idea to them, and as dangerous to trust, as the notion that you can base your future on weaving, or cooking artisanal food, or growing heirloom wildflowers.

Eva, a young writer whom I mentor, is a spunky, fast-talking twenty-four-year-old Hispanic-American with a sprightly expression and curly black hair. When I first met her, through Madeleine, a young woman I had taught at our leadership institute, Eva was burning to begin her life as a fiction writer. I had felt an immediate bond with Eva. She was like a female Holden Caulfield, without the wealthy parents: wry, bright, scrappy, undeceived, and hopeful. She was truly broke, had no health care, and was looking after a sister who was ill with diabetes, but Eva woke up every morning trying to make herself be happy, and willing to get to work. I felt for her situation.

We had been e-mailing each other occasionally about how she could approach her work. She wanted to start publishing fiction. The trouble was, I sensed, she had not yet found her own voice; or rather, I suspected, she had found it but was scared to let it sing. When she spoke about her fiction, from time to time you could hear the true Eva, but you had to get past other voices standing in her way. I had a sense of seven pretentious young men and one pretentious male writing professor standing around the woman, interrupting her when she tried to get a word out, and refusing to laugh at her jokes. Sometimes, I sensed, the overbearing voices were those of the trendy young men who were now writing in the little magazines, with their ironic, detached style. Eva's true voice, I suspected, was very funny and very smart but not at all detached. I wanted her to have confidence in her own voice.

What could I do? I felt I was in over my head. I thought of turning to my father for professional advice—something I had done only in the face of internal resistance for the last fifteen years. As Leonard had been talking me through his lesson plan, I found that I had begun more directly to reach out to him for guidance, especially when I was stymied in my role as a teacher. I took a deep breath, checked my ego outside for the night, and called to ask for his help with urging Eva to get, as he put it, "to the heart of her matter."

She sent me a pitch letter; it was detached. I read Leonard some of her passages over the phone. "Where is Eva in this?" my father asked. "Ask her: 'What made you—you, Eva, personally—feel strongly about this subject, strongly enough to want to write it?' Tell her to forget her audience and ignore the little magazines. Think about Wordsworth—'emotion recollected in tranquility.' She needs to remember how she first felt when she realized she was having an experience or insight that moved her enough to want to write about it.

"Students," Leonard continued, "need to become alert to the individuality of their own speech; they also have to become aware of their own impulse toward redundancy, and the degree to which they are prisoners of the cliché.

"I write over and over, on their essays, 'cliché, cliché, cliché.' But I praise them when they slip into something all by themselves that is true."

I passed along Leonard's advice. Eva, to my surprise, was not offended at all; she got it at once, and began to write.

She had become excited about the thought of writing the nonfiction article. It seemed there were experiences she wished to put into words, experiences that she had not taken seriously when she was writing as if to please the cool young men in the literary magazines. She wanted to tell the story of a friend with a blood disorder who wanted to have cosmetic surgery and was willing to undergo treatments that could jeopardize her life.

Again, Eva e-mailed me her pitch letter. Again, she was struggling with someone's else's language; this time the language of the academic feminist theory she had encountered in college. "Why would women subject themselves to these cultural processes?" her pitch letter wondered.

I bit my lip and called my father once again. With each call, my awareness shifted a bit away from my psychodrama with him—my resistance to becoming his student, or *a* student, for that matter—and toward the challenge at hand, which became more and more absorbing. It was feeling better and better to learn from my father this valuable material. I felt, with the second call about Eva and how to teach her, that we were doing something very collegial, very concrete, and very interesting— like standing side by side in a garage, absorbed in diagnosing the workings of an engine. Who knew more did not matter; what mattered was understanding and fixing the problem.

It hit me: when the teacher-student relationship is working as it should—as when the creative gesture is working as it should—the ego fades, absorbed, along with everything else, in the fascination of the subject.

"She should trash this letter and start over," my dad suggested. Then he taught me the best trick anyone has ever given me to cut through layers of "shoulds" and inhibition, to guide a student toward her own real voice. "In her new letter, she should express herself as if she is talking to a good friend. She should even write the friend's name—'Dear Madeleine"—at the top of the document. Then she should just write her feelings and thoughts about the subject to her good friend, directly, from the heart. When she is done, she can edit; then she should delete the heading and replace her friend's name with that of the editor."

A few days later, I was pleased to get the following, which I copied to Leonard:

Dear Naomi:

My friend, Anna, has longed for surgery to correct a slight cleft lip all her life. She is a schoolteacher in a solid marriage, and she is about to turn forty. She also has a rare blood disorder.

My friend's feelings have recently become unbearable: she walks the streets, and when she sees her reflection in a window, she is in so much pain she has to look away. Last January, she decided it was worth risking her health to try the surgery . . . I am horrified at her decision, and her mother is distraught. But I also understand it a little. To understand it more—and to understand the decisions of hundreds of women like my friend Anna who long to correct an imperfec-

*tion so powerfully that they are willing to take medical
risks—I would like to write a piece of 2,000 words . . .*

"Right on!" I e-mailed back. "Eva, you rock. Replace the
header. Enclose a self-addressed, stamped envelope. Send it out."
"This lesson," my father said, as we discussed Eva's work
that weekend, back at the dining room table upstate, "is: 'Speak
in your own voice, from the heart.' You need to persuade your
students that there is a voice in each of them that is unlike any
other, and there is a message, in each of them, unlike any
other. Fear, scolding, professional jargon, and listening to the
outside exhortations can all dim it or smudge it. Yet when this
voice comes out, there they are, compelling, original, in focus.
When students find their own voices, you can see the light in
them leap up," said Leonard.

The young women at Woodhull to whom I teach public
speaking, during an exercise in which they have to name their
accomplishments, will often reach for jargon at first: the nonprofit workers use nonprofit jargon: "marginalized," "imple-
ment"; the academically trained young women use academic
jargon: "nondominant," "hegemonic."

Some of their reluctance to speak about their own lives in
their own voices comes from fear of standing up in front of a
group, but some of it comes from the layers of alien voices that
already, at age twenty-three or twenty-four, have overlaid their
true voices like layers of paint over good wood grain. Those
who wish to please others more than they have learned to know
themselves will have voices that are trapped in their throats,
making them sound unnaturally high-pitched and girlish. Those
trained as corporate presenters tend to speak with false polish;
those trained in the political world often speak with an artificial

sense of uplift. Those from cultures in which women are not supposed to reveal their power will sometimes speak with an artificial humility. When I ask them to try dropping their voices and speaking from the diaphragm, which is their natural register, they will be startled by the voice of the real, adult woman, with its range of feelings—pain and rage and strength, as well as the prettier emotions—that emerges from inside them.

The jargon or the cliché, or the pleasing persona, seems to serve as emotional protection. I do understand that there is little that is more exhilarating, but also little that is scarier, than telling your truth.

Some of the students show their fear physically. When my brave, brilliant student Eva undertook this exercise, her body became very still, her brown skin went pale, and her black eyes widened. Some of the young women, as I mentioned, weep. We keep Kleenex handy. Though for some of them the fear had to do with the exercise, for others it had to do with the teacher. As I was working with my father, I suddenly reheard, as if for the first time, what I had thought was a joking introduction at a gala by one of my students: "Woodhull gave me many things—including the fact that I can say I have survived being yelled at by Naomi Wolf."

When I do the work well, or when I am temperamentally in tune with a young woman, I operate on a kind of intuition about what she needs and what I should say to her; what I should reveal about her and her potential. That intuition was so different from the analysis and argument that had defined my professional life for fifteen years. I wanted to strengthen it.

But when I am not in tune with a student, or when she needs more patience than I have, I challenge her to speak in her true voice, just as, I realized, I challenged her to be confident, in a way that can be far too rough for her. Not mean, but impossibly demanding.

I realized that in that way too, I had been too abrupt with my expectations for these particular students and their particular, more hesitant beauty. "Say it from your heart!" I have sometimes reiterated to them—as if it were that easy for everyone to do such a thing. "Try it again," I've insisted. "Try it again."

At those times, I feel my intuition close down and my ego—my argument mind ("Jeez, how hard can this be?")—take over. The part of me that was sure I was right, that had made a career out of "rightness," shrugged off my colleagues' advice to be more gentle as specific to their field: mushy, girly, therapeutic overprotectiveness. The part of me that was not good at listening—the part that talked down men twice my age in national TV debates—did not want to be open. The portcullis of my rightness had descended firmly.

My conversations with my dad, though, were getting through to me. If I was going to be a good teacher, I had to take all my students—not just my favorites, not just the ones who happened to share my own temperament and abilities—with compassion. I would have to learn a kind of unconditional love to go with the particular grain of each.

I had to go to where they were—all of them—and not demand that they somehow get themselves to where I imagined, in my arrogance, bright young women whom I had helped select *should* be. I would have to bring them along not at my own personal pace, not at an idealized pace, but at their own real pace, step by step, with my full, patient support.

I would have to get my ego out of the way.

Damn, I thought as the magnitude of this began to sink in. To be a decent teacher, I would have to grow up; I would have to become another kind of person.

The change would be worth it, though, I hoped. The amazing thing is that, when I get it right and reach them, when they break into their own true voices, "the light in them" leaps out: they change, even physically. It is a kind of miracle. The air around them becomes clearer, and a radiance amps up in their eyes and faces. Those who were distant become charismatic; those who were dimmed become easier to look at; those who were muffled become compelling to listen to. Speaking in their own voices, they become, if only for a moment, what they were put on earth to be.

It occurred to me one day that when I was cheering them on as they hit something true, I was simply channeling the teacher who was my dad. It occurred to me that he would be there for them as a teacher through me as a teacher, after his death; the fact that someday he would die was, in this regard, immaterial. He had successfully transmitted his art. That was a kind of immortality. Then I had a glimpse of something bigger: that anyone who lives out his or her art or creative mission lives, in a way, forever.

Finally, I had a shiver. It struck me that if I really did learn to become a teacher, one of these young women might cheer on someone else to speak in her own voice, long after I myself was dead.

MY DAD believes what he does about the universal humanist story, and the power of the individual voice, because of his formative experience in America's postwar Bohemia. He came of age in a time when the Western world was being renewed by the power of the individual imagination.

In 1945 the young men came back from the war, and the young women came home from the universities and the factories.

In the war, the young men had seen everything.

The country they returned to was closing in and settling down. It was a time of consolidation: many individual voices were becoming fewer, monolithic voices. By 1949, radio had been eclipsed by television as the main medium for family-oriented news and entertainment. In 1953, a developer named Eugene Ferkauf created the first suburban "mall," Korvettes, on suburbanizing Long Island. In 1954, Kemmons Wilson, a homebuilder in Memphis, had decided to expand the new franchise called Holiday Inn, replacing the one-of-a-kind motels along the region's roads. In 1955, the Philip Morris cigarette company invented the Marlboro Man. In 1956, the massive federal highway program was passed, beginning the building of the interstate system that overshadowed the rural byways. A national discussion of "conformity"—symbolized by the 1955 novel *The Man in the Grey Flannel Suit*—acknowledged that postwar affluence and homogeneity was a threat to individualism. The regional landscape— the prewar South as described by William Faulkner and Thomas Wolfe, the prewar West of Ansel Adams and the prewar Northeast of Robert Frost—was starting to change, to become homogeneous. In these postwar years, soap manufacturers began to sponsor television variety shows; women were being encouraged to seek transcendence not in art but in appliances—to take up full-time housekeeping and consumerism.

But during this same era, in Los Gatos, California, the artist Carolyn Cassady was setting up her home with her husband,

Neal Cassady. He was sometimes working on the freight trains, and sometimes disappearing for binges across the bay, and always serving as a Beat muse. Occasionally, the couple was housing Jack Kerouac, the French-Canadian ex-football player who came to sleep and work in their attic. Writer Herbert Gold was carousing in the bars of North Beach, seducing women. Charles Bukowski was living as a drifter, working in a series of menial jobs, writing short stories and drinking. All turned their backs on the conformity settling into the culture.

This was what was in the air when Patricia and Leonard moved to Big Sur, and when Kerouac started hitchhiking west. Kerouac was not just looking for America; he was looking for an America that was already disappearing.

Many of the brightest of the immigrants' children wanted to escape to Bohemia. They caught glimpses of another kind of life, completely different from the backbreaking, prudent, sexually restrained, often religiously orthodox homes in which they were growing up—and different, too, from the increasingly affluent, uniform culture that they saw taking shape around them. In that imagined life, the artist or poet lives for the moment, in pursuit of what essayist Walter Pater called the "hard, gemlike flame": disdaining material well-being, flouting social convention, living on the edge.

"In the prewar era," said Leonard, "everything was black and white. There was no room for subjectivity: you were against Hitler; you were for defeating fascism. But after the war, it was as if everyone breathed a huge sigh of relief. We longed for emotion; we felt that it was time to announce to the world that the heart was as important as the mind. We felt that those who called forth their emotions were the true heroes."

In the memoirs of this generation, 1946–49 was a watershed time. In New York and California, new voices were entering the creative ferment. According to Jan Morris's *Manhattan '45*, half of the city's residents were either "foreign-born, or the children of foreign-born parents." One in five was African-American. The rich ethnic immigration to California, the second home of postwar Bohemia, was similar: Chinese immigrants had come to build the railroads in the previous century; Jews had crossed overland to do retail business with the growing populations and, during the war, to seek new opportunities in the urban areas and in the film industry. Now new settlers from all backgrounds poured into Los Angeles, San Francisco, and Oakland, having sought out high-paying war work. Culture itself opened up in California: to jazz, to film, to new rhythms of speech. The two coasts created very different countercultures. While the small world of the *Partisan Review*, the Village salons, the University of Chicago, and Wellfleet all maintained their well-documented postwar conversation, something very different was happening on the West Coast, which was so much less centralized. After the war and into the 1950s, Ruth Witt-Diamant was initiating a salon for poets at San Francisco State University. Buddhist texts were influencing the Bay Area poets. The connections were looser among these writers—for some there was no direct connection to a larger world of writers at all—and the interior voices were more eccentric and subjective.

The GI Bill—the 1946 Readjustment Act—changed everything for the moneyless poets and writers of this generation. These children of the immigrants could only now, economically, make plans for a life of the mind.

My father's father had been an often unemployed glazier, and yet, on the GI Bill, Leonard became a professor. Poet

Diane di Prima grew up in what she called an underclass. She read *Cyrano de Bergerac* and Dante's *Inferno* as a teenager at Hunter, the public high school, when "the winds of change were blowing. Schools were tailoring themselves to the postwar influx" from the GI Bill. Ted Solotaroff went to the University of Michigan on the GI Bill.

While the New York intellectuals such as Norman Podhoretz and the *Partisan Review* crowd consolidated cultural norms, in other regions—in Berkeley and Big Sur, in Wellfleet and Provincetown and Cambridge, and in Greenwich Village—their counterparts were striking out for a counterculture where the norms were less definite.

Over the next few years, my father would encounter teachers and writers ranging from Delmore Schwartz to Dylan Thomas, Josephine Miles to John Berryman, Karl Shapiro to Robert Lowell and Marianne Moore. Each, for a time, was an exemplar to Leonard about the life of the writer, the transcendence of the unique voice, as opposed to the career of the writer.

"At the end of the war, there was a psychic liberation," said Leonard. "Because of Henry Miller and how he talked directly about sex, the word 'honesty' came into its own. It was a time when they were beginning to honor people for being truthful: psychoanalysis was becoming prevalent; there was a call for more emotional honesty. Where we lived, the Berkeley atmosphere maintained that you had to 'utter yourself.' And then the difference between the outsiders we wanted to be and the bourgeoisie was that they were supposedly hypocrites, and the outsiders or Bohemians, and later the Beats, told it as it was."

Creed's Books, on Telegraph Avenue in Berkeley, right at Sather Gate, was the place to hang out if you were young and looking for intellectual life in 1946, and the Log Cabin coffee shop down the street was where all the young, broke writers went after they had bought their paperbacks, to talk. Creed's, owned by a Mr. Schilling, a man with a Vandyke beard, was "the classic bookstore as imagined by avant-garde people—a wonderful dark place that smelled of the ten to fifteen thousand used books it had on the shelves, in no apparent order."

"We were all reading Sartre," my dad recalled. "And Henry Miller, and Camus—even as we were all still wearing our khakis from the war.

"Schilling, the owner of the bookstore, was portly, and he had a wife twice as portly, a huge beautiful woman who looked like a fringed lampshade, or like the Red Queen in *Alice in Wonderland,* as she came sweeping in to collect the money from him. Schilling was the pseudo mother to all of us. He would slip money to the broke poets . . . and we were all broke. A dollar here, one there. He would allow you to owe him money . . . When I had been about to marry Patricia, Schilling asked me, 'Do you have a ring?'

"'Oh, God, no,' I replied.

"'Do you have money for a ring?'

"'No.'

"So he slipped me a twenty to buy a ring.

"We would work there and wouldn't be paid. The conversation was enough.

"We talked about the weather; about politics, because the world was settling down from the war; and about who was writing."

BOHEMIA is a place in the mind, as writer Herbert Gold put it in his history *Bohemia: Where Art, Angst, Love and Strong Coffee Meet.* Bohemia had flared and sputtered, and migrated from country to country, for two centuries. "Although Bohemia took its modern name and form about a hundred and fifty years ago in Paris, when *la vie bohème* was immortalized by Henri Munger," writes Gold, "the practice of breaking class restraints in something like the Bohemian manner runs as a continuous thread in history."

Byron and Shelley, with their tempestuous sentiments and their wanderings and their illicit loves, were among the first Bohemian celebrities. In Second Empire Paris, in the quarter of Montmartre, the inexpensive cafés and flats attracted demi-monde women, writers, and artists. Montmartre set the tone for Bohemia in Europe for the rest of the nineteenth century. In the early twentieth century, the center of Parisian Bohemia had shifted to Montparnasse and the Latin Quarter.

By then all of Bohemia's hallmarks had been established: free love, the rejection of conventional morality, an abundance of absinthe or wine or other stimulants, the fellowship of one's peers, and the pursuit of the transcendental experience at all costs.

By the teens and 1920s, even America, that young, strait-laced country, had developed its own Bohemia in Greenwich Village. Margaret Sanger preached free love, while Edna St. Vincent Millay composed her sonnet sequences devoted, scandalously, to love's pleasures. e. e. cummings broke apart formal poetic syntax. Those who sought an experience outside the conventions flocked to the narrow streets and basement dives of the Village. South of Fourteenth Street, Bohemia was at its height: homosexual gathering places, where men wore makeup and women wore suits, were tacitly accepted by the authorities; tourists came downtown to marvel at the wild lives of Village habitués.

In Europe, Ezra Pound and T. S. Eliot were picking up

where Whitman had left off. The 1920s generation, the famous literary expatriates, famously took the party to Paris's Left Bank as well.

Then came a retreat in the hardships of the Depression, when even such established poets as W. H. Auden and Stephen Spender felt the need to become political commentators. In the face of the struggle against fascism, the individual experience and the transcendental moment seemed less than relevant. To the new generation of Marxist poets and writers, transcendental humanism seemed downright counterrevolutionary.

But, after the war, the next generation came of age to seek it out again: in 1943, Alfred Kazin had published a path-breaking book, *On Native Grounds,* which spelled out his generation's emerging appreciation for the transcendental: "The radiance in Emerson, Thoreau and Whitman . . . had been a last effort to keep something alive in a society that was losing its sense of history as an ongoing spiritual effort, that was indifferent to anything standing in the way of its newer faith in progress." What they did with that radiance, when they came home from the war, was something new.

In the wake of the horrors of political isms—Nazism and Stalinism—this generation rejected the older poets' insistence that realpolitik was the only answer. Collective solutions were obviously not the simple path to a better world. The French existentialists began to have an impact on the thinking of the postwar generation: some answers would have to come from the individual, from personal conscience and vision.

"Nineteen forty-six was a good time—perhaps the best time—in the twentieth century," wrote the late critic Anatole Broyard. "The war was over, the Depression had ended, and everyone was rediscovering the simple pleasures. A war is like an illness and when it's over you think you've never felt so well. There's a terrific sense of coming back, of repossessing your life."

In this moment, as Kazin put it in his memoir of the postwar years, *Writing Was Everything,* the immigrants' children were entering the world of ideas. Many of those who were Jewish— coming from a tradition in which language was actually sacred—were bringing with them a sense of the numinousness of words. Kazin writes of that transition from the political to the transcendental: he had grown up in "darkest Brooklyn, where my friends had no small talk and only got together to chew each other up in radical political argument . . ." Yet he'd had an epiphanic moment postwar, when he found, in a Charing Cross bookstore, "in the exhilaration of that perfect May when the war finally came to an end and couples were openly making love in Hyde Park," a quote from George Bernard Shaw: "Only in books has mankind known perfect truth, love and beauty."

Broyard, too, was an outsider to the older literary establishment. Like many of these young people, he was the first in his family to believe he could live a life of the mind. He was descended from African-Americans as well as Caucasians but "passed," during his professional life, as Caucasian. In *Kafka Was the Rage,* his memoir of his life as a young Bohemian in postwar Greenwich Village, Broyard remembers that feeling his peers shared, of seeking the sublime in reading and writing and art: "Culture in those days was still holy . . . I went to [Meyer Schapiro's class on modern art at the New School for Social Research] as students twenty years later would go to India . . . Reading had turned [Schapiro] into a saint or angel of scholarship . . . Then, only forty years ago, artists were revolutionaries; we still believed in revolutions . . . Color was salvation . . . the world was warmed by art, like fire."

Broyard recalled: "in 1946 in the Village our feelings about books—I'm talking about my friends and myself—went beyond love. It was as if we didn't know where we ended and books began. Books were our weather, our environment, our clothing. We didn't simply read books; we became them. We took them into ourselves and made them into our histories. While it would be easy to say we escaped into books, it might be truer to say books escaped into us. Books were to us what drugs were to the young men of the sixties.

"They showed us what was possible."

That was the intoxication, the world of sense and ideas and dreams that shaped my father and what he believes about art and poetry and how it saves your life.

With the new sense of a Bohemian possibility on the American margins, Leonard was able to shift his attention away from a country growing ever more homogenous—a country in which a strong animus was growing against the left, and the pressures to conform were growing stronger by the day. The loyalty oaths imposed on federal workers had been instituted by 1949; it is not hard to see why Bohemia would have exerted a stronger and stronger appeal.

Bohemia was waiting for Leonard. In the two years after the war, Leonard flunked out of Berkeley—he had failed *Beowulf.* He lived for a time in Carmel, where he found a job as the houseboy for Jeanne D'Orge, the pseudonym of a wealthy, middle-aged painter and poetess.

"Jeanne d'Orge's first marriage had been to a respectable Ohio politician; a few years later, the proper society matron had eloped with Carl Cherry, an inventor. Cherry became hugely wealthy for inventing the exploding rivet," remarked Leonard. "Before the invention of the exploding rivet, the aerospace industry had had to hire midgets to crawl into the diminishing space of an airplane's tail, to hold the rivet from within, while on the outside, someone with a riveting hammer hit the rivet in place. With the invention of the exploding rivet, the midgets lost their jobs."

"We say 'little people' now, Dad," I remarked.

"Right. Well: Jeanne d'Orge and her husband received one-ten-thousandth of a penny for every rivet; they were sold in the billions." The scandalous couple built their house in romantic Carmel with skylights but no windows, so that the neighbors could not see in.

In exchange for a stone cabin in the woods, Leonard cooked for the widow, writing and socializing the rest of the time. Patricia went around the world alone as a stewardess on a merchant marine ship.

"But you were married!" I said.

"We thought of ourselves as free spirits. She wanted to have an adventure," he explained.

Patricia returned from her journey, and Leonard left his work as a houseboy. The couple moved into an apartment on Piedmont Avenue in Berkeley. Leonard worked as a waiter, a janitor, and a short-order cook. He drove a 1930 Studebaker Dictator with wooden spokes in the wheels.

Patricia and Leonard created a poetry evening every Friday at their apartment. The "Berkeley Circle" of poets gathered there: Robert Duncan, Jack Spicer, and William Everson, who later became Brother Antoninus. Dwight Macdonald visited from New York City, E.M. Forster from London, and other, lesser known poets and writers gathered there as well. "Our literary gods were Kenneth Patchen—almost unknown now, but who was a really avant-garde poet—and Kenneth Rexroth."

Robert Duncan lived in the Berkeley flatlands in what we would now call a commune, a huge old house with eight or ten other young men, most of them homosexual. It was a run-down Victorian house, considered unfashionable at the time, with wooden siding. In a bay-window alcove was a Salvation Army couch where a friend could collapse for the night. Poet Jack Spicer, my dad recalls, never had any money and looked as if he were actually homeless.

Eudora Welty came through town, a pleasant, homely lady; my father took her to see the Japanese Tea Garden. The poet Josephine Miles was Leonard's mentor; she had an advanced form of arthritis that had immobilized her limbs from the neck down and, it being before the invention of motorized wheel-chairs, she had to be carried from place to place. Later, at her home, my father met Allen Ginsberg, whom he remembers as a slight young man with intense eyes. "Since I did not have sensors about gay people then—the word 'gay' was not yet in use—I never thought of him as gay, but only as this person who had made quite a name for himself."

Leonard sometimes met Ginsberg when Ginsberg was working as a baggage handler at the Greyhound bus station in downtown San Francisco. My father and his friends would go to drink bad coffee with him at the station café. (Years later, my father and the Bay Area poets of his generation would read *Howl* in the City Lights bookstore, before crowds of people, as a protest against the poem having been seized by the police.)

These young people had what my students lack: a time in their youth when they could be without accomplishments or obligations—stateless, in a way, to think and dream. Most of all, they had, as my dad put it, "what many people really need to have to believe that literature can change your life: a community of people who really believed in writing. The ones who came to Patricia and my poetry reading evenings were of two kinds: the authentic dropouts, and people who lived in a peripheral relationship to the university—Duncan and Spicer, for instance.

"Others were enrolled in classes but thought of themselves first as writers. We all bought the package that we had to be poor and unknown, and that was our mark of distinction; we were Bohemians. We were replicating Paris . . . on the Bay. We tried to get published, but we did not talk about publishing. I have no memory of anyone telling you how to mail a manuscript or to whom; no one bought writers' guides or talked about agents or who is up, who's down. We wrote because we were writers and that was what writers did. It was, on the one hand, profoundly idealistic, because there was no question of making money. On the other hand, it was stupid; but I think all young people need a time to have that kind of crazy faith in what they are doing creatively.

"We had a sharp sense that, above all else, we had to see poems in front of us; we had to see text. The poem was the thing. Our relationship to the work was probably a replay of the early Romantic movement in Europe, that insisted it was in poetry that the human spirit was most concentrated."

BECAUSE he was blessed to experience a time when anyone could expect to be an artist if he or she was willing to sleep on someone's couch and do the work, my dad still tends to feel, wherever he is, that he is in a community of artists. He addresses the artist in the store clerk, in the landscaper, and in the flirtatious widow.

I got to see Leonard's faith in this possibility come alive when he met Mr. Christian, the man who had the yellow bulldozer that Joey had loved.

David Christian grew up in Queens, but as a boy, he often visited Columbia County with his father. As an adult, in spite of being one of the few African-Americans in the region, David decided he never wanted to leave. His sense of the land and its potential is deeply rooted. When he first arrived with his coworker Cathy, a retired social worker with a long white ponytail who startles the local farmers by hauling lumber herself, Mr. Christian had the slightly tense air of a creative person who worked as much with his hands and his machines as with his creativity.

After Mr. Christian had been at work for a few hours, we all climbed up the man-made berm that had emerged after Mr. Christian had cleared it of dead wood and thorn canes.

It was exhilarating simply to be able to get into the forest. The berm turned left onto a man-made trail that had been built originally to run alongside the disused nineteenth-century railroad tracks. This path was still overgrown. We picked our way under the vines—"woodbine," explained Cathy—and toward what I wanted to show my dad, Mr. Christian, and Rosa: a place where I believed a meadow lay under the brambles, with a tree that would be perfect for a treehouse.

We hacked our way to the area I was thinking of. The tree was too overgrown to reach. It had a trunk about four feet around, and a heavy, solid bough that reached almost horizontally about six feet up from the ground. The tree had another bough, not quite as heavy but still good, thirty degrees away from the first one. This fork, I thought, could support the base of the treehouse.

"Looks good," said Rosa hesitantly. She was being polite. She could not get within ten feet of the tree to see it clearly, because of the chaos of thorns.

But Mr. Christian was gazing out from the edge of what I thought would be a meadow when the brush was cleared. My father stood beside him and waited patiently. The two men looked out over where the land seemed to slope down.

Mr. Christian started to talk. If this lower-level configuration was really there under the brush, he said, it would make a spectacular vista for the treehouse to overlook. I tried to see what he saw, but the brush obscured everything. It was the result of a generation's worth of neglect, David Christian had said, since the land had been left fallow in about the 1950s. The growth made the contours of the land as indistinct as a painting darkened by smoke.

David Christian kept talking. If you clear the brush and leave those big trees, he said, you will have a vantage point in the foreground and a beautiful view in the background.

I overheard my father reply, "Yes; that would look just like the eighteenth-century ideal of the sublime."

David Christian gave my dad that look people give him when he has surprised them by acknowledging the artist in them. Dad gets that look from people just before they let the artist—often the most vulnerable part of themselves; indeed, often in hiding—speak back.

David Christian and my father started talking about the problem ahead of them, artist to artist. In the tangle of wild grapes, poison oak, thorns, marsh grass, bulrushes, and wild fern, Mr.

Christian pointed out to Leonard the massive trees that were only just visible. Leonard looked carefully. The two men considered Mr. Christian's suggestion that he make a path down from the upper meadow to the one we thought might be under the brush below, and to clear around the trees in the lower acre to create perspective. Under Mr. Christian's eye, with my father deeply, actively listening—a kind of listening that, I realized, I did not yet know how to do—a spectacular vista emerged out of the Jackson Pollock–like mess of thorn and weeds. As David Christian described what his imagination already saw, it was clear that he loved the way wild landscapes behaved when gently shaped by the hand of man. He described how, from the vantage point of the treehouse, you could get depth and perspective by establishing one striking point from which your eye would depart to take in the larger scene. I loved that he believed a seven-year-old should be granted the most compelling perspective from her treehouse. More than that, Leonard and I saw what he could see, and it was remarkable.

Mr. Christian's vision *was* the eighteenth-century ideal of the sublime in painting. The first-century A.D. essayist known as Pseudo-Longinus defined sublimity (from the Greek *hypnos*, with the same root as "hypnotic") as "the echo of greatness of spirit"—the effect of the moral and imaginative power of the writer on his work. The essayist called a work of art sublime if it had the power to provoke ecstasy. The sublime in art derived from "flare-ups of genius that rules alone could not produce."

This departed from the classical view, that technical skill explains the success of a work of art. This essay, ignored for centuries, became influential in England at the end of the eighteenth century. The new fashion for the sublime moved British poets and writers away from the rationalism of Enlightenment classicism and toward the emotional richness of Romanticism. Painters of the sublime, especially in vast landscape paintings, did all they could to provoke feelings of awe in their audiences.

They did it the way David Christian was describing. An eighteenth-century painting in this style will typically show a human figure in the foreground, then use vaster scale, deep perspective, and dramatic light effects to reveal an inspiring natural panorama as the background. The treehouse would be the human reference point in the foreground, and the cleared lower meadow, the standing great trees, and the light dappling through would provide the classic panorama in the background. Mr. Christian was describing planting some turfy grasses on the floor of the foreground meadow; that would be part of his frame.

As the two men stood knee-high in thorns, imagining the buried panorama, it was a David Christian that he and my father were seeing together, and it was as distinctive and stunning as a Turner.

THERE WAS no stopping Mr. Christian's imaginative drive after that. He would come in the rain, bringing with him purple butterfly bushes in deep pots to draw a more pleasing contrast to the unattractive gray siding of the house. He found florists' tubs for the nasturtiums, which he suggested we put under the windows so they could entwine around and soften the raw lines of the side of the house; he carried raspberry canes to set against the garage, which would bear fruit in the second year.

One day he came up the driveway, his overalls caked with mud and his boots covered with dust. He was carrying a crate. He said excitedly, "I found something perfect to put down there—not grass. Grass, no offense—grass is boring. We need something that belongs in the forest. I found something that will spread and grow low down, so you can walk over it, but it is wild; it belongs. The leaves are a beautiful shape. I found"—he gestured with the crate—"the most amazing *myrtle*."

He had an eye not just for the big picture—his major work in the forest—but for more minor illustrations: what the eighteenth-century fashion for the sublime in gardening called "follies," to delight the children. We could drop swings from this tree; we could dump sand by the river and build a four-foot beach; we could hollow out the choked-up stream to make it into a proper pond, and fill it with goldfish. Sand would arrive mysteriously in Joey's sandpit, and additional arcs of clearing in the trees—off-script, like an improvised note—would emerge from week to week.

I laughed and had to tell Mr. Christian that we could not afford his suggestions. I kept trying to ask him to stop, and he kept reassuring me. When the bill finally came, it was clear that he was scarcely charging us for his expenses.

Mr. Christian's yellow bulldozer dug ever deeper into the tangle of the forest, carving out lanes between the trees into which the sun fell in rays, until it looked exactly like an eighteenth-century engraving. He discovered that there was indeed a meadow. To add his signature touch, he cleared around stands of bulrushes, leaving them intact.

I had not expected Mr. Christian to get involved with the treehouse—I thought he would only clear away the land around it. But one day he saw something that took our treehouse to a whole new level.

He glanced down at two wooden pallets that had been sitting, on the lawn, left over from a delivery of slate. They measured about four by five feet each, with two wooden sides that went up about three and a half feet into the air. I had thought they were useless and ugly: there were bare patches between the boards, and they were caked with dirt. They were also enormously heavy. I mentioned to David Christian that I did not know how to get them to the dump.

"They are part of the treehouse," he said with unhestitating confidence. He pointed to the first pallet. "That is the entry area," he said, and, pointing to the second pallet, "that is the sitting room."

I stared at him in admiration. Of course, Mr. Christian was right.

LESSON FIVE

Identify Your Heart's Desire

There is a wonderful fairy tale in which you can't kill a giant without finding the rock underneath which lies his heart. The hero's heart, too, may be under that rock.

IT WAS THE END of June; dragonflies that looked as if they were carved from jade-colored enamel were hovering over the lawn. The maple and ash trees were heavy with soft green leaves. The air was moist. My dad was dressed for the heat as a Midwestern tourist: he was wearing a visor, khaki shorts, and a T-shirt that had found its way into his laundry somehow. It said THE BIG APPLE. He was back to black coffee again.

My dad believes that in order to be a fully realized person, you need to have your heart's desire. He believes, too, that your heart's desire often appears to you first as a symbol. To discover your heart's desire, he feels, you should notice what symbols you are drawing into your life. Those symbols can reveal you to yourself at least as clearly as a psychologist can.

Symbols are sometimes more important than concrete reality. Do you keep tuning your radio to cowboy music? Pay attention: Is there something you need to be free of? Do you keep lingering over herbs in a grocery store? Pay attention. Has something in your life lost its savor?

Was the little house, for instance, real estate or a state of being for me? What did a treehouse mean to Rosa? Simply a place to play, or a place to start becoming the person she was going to be? My father believed that if you could learn to read the symbols in a poem or a story, you could also learn to understand the code of symbols in your life narrative. "The way it works," he said in the red dining room, as he explained how he taught his students to read the symbols in a story or poem, "is that you have to understand the psychological dimensions of the object: the thing made is capable of giving off symbolic meaning.

"In the real world," he continued, "there is nothing that can be regarded as purely objective. All things, everything, can stand for something else. It is at this point that I hold up a pencil and break it. Then I hold up the two sticks and I ask them, 'What do you see?'" My father held up his forefingers as if holding two sticks side by side.

"They all nod and say, 'Two sticks.' Same two sticks . . ." Now my father put one forefinger perpendicular over the other: " 'What do you see?' They say, 'The cross.' I say, 'No, you don't . . . you still see two sticks, but the perpendicular sticks have acquired the meaning of the cross.' Culture does that; history does that.

"Any object in the world can represent something other than itself: an apple can be a fruit off the tree of knowledge or an apple for the teacher. A gear can be the kind of gear that moves machinery, or you can get caught up in the gears, as in the bureaucracy. This lesson, about signs and symbols, tries to move my students to a recognition that language is fraught with meanings—some of them dangerous, some of them glorious; that there is no such thing as a simple word. The language of their life choices is fraught with meaning.

"Finally, I explain the difference between the thing itself, the sign, the symbol, and the allegory it can be part of.

"At any given moment, we can experience things on all four levels: say someone breaks a mirror. First, the mirror is a thing in itself; second, it is a *sign* for a reflection of yourself; third, the mirror can be a *symbol* of, say, egocentricity; and fourth, the broken mirror can be part of an *allegory* about the loss of the self. We instinctively experience life all the time on these four levels.

"Outside our apartment, for instance, the city has planted a tree. If, one day later, a car ran over the tree, we would experience that lost tree on all those levels.

"In all your relationships, every day, a literal exchange is taking place, but so is a symbolic one. This is why so many people are confused about their heart's desire. They are paying attention to literal meaning—say, the size of their paycheck—but ignoring the symbols that are crowding around them: say, the fact that they keep gazing out of the window at birds migrating. Where are those birds migrating to for you? Believe me, you will find your heart's desire there. But you won't be able to identify the direction unless you notice the birds, and notice your own interest in them, as living symbols in your life. You ignore those things at your peril."

When we were growing up, things often happened, as my father had just described, on both a literal and a symbolic plane at the same time. Most people grow up with a sense that the world becomes less luminous and more literal as the days of childhood pass. But for Aaron and me, the childhood sense that we were in the middle of a weird signature dream—that the smudge of sealing wax that Aaron had left on our bedroom windowsill looked like a rampant lion and *meant* something—was never corrected by the adults. For better or worse, it was affirmed. If we thought it meant something, according to our dad—and heartily endorsed by our mother, who had her own attachment to the world of the imagination—it meant something.

I remember the time we celebrated Hanukkah on a sandy beach in which pink clams lived, in Guaymas, Mexico. I was five. "Of course clams are forbidden to Jews, but that doesn't matter," my dad had said placidly as we dug up the clams with sticks. We collected and cooked and ate them, and then we crawled inside the tent and lighted the Hanukkah candles in a hanukiah my mother had made out of twisted tinfoil.

I remember the feeling I had then: that this was real life, but it was also a story with magical aspects, because we were agreeing to be enchanted together, and to notice our enchantment, and to eat things we had dug up with our own hands, as a family.

The night grew dark, and the warm wind whipped up. What we were eating was probably disgusting to a child's palate (come to think of it, it may have been disgusting to the adults, too; more weird food from our family album) but the adventure, the fact that we had done it together, wedged those clams from their holes like the Swiss Family Robinson, and that my parents were there with us, willing to make a feast out of these clams on Hanukkah—made it delicious. I ran outside as dusk fell, and the light from the candles glowed through the tent. A feast of hand-dug clams on Hanukkah? It stayed with me as a symbol of what I loved about our family.

"If you can understand the myth you want to make out of your own life," explained Leonard, "you can identify your heart's desire."

LEONARD has always worn his own personal mythologies on his sleeves; he has a complex wardrobe. Once in a while, when I was a child, someone would make the mistake of asking, "Leonard, you spend all day at a desk. Why do you need another red flannel Basque shepherd's shirt?"

My father would draw himself up to his full height, look slightly insulted, and start to quote from *Lear*. "'Reason not the need,'" he would declare firmly. "You've read *Lear*," he would say to his interlocutor, in the same tone of voice someone might say, "You've met Jim"—as if King Lear were in the next room, taking off his coat. The questioner would become uncomfortably aware of not having read Lear recently enough.

"You know how his daughters and their husbands chide him when he is no longer the king but has still kept his retinue?" my father would ask. "And they ask him why he still needs the retinue, since he is no longer on the throne? And he gives that speech urging his daughter to reason not the need. He is still a king in his own eyes. That matters."

"Reason not the need," Leonard taught us, all of our lives. In Betty Smith's classic, *A Tree Grows in Brooklyn*, the mother of Francie, the young girl at the center of the story, encourages her daughter to pour the expensive leftover coffee into the sink instead of saving it to be reheated later. The impoverished mother reasons that if there wasn't something the family could afford to waste, they would not only *be* poor, but, far worse, they would *feel* poor.

My family had very little money when we were growing up, and a lot of financial worries. Nonetheless, my dad was always encouraging us to do the equivalent of pouring the perfectly good coffee down the drain. It was when the bills were pressing and we could not be sure of making it through the month that at least one grand gesture was necessary, if only to keep our spirits up. His hierarchy of needs was not the same as that of other parents. All families have rules: you can't buy a luxury item, for instance, unless all the basics have been accounted for. Or: save the pence, and the pounds will take care of themselves. Or: the Johnsons never raise their voices in an argument.

We had rules, too, they were just weird ones. If you saw something your heart went out to—no matter how broke we were, or rather, *especially* if we were broke—*you had to buy it.* It's not that, if your heart went out to it, you *could* buy it; you *had* to. You had to the way, in other families, you had to finish the chicken on your plate before you could have dessert.

All families send unspoken messages about what a genuine misdemeanor is: waste, or laziness, or unkindness. This insistence that we had to honor our innermost inclination—and the phrase was always "If your heart goes out to it"—sent the clear message that it was actually naughty to disregard what Yeats calls "the deep heart's core." I discovered only when I was older that this insistence is exactly what many children are strongly cautioned against.

Yet children get it; they know there is such a thing as one's heart's desire—that is why they howl with real grief for some things denied them and not others, and it is more likely, at first, to be to take home a sand-crusted stone from the beach with a particular jagged stripe rather than to have the biggest toy on the block. Children know that if you listen, especially when you are young and have not been told for years *not* to listen, your heart does speak to you. Contrary to conventional wisdom, my dad believes, it is not usually crazy or dangerous to let a child follow the heart's true impulses. His view is that these impulses are usually sensible and wise. One's impulses become crazy or dangerous later, only as overcompensation, if the heart's desire in childhood has been spurned again and again.

But if you are firmly instructed to listen to what your heart goes out to, it turns out that your longing won't necessarily go out to what is in TV ads. If you are an adult listening to your heart's desire, you will surprise yourself, too; it may not be vacations, jewels, or cars that you yearn for, but things unique to your own creative vision.

That is how, in our family, we acquired some strange objects. When we were really and truly broke, when I was eight, we bought a costly hand-turned ice-cream freezer from Sears that we used once. My heart had conceived the idea that our family had to make its own ice cream. No one pointed out that we could buy ice cream more easily and with less expense. No one warned me that I would tire of turning the hand crank, and then what? We'd be stuck with the thing.

When I brought up my wish, my parents asked me only one question. "Does your heart go out to it?" They asked with the same careful adult attention that grown-ups, before a long car trip, give to the question—because only the child can answer accurately—"Do you have to go to the bathroom?"

We bought the cumbersome bag of kosher salt and the bag of crushed ice. We poured cream and sugar in the dark, sleek well in the center of the machine. We layered the crushed ice, the salt, the crushed ice. We turned the damn crank. We took turns. We had one irksome, blissful experience of making ice cream.

It was tiring and boring, but it was also fascinating and magical: the ice, the salt, the layering, the turning, the tedium, the four of us, two adults and two children, working together, not speaking much, the slow alchemization of cream and crystals and sugar into ice cream.

I never wanted to do it again, of course. But that was all right. The set—which we could not afford in the first place— was put away forever, and no one mentioned it again. It sat above the refrigerator, gathering dust, for the next ten years. I was not scolded for having wasted money on a costly toy, or berated into using it again against my will.

Same thing with Aaron's twenty-four-hour venture into ice hockey. A weedy Jewish kid with braces who was not yet the popular teenager he would become, at twelve he longed to be tough and fast and part of a team. He wanted to play ice hockey. The same process on the part of our parents—the question about true longing and then the purchase of the entire array of equipment—led to Aaron getting fully fitted out in a way that turned the thin, dreamy *Spider-Man*-reading kid into an apparently husky young Quebecois out to club a baby seal for sport: shoulder pads, elbow pads, knee pads, helmet, breeches, heavy curved stick, and murderously sharp skates.

Aaron went out on the ice with a team just once, long enough to enter fully into his dream world—and to find out for himself that that zooming thug with a stick was not who he really was. He was more Spidey than the Incredible Hulk. The whole kit came off, never to be worn again. Our parents undertook the installment payments without complaint, understanding that it was worth every penny for Aaron to know at that stage of his life that he could, *if he chose to,* just about kill someone, in a manly way, on the ice—if that was who he really wanted to be. It was worth, indeed, twice what they had paid for the hockey getup for Aaron to know that his basic gentleness would be a choice made out of strength and not an accommodation.

It was understood by the grown-ups that the longing and the fulfillment of that impulse toward magic—not the ice cream but the ice-cream *magic,* the hockey-player *magic*—was the point of the purchase. You may not have to summon the magic twice. If the heart's desire was fulfilled by one experience, so be it. The point was not to amortize the item over time and adequately use an expensive investment in a child's whim. We had done it: my heart's desire, Aaron's heart's desire—both of which were symbolic—were fulfilled.

So, too, with my dad's collection of astrolabes. It would have been *correct* to say that we did not need a medieval astrolabe, we needed a washing machine—but would it have been *right?* My dad taught us that it was better to be slightly grimy than to give up the notion that you might have, at any moment, a need to navigate a vessel by the stars.

My parents' hearts' desire? One day it was two plums. They often tell the story of how, when they were completely out of money in France, they took a bus with their next-to-last change to the market at Monte Carlo. There they bought all they could afford: two perfect green plums from a fruit stall. They enjoyed the plums slowly, leaning against a wall, looking out at the sparkling ocean. It was a feast.

From my father, I got the idea that wealth was not a specific figure or a set of luxury items. That wealth was the ability to buy two ripe plums and enjoy them so fully that the memory of how good they were could last you forty years.

*   *   *

THE LATE-JUNE sun had begun to beat strongly down on the garden by the middle of the day. We had killed several species of annuals, but the lantana were surviving well and actually spreading. We had a visit from my friend Teresa and her daughter Clara, who came every summer from London.

Teresa is a research scientist. She is earthy, broad-shouldered, witty, and freckled, with a milkmaid complexion and copper hair that flies all over her head in luscious curls. Her eyes are almond-shaped, hazel, and always laughing. Her hands and feet are shapely.

After her divorce of three or four years before, her lovely shoulders had slumped a bit; she had not yet returned to her former proud posture. She was at that time someone who seemed to be waiting for permission from herself to identify and unearth her heart's desire. Right now duty seemed to be directing her.

Teresa had the figure of a 1950s European movie star; she was an attractive, voluptuous woman with a sensuous curl to her smile. But now her body language was saying something slightly different.

I had met Teresa about four years before, when Rosa was in preschool and when Teresa and her then-husband were in the U.S. on parallel research fellowships. Teresa and I used to sneak off to the California Pizza Kitchen after dropping off our daughters and confide in each other about how noxious the whole preschool-mom set of expectations was. We also enjoyed comparing notes about the U.K. versus the U.S. since we loved and hated similar things about both countries.

"McVitie's biscuits! Marmite! Devon cream!" I would reminisce.

"Fried Mars bars . . . kebab vans on a Saturday night . . . curry . . ." she replied longingly.

"Reading the papers on Sunday morning by the fire . . . *The Guardian* . . . there's nothing like it here . . ."

"BBC World News. On the other hand, the minute you open your mouth, you're pegged into a class system . . . But when I'm over here, I miss being around people that you can't shock."

"Hmmm . . ."

"On the other hand, when I'm over there, I miss Target. And the UK has the Gap now but it costs twice as much," she said.

"When I'm over there, I miss accurate newspaper reporting."

"Cheap petrol," said Teresa.

"Chunky peanut butter," I said.

"Chocolate-chip cookies," she said. "And men with straight teeth."

"Hey, how about representative democracy?"

"Right, so important," she laughed. "How about those men with straight teeth?"

And so on.

As we caught up with each other in the yellow parlor, I felt that Teresa's emotional life had been put on the back burner. She seemed to me very profoundly focused on her work and her child; I felt that other parts of her were, for the moment, dormant.

The first day of our visit, Rosa and Clara gleefully pounded nails onto the pallets that would be the base of the treehouse. Their faces flushed with exertion.

Rosa is dark-haired and pale and ironic, and Clara is golden-haired and golden-skinned and a bit fiendish, like a slightly demonic cherub. With their subversive communications as they tried to evade the scrutiny of the moms, and in their striped sweatshirts, they had the expressions that day of two miniature partisans who had penetrated Vichy lines and were passing intelligence back and forth.

We had taken them out to the clearing where we hoped to put the treehouse, and where David Christian had been planting his myrtle. ("Look at this, Naomi! You can move the wild ferns from the marshland and arrange them under the treehouse. You can save the bulrushes! Look at how this ground cover blooms, it will look like a carpet.")

With my father's help, Teresa and I showed Rosa and Clara how to saw the pine two-by-fours into four-foot-long crossbars. We positioned the crossbars against the trunk of the big old gnarled tree for the two sides of a ladder. We taught each girl to hold a twopenny nail with one hand without flinching while the other girl hammered it in. The nails went in finally, though each one was a bit askew. With enough banging, we managed, by the end of the day, to put three boards horizontally against the two crossbars on the tree trunk. It leaned and buckled, but it held.

By dusk, the girls were able to climb up the ladder to the bough of the tree. They shimmied out onto the edge of the bough; they dangled their sturdy legs off the branch and looked into the leaves.

Teresa and I stood down on the matting of David Christian's myrtle, now growing up from the once-raw earth. We watched our daughters' silhouettes darken in the tree against the streaming light from the sun that was sinking behind the mountain. We were proud of the girls, but we were quiet together, down below.

Teresa and I understood that our children, no longer so
small, had forgotten us for a moment in the leaves, and in the
pleasure of their own independence. We felt the rush of the
evening's wind against us, thinking as we were about this first
time that we scarcely mattered, which would, no doubt, be only
the first of many; and about how our girls had managed to
make a ladder for themselves that would carry them, but that
we, their mothers, were already too big to climb.

ROSA AND CLARA continued to be preoccupied with working
on the treehouse. Now that the ladder was done, they could
not wait to finish the pallets and have Mr. Christian lift the
platform up into the tree, where we assumed they would connect with the ladder. The girls wanted to decorate them.

Teresa and I explained that it made better sense to complete the nailing of the slats before we decorated them, but
their hearts' desire was to decorate as they were building, so
they begged us to take them to the big Herrington's in Hillsdale. Once there, while Teresa and I looked at wood glue and
hammers and circular saws, the girls disappeared on a quest of
their own.

After almost forty-five minutes, we tried to track down the
children and see what had so engrossed them. We found them
seated in a corner, counting piles of seed packets like traders
adding up change in a bazaar after a long day.

"Look," said Clara, in her English accent—half Carnaby
Street and half Balliol College—gesturing at a pile of items, "oh,
Mummy, Mummy, please, please. The treehouse *needs* these."

Teresa and I thought we knew the components of a treehouse, but we had no idea. What was Clara's treehouse made

of? When Clara was three, she loved to twirl around in a white gauze fairy gown, bearing a sword and looking like a fierce escapee from a production of *A Midsummer Night's Dream*. Her heart's desire, when I had first known her then, had involved sequins and drama and dragon scales. Now eight, Clara had collected in the hardware store a cache of similar kinds of treasures: she held out to us a set of foot-long wind chimes, and stood up on the tips of her sneakered toes to give them room to sway. They emitted a low tone, like a harp underwater. In her other hand she held up, like an oversize lollipop, an eight-inch piece of straight wire to which was attached a round red circle of reflecting plastic. This was a device meant to be staked in the ground beside a mailbox, to reflect oncoming car lights.

Clara held the red plastic circle up to the fluorescent lights in the ceiling of Herrington's. The grid sparkled, the light moving in a checkerboard pattern across the circle in a magical way, like the scale of a red dragon.

"Please, Mummy . . . please, Naomi," Clara begged. Teresa and I looked at each other and laughed.

What did Rosa's treehouse look like? She was a different child from her friend. Rosa's heart's desire had always involved rope swings and dogs and jungles. When she was three, she turned over rocks to stare at slugs, and liked bugs and rocks. Now she had chosen a piece of plastic-coated copper tubing that, she insisted, could be used to make a rope swing like the one she had seen in *Tarzan*, that could let you swoop from tree to tree. She also held up a U-shaped bolt that she thought could be used to make a pulley to attach to the rope. She showed Teresa and me some seeds—blue morning glories and green-and-yellow-skinned watermelon. She would like to train the morning glories up to and around the treehouse, for shade and decoration, and to plant the watermelon on the ground below, so she could hoist one up with a pulley whenever she was hungry.

We bought some of the necessities—chimes, seeds, and re-flector—and said no to the others.

On the ride home, the girls fanned out an array of paint chips. They separated out the essential colors from the nonessentials. Yellowtail, Claret, Morning Mauve, Sunday Toast, Taupe, Sailor Serge, and Amethyst hit the floor. Left in Rosa's lap after the editing process were: Olive Drab, Easter Bonnet, Ice Blue, Magenta, and Duckwing Teal. Left in Clara's lap were: Butterscotch, Candyland, Grosgrain Pink, Rose Red, and Violet Ever After. In each girl's pile were the colors she had to have to complete her own vision of her treehouse.

The girls were no different from the adults. Each of us had a heap of colors, of symbols, in our laps. What did we each really need? I wondered as I lay in the yellow room after the children were finally asleep, and looked out over the tops of the trees to the darkening mountain.

We all longed for something different to symbolize our hearts' desires. I thought of Sophia, whom I had recently seen in the city, and who was looking different every day. As she began to face the end of one love, a kind of self-love was strengthening in her.

Her hair used to be expensively groomed, blow-dried regu-larly into smooth corporate tresses. Now it was wild. She used to wear heels all the time; now she slipped into sandals or ballet flats immediately after work. Sophia used to get a manicure every week, a deep plum-brown, a sophisticated look; her nails were uncolored now. She slicked them herself with clear var-nish. The heavy, huge diamond on her left hand, the family heirloom, looked increasingly like it belonged to someone else.

She was not saying any of this to Malcolm with her words, but she was saying it with her appearance; the symbols of her heart's desire were all around her. She needed Malcolm to let her just be happy.

Teresa . . . what did she need? I could not tell. Perhaps, I thought, the time wasn't right yet for her to know. But I was sure that her intense focus on work and mothering could not provide everything she needed.

Clara and Rosa needed room to be different: each needed to be able to see a dragon's lair or a jungle platform, and each needed to grow without being forced into someone else's vision.

You should treat every loved one every day as if he or she will die the following day, my father always said. I knew that I really needed to learn my father's craft now, this summer, while he was here; not someday. I needed to let him—and all my loved ones—know what they meant to me while there was still daylight.

Leonard had said, "Notice the symbols in your life." Here I was at forty, heavily scheduled to talk abstractly in various venues, but completely preoccupied with constructing a child's treehouse. What was that about? I should, I realized, take my dad's advice for myself and be curious: why a treehouse—why now?

The treehouse—and Dad's lessons—were about everything I was not doing in my life. They were about everything I needed to learn.

I had to face the fact that there was not one more thing I could learn in my life from one more plane trip, one more opinion piece, one more argument. My focus on talking at the expense of listening—my well-rewarded *rightness*—had, if not hurt, certainly shortchanged my loved ones.

If I was going to grow, I would have to stretch a part of myself that would continue to ache: a part that was new to me, that I was unskilled with, in order to become a teacher, not to mention a better wife and mother; the part that listened and took things in; the intuitive part—the soul part. The change in my life was going to hurt; there was no way it wouldn't. That's why I was so scared.

"Two roads diverged in a yellow wood . . ." I thought of the Frost poem. Which road? One was easy and smooth, but it was taking me in the wrong direction. One was full of difficulty and uncertainty, but it might take me, in every way, home.

I couldn't hold a hammer well. Why did I so want to hold a hammer? Because I was so bad at it; carpentry forced me to be an honest learner again. I, who had resisted for so long—*on principle!*—sitting at anybody's feet would have to sit down, a student, and pay attention—*which I hated*—if I was going to help those who depended on me.

I had to feel my least comfortable feeling, humility, now, if I was going to learn anything; to learn from Chris about drills, or from Dave about ground cover, or from my father, after rejecting his authority so well, for so long, about poetry—and about how to help the young people who came to me to believe in their own light.

If I was going to grow up now, in this way, it would be like slowing a comfortable, speeding car on a highway, in which the temperature is so neutral you don't feel much anymore, and pulling over and stopping; taking off warmly lined boots; and stepping out barefoot onto ice that may or may not hold you up.

Do Nothing Without Passion

Western wind, when wilt thou blow,
That the small rain down can rain?
Christ, that my love were in my arms
And I in my bed again!

This anonymous quatrain has lasted for five hundred years.
If you don't feel that feeling about where you are in your
life—change your life.

DAD LEANED BACK in a rattan armchair on the sunporch. It was the middle of June; a warm wind was blowing. The pond had filled up with silt and water plants, so that only a trickle of water fell into the stream. The impatiens had proliferated, though the lamb's tongues had died. The air was thick with mosquitoes.

Sophia was at the house again, too. She was sitting in a rose-colored T-shirt on the sunporch, reading *Manon Lescaut*—a novel about obsessive love—at my father's insistence and, at the same time, half-listening to our conversation.

It was the height of berry season, and there was a fully

stocked supermarket in Hillsdale. But Dad thought that since we were roughing it in the country, we should never be without dried provisions, so we were eating the dates and dried figs that he had packed to bring up for us. He often told the story of how, when he was living alone in a hut in the woods after his divorce, and he had run out of canned goods, he had killed, cooked, and eaten a rattlesnake. I was relieved it was only dried fruit that he had brought us.

To give me notes for the sixth lesson, Leonard was dressed from the waist up like an urban 1950s hipster, wearing a fine charcoal T-shirt that my mother had given him. From the waist down, he was 1980s rapper; low-slung jeans from a discount store, and huge sneakers with Velcro straps that he had acquired from a street vendor's bin on the sidewalk. "These are the most comfortable shoes I have ever worn," he said proudly.

"Nice. And you look so fit!" I complimented him.

"That's because I got a haircut," he explained.

He had brought us a house gift: a homemade woodburning set for etching designs into scraps of lumber. If our kids played with it, it would mean teaching them to heat a sharp tool and then dig it into the wood till everything smoked. When I was five or so, he had let me use a white-hot icepick for this purpose. My parents' apartment in New York was still littered with scraps of wood into which he had engraved small animals, cartoon characters, and tiny icons; family and friends would receive them as presents. I decided not to bring up any problems with the white-hot tool I envisioned in our three-year-old's hands—I would just pray inwardly.

"In Lesson Six," said my father, shuffling his papers, "I talk to my students about passion. I read to them from Chaucer's *Troilus and Criseyde*. Chaucer writes, about Criseyde, 'Men

seyn—I not—that she yaf hym hire herte.' Chaucer is letting
you feel the shadow of doubt there. Pay attention. If you feel
that shadow of doubt in whatever you are doing, it is an important sign you are in the wrong place. Never ignore it.

"Criseyde has been held prisoner in Troy and fallen in love
with Troilus. Her father arranges to give up Trojan prisoners of
war in exchange for Criseyde. But Chaucer writes that, after the
exchange has taken place,

> . . . God it wot, er fully monthes two
> She was ful fer fro that entencioun [to return to Troilus];
> For bothe Troilus and Troie toun
> Shal knotteles throughout hir herte slide
> For she wol take a purpos for t'abyde.

"After the lovers are separated, you see, and only two
months have passed, in spite of her intention to remain true to
Troilus and return to Troy, Criseyde begins to lose her attachment to her lover. She begins to find Diomede, a Greek warrior,
interesting. Troilus and Troy town," Leonard said excitedly, in
that urgent tone of voice he uses when he wants you to really
notice something, "slid, Chaucer writes, *knotteles* through her
heart . . . Pay attention to that: it says everything about how you
can tell whom you should marry."

Sophia looked up from her book and stared at my father.
"Why?" I asked.

"Well, he slid *knotteles*. Chaucer is saying that after a while,
Criseyde felt no pain at the absence of Troilus. If a string with
knots was pulled through a heart, it would hurt! No knots, no
pain. You marry someone if you literally cannot live without

them; if they have made knots in your heart that cannot ever be released, by time, by distance. About marriage, it means, in plain words: if there is no passion, forget it.

"The knots: if there is no passion about your love—or your work—you have to face the fact that you are in the wrong place.

"Rilke gave famous advice to the young person who asked, 'How do I know if I am a poet?' He said: 'What would happen if you were not permitted to write? If your answer is "I would die"—then you *might* be a poet.' The interior dynamic about either love or work is that you need to see passion not as some hoped-for but dispensable luxury, but as the main thing."

No matter how much money your job pays, Leonard explained, if it does not fire you up, you should leave immediately. No matter how impractical or obscure another life task may be, if you become passionate when you think about it and talk about it—well, you had better change your priorities so that your life energies go in that direction.

Leonard does not think passion is inert. It is not enough to feel the spark; it is your responsibility to tend it as well. The care and maintenance of your passion—in love, in work—should be, he feels, your highest priority.

The conventional wisdom is that marriage erodes passion. My father would say that is a choice, and a foolish one. When we were growing up, Leonard and my mother made an ongoing demonstration out of absurdly, dramatically romantic love. My parents have been flagrantly—irritably or peacefully—in love for decades. It is not that mellow, comfortable, mature love that we are told is the best we can hope for in marriage if all goes well.

Their marriage is far—very, very far—from perfect. Both say there have been disastrous times. My father comes from the generation of roués, scoundrels, and womanizers. But their relationship is now like a four-decade-long third date: the two are alert to each other; their feelings are fresh. They are still courting; they can still be hurt by each other. They still storm off and still make up as if for the first time. They are still trying to please each other, they dress for each other, they try to make each other laugh, and they give each other room for separate journeys. My mother will start laughing uncontrollably in a phone conversation with me while watching my father wander around the apartment to find a place to put a statue of a horse's head. My father will ask my mom to dance as if there were still a possibility that she might turn him down.

As I was growing up, I would observe my dad giving my mother this leaven of romance, this daily *noticing* of her as a woman.

"Isn't she gorgeous?" he would say, interrupting himself in the midst of a sentence to a group, as if simply swept away by her loveliness. "Isn't your mother *cute*?" he would say to us kids, looking at her admiringly—at thirty, at forty; it was never going to end. Leonard always said, about romantic love, paraphrasing Rilke again, that it is the greatest risk, but the risk most worth taking.

I watch my dad, still hopelessly besotted with my mother today. In spite of his many imperfections, Leonard taught us that this kind of besottedness over a long lifespan is not just possible; it is necessary. If you start with the spark, you can choose to tend it.

It used to embarrass me. Now I admire the secret he knows.

My dad has been pursuing the permanent courtship of my mother since they met. To Leonard, marriage is not the end of courtship or a time to drop the strategy; every day of married life is a chance to pursue the girl afresh.

Freud asked, "What do women want?" I think Leonard has figured it out. Women, perhaps, want their marriages not to terminate their status as the prize, but to consecrate it as a continual beginning. To be courted and won and courted anew, again and again.

To do this persuasively, you need to use your imagination; to see not only the object of your desire in a romantic light, but yourself as well. You must view yourself as a romantic lead and follow through, but every single day. Quixote needs his Dulcinea. But as soon as Quixote takes Dulcinea for granted, she will no longer be Dulcinea. Men, dad believes, do well to remember that the minute Dulcinea is just a middle-aged housewife, Quixote is no longer Quixote.

It goes the other way, too, of course. Just as the grown-ups believed in the children's weird feasts and journeys, so my mother is willing always to believe anew in my father's status as a troubadour in corduroy, or in Velcroed tennis shoes. He courts her every day, and she admires him every day; it may be old-fashioned, but it works. I tease my mother by referring to her "geisha etiquette"; but because of my mother's geisha etiquette, I am viscerally horrified when a wife disparages a husband in any way. Don't do that! I think instinctively. His armor will vanish!

Leonard, after his years of womanizing, had discovered an alchemy about passion in marriage. Like the Buddhist notion that cultivating kindness makes you kind, it seems as if cultivating passion makes people feel passionately. His example has suggested to me that words between lovers, especially married lovers, have magical power over time, to help or hurt passion. My father decided that my mother was going to be eternally beautiful, and he told her so, so my mother somehow grew older in this way.

Leonard also refrains from scolding her. In our house, there was a rule that you were not allowed to guilt-provoke. "You know the wonderful koan from the *I Ching*?" he explained. "All it says is: 'No blame.' Do you want to know the secret for a happy marriage, honey? 'I would rather be happy than right.' If someone spills something, the only admissible reply is: 'Where's the mop?'"

My friend Rhonda jokes that she and her new husband heard my father say this once. Now, whenever they start to get into an argument about who is to blame for something, one of them will say: "Where's the mop?" They will both start laughing and drop the blame in favor of solving the problem.

Because of all this, my mom forgives a *lot*. She discovered, for example, that my father has a son, conceived before my parents met, whom he had never told her—or us—about. She discovered this when my half brother, Julius, contacted us, and after her initial disbelief, she took my father's son as being a natural part of our family. I did not understand how she could be so calm about his having kept this a secret from her for so long, but I think that because Leonard gives her so much adoration, she gives him a lot of room to be flawed; even very flawed.

My mother's relative serenity in the face of Leonard's very real and even dramatic imperfections has, I think, to do with the power of the verses he leaves for her around the house.

My eighty-year-old dad still leaves poems about my mother, who is no longer eighteen, on the refrigerator, on her desk by the computer, and on the front door when she comes home from a trip.

Posted on their refrigerator is the usual list of mundane tasks that comprise married life: "Call about the wiring. Recycling Thursday. Buy orange juice." Next to the list, my father has written, in black marker, for my mother, an echo of William Carlos Williams:

> *How sweet it was*
> *To find your little shoes*
> *Beside my bed*
> *When I awoke*
> *This morning.*

That is why my mom, when she was an undergraduate at Berkeley, abruptly broke off her engagement to a respectable Jewish doctor who had been teaching her to fly his airplane. "He was presentable, but I knew something was missing," my mother told me.

The doctor had invited her to go to a wedding reception in San Francisco. She went, she said, so she could get a good meal. Everyone there would be older. She dressed in her fancy clothes—including a girdle—and put on a hat with a big brim and tottering spike-heeled shoes. "This being Berkeley," she recounted, "I had not worn heels for a year, and, out of nervousness, I just kept sipping champagne. I am sure I was a little unsteady on my feet.

"A woman asked me if I'd like to meet Leonard. He was across the room and looked handsome and haunted—he still does. He was also older. I knew from one glance that I couldn't handle him, so I declined.

"Later, I tried to walk across the floor. I caught my heel on the tassel of a rug and started to fall. Just before I hit the ground, Leonard turned away from the group he was talking to, caught me, and put me on my feet. Then he returned to his conversation."

"He told me later that, as he picked me up and our eyes met, he knew he would marry me."

My mother, for her part, knew she wanted to be with him forever on the day they drove back from a trip and she sang, off-key, the whole way, and Leonard loved her singing.

A month later, Leonard gave Deborah a Prothalamion—an engagement poem, like Spenser's. (When they were married, he gave her an Epithalamion—a wedding poem, like Spenser's.) In February, when she was already pregnant with Aaron, Leonard asked Irving Goleman, Deborah's father, for her hand in marriage.

Sophia listened to my father describe his feelings for my mother with a sorrowful expression.

"How do I know if I want something I am being overly romantic to wish for?" she asked Leonard, and put down her book. "I have a nostalgia for something—for a feeling—that I don't have in this relationship . . . even though I have never had it before, either."

"Life," my father said to Sophia, "is full of nostalgia for an experience we have never had. Just because you don't know whom you are missing doesn't mean you are not missing him. My guess is that it is passionate attachment itself you are feeling nostalgic for."

His remark made me think with concern about my students. They come to love relationships with a checklist of attributes that a partner should have, or else they set themselves a "sensible" mission to "settle" for a realistic arrangement. Many of my students have received the message that passion is misleading or fleeting, and that marriage outlives it. No one tells them that these are some of the most destructive approaches to love.

Leonard expanded on his theme, his face growing brighter. "I'll be sitting in Jerry's coffee shop. I look up, and a beautiful woman is coming toward me—and it turns out to be Deborah! I feel this extraordinary rush of delight.

"Now, that doesn't happen every minute of every day. What I would suggest to you, dear, is that it has to happen sometimes, to remind you that you are linked to this person in this profound way—if you are. Otherwise, if it never happens, even if you have a 'good relationship,' you can't be truly happy.

"Dear Abby says to ask yourself, 'Are you better off with this person or without?' That is *not* the question to ask; don't aim so low. Rather, whatever your struggles together are, if you close your eyes and ask yourself, 'What if I never saw X again?' and you know something terrible would happen, then you know that bond is there."

Sophia wanted a family. She wanted the stability of marriage, as a woman who wants a family often does. She also wanted a marriage in which she could feel deeply at home. Malcolm was not keeping the spark with Sophia alive, and it was dying. Sophia feared to acknowledge even to herself that it could already be dead. Malcolm, needless to say, met most of the items on a checklist; he was a "catch." It was only the passionate connection that Sophia needed some sense of, to touch—if only just a little bit—in order to stay.

"How do you know," she asked my father, "when to leave? How do you know if you are supposed to stay?"

"Well," my father said thoughtfully—questions such as these never surprise him or make him uncomfortable, since he thinks it's quite normal to think about either love or art pretty much all of the time—"how do you feel about him now, dear?"

"How do I feel . . ." she murmured.

My father settled more deeply into the couch and adjusted his legs. One did not rush a conversation about the heart; besides, talking with a beautiful young woman in distress, whom he might be able to help, was one of his favorite activities.

"I feel . . . I have cared about him for a long time. I feel responsible for him. If I am being completely honest, I also want all the things that go with being married. I am scared to end something so secure. He gives me this complete life full of everything I think I want . . . just about. He is so smart; we have wonderful talks a lot of the time. We share so many values. I love his family. I want it to work."

"You told me all the reasons you want to make it work, and they are all perfectly understandable. But how does he make you, Sophia, feel?"

"I don't know . . ." she said, staring out at the trees. "I don't know."

"This is all very subjective," Leonard said slowly. "But for what it's worth, I have discovered that without passion, whatever else is right or wrong about the relationship, there is no point in forcing it. You can work on what you need to work on if there is passion—and I don't mean reductively sexual passion. I mean a passionate recognition; a spark. Do you love him?"

"I . . . love him," said Sophia uneasily, not meeting my father's gaze.

Long after she had left Malcolm, she told me that when my father asked her that question in that way, she realized in a flash that she did not love Malcolm in the right way. But since she was not yet able to leave him, she did not want to tell my father, or herself, the truth.

Nonetheless, she confessed later, it was a turning point.

*   *   *

SOPHIA brought Malcolm up before Christmas. She wanted to show him the house, and she wanted to try to share with him some of the magic she felt there. She thought she could take him away from the city—from his work and his anxieties—and bring him close to the river and renew the relationship. Maybe even begin to plan the family.

But Sophia had been changing and growing. Malcolm was not completely happy about it.

It was about eight weeks after her last discussion with my father. She had worked on the marriage with steely discipline. The couple had managed to go together to counseling; when the therapist suggested that there were things Malcolm was reluctant to look at in himself, he refused to go again. Sane people didn't do therapy in his world.

Sophia's eyes looked more and more haunted. Some days she forgot to eat. But she was loving and gentle with Malcolm. As her friend, I struggled with what I was seeing. She told me she wished she had never asked my father about passion. The conversation was not helping her. It was agitating her.

Malcolm and Sophia arrived on a Saturday morning. I tried to make both of them comfortable. But the house, which had embraced Sophia, seemed almost alchemically to resist Malcolm. He shifted from couch to chair in the sitting room and unconsciously brushed dust off of a side table when he put down his tea.

THAT SUNDAY we went for a drive up the mountain road to a diner on Route 22, at the base of the Berkshire foothills. It was an old truck stop, unchanged from the early 1970s. Its wallpaper was smoke-tarnished silver, and the countertops were made of silver Formica. It was a meeting place for truckers driving produce through the mountains, for dairy and corn farmers, for homemakers with toddlers coming out for a snack, and for men looking for gossip about work, now that the paper mill in nearby Ancram had cut back on jobs.

I knew our waitress. She was an efficient single mother, petite and pretty, with carefully set yellow-blond hair. She came to our table and gave us a warm smile. "What would you all like to drink?" she asked.

Sophia smiled back. "May I have coffee, please?" she replied. I asked for coffee as well, and started to look at the breakfast menu. As Malcolm studied the menu, Sophia gazed hopefully out the window. I knew what she was thinking: it was going to be okay. She was looking at the green flank of the mountain, happy to be here with her friends and her man, about to enjoy toast with butter in a warm diner.

"Do you have cappuccino?" Malcolm asked.

"No," the waitress replied. "Sorry, we do not."

"I can't believe," Malcolm said, looking away from the waitress as if she were not standing there, "that I am going to have to try to wake up in a place where you can't get a decent cappuccino for miles."

I knew the look I would see on Sophia's face, and I could guess the look I would see on the waitress's face. So I stared into my empty coffee cup and I did not look up.

AFTER THAT, Sophia came up alone to help me paint a room in the little house; we had given up on finishing the downstairs by ourselves, but we thought we could manage to finish one or two of the small bedrooms. We wanted the second floor to glow like a jewel box.

We painted the smallest of the bedrooms together. Sophia still believed that her marriage was going to work, and that she could have a baby with her husband. She needed and tried to believe that. But of all the rooms we could have chosen to paint first, Sophia suggested we start with the only bedroom small enough for just a single person.

We chose a subtle lilac. As we painted, she sometimes wept. Sometimes she talked to me while she painted; sometimes she took breaks to go on walks with my father down the country lane outside, gathering blackberries for Joey and Rosa.

While we worked, the swish of the paintbrushes calmed us; it seemed to help her draw to the surface the agonizing emotions she needed to look at. The house, in its slow transformation, also seemed to help her: the lilac bedroom, when we were done with it, eventually became her bedroom whenever she came up.

After we finished painting, we dragged in a small Edwardian dresser with a mottled oval mirror, perfect for a thoughtful young lady. A full-size Victorian bedstead, with an oak headboard carved into simulated bamboo, had come with the house. We covered the ugly plywood frame and the foam mattress with pale blue cotton sheets, and spread out a white quilt printed with lilac flowers. We placed a low table for books under the window, and hung lilac cheesecloth curtains. We unrolled a rug that looked from a distance like needlepoint, lilac flowers on a black ground. We set a lamp by the bed and painted its white paper shade with a lilac pattern. Finally, we hung postcards of lilac- or lavender-colored flowers that we had placed in dime-store frames that we had painted silver. A Victorian slipper chair had also come with the house, and we put a lamp behind it. If you sat in it, you could read and look up from your book out to the mountain.

When we were done, Sophia had become so attached to the room that I had to intervene when Rosa asked if she could sleep there, because I knew how Sophia felt about it.

As her marriage unraveled, Sophia would come back to talk to my father and spend time in the lilac room. She would talk to me, too, on the bed late into the night, sleep heavily, and feel more solid in the morning. When she went back to the city, she would feel, not better, but stronger.

But when she went back to her marriage, the conversations with Leonard and the lilac bedroom—how peaceful she felt in it, even with her loneliness—went with her, changing her little by little. In the lilac room, Sophia was a thirty-four-year-old woman without a big diamond ring, or a husband, or a child, or the status of her job. But even after tears, with nothing but a book, she understood that she was still happy—even happier.

The room had become a room in her imagination.

LESSON SEVEN

Be Disciplined with Your Gift

Don't wait for inspiration, but sit down quietly, and begin; once you have gotten to work, shut up, even to yourself, about writer's block; use your imagination; and keep work- ing. That is your draft. The first one will always be terrible; don't worry about that; keep working. Cut anything that is not in your own voice or anything about which you do not feel passionately or anything that is not true. If you have taken a wrong turn, go back; that is part of the process. Then edit, edit, edit. Finally, know when you are done.

Of all these, "get to work" is the most important.

A T THE END of July, when it was warm enough to sit out on the screened-in porch from early in the morning onward, Leonard gave me Lesson Seven: "This lesson, honey, is: BE DIS- CIPLINED with your gift."

It was now after breakfast. Leonard looked like a camp in- structor: he was wearing a lime-colored linen shirt, bright as a popsicle; khakis; and rubber river sandals. I did not think he was aware that the footgear that was a dashing part of his ensemble was intended only for hiking through riverbeds. I decided not to mention it. He crossed his feet at the ankles and admired his sandals before speaking from his notes. Butterfly bushes had put out heavy blue-purple blossoms, and yellow butterflies were flitting through their leaves.

Leonard had made himself a bowl of groats. His doctor had suggested cereal for breakfast instead of eggs; so, rather than just pouring out some Special K, Leonard had decided he had to cook various grains—many of them nearly obsolete, in marketing terms, or at the very least arcane—on an alternating weekday basis. You would hear a rapturous paean to Cream of Wheat, for instance, if it was Monday: how shameful and wrong it was that Cream of Wheat was no longer a breakfast-table favorite. Today was Tuesday, so the kitchen was filled with the horse-market scent of cooking groats. "Kasha. Nothing better with milk. Have some," he would urge every Tuesday I was around, and every Tuesday that I was around, I would back off as politely as I could from the equine smell emanating from the mush in the wooden spoon.

But he was done with breakfast, and the steam from the kitchen had mercifully cleared. He riffled his papers.

"I told you earlier: it is not enough just to feel; you need shape and form. I got my respect for form from the New Critics. They did not believe in just putting your feelings out there; free verse was anathema to them unless, like Ezra Pound, you had mastered the form so well it was like an invisible structure underneath your free verse.

"In the late 1940s, the cry from the heart was entering fiction. At the very same time, some academics—I. A. Richards, F. R. Leavis—were talking about how important form was. The southern renaissance poets—Allen Tate, his protégé Robert Lowell, and John Crowe Ransom—were writing measured, formal verse. I became convinced that these two currents—discipline and emotion—best informed a poet, or a life, only when they were in balance. The heart alone was not enough without technique, and technique alone was ice-cold without the heart."

That was the mixture that influenced Leonard at twenty-three: the marriage between emotion and rigor; the discipline of form holding the content of authentic feeling. He always maintained that transcendence alone was not enough. "Look at Ransom," said my father. "The freedom comes about in the line because the form is so beautifully mastered. You won't have meaningful freedom if it is not in the context of discipline and restraint."

I looked up from my note-taking to the garden, which was wavering in the heat. Inspired by Mr. Christian, I had begun to tackle the garden. The poor strip that ran only along the front of the house seemed to have been planted by someone who actively disliked things that grew. The plants had been chosen on the basis of ease of care: rows of razor-sharp decorative grasses marched along, and hosta—whose greatest charm is that you can ignore them and they still live—crowded the borders. Conical evergreens grew too close to the little house. A scrub tree with sharp-edged leaves overhung the main door, casting shadows on the interior. The only color in the garden had been from the purple of the bleeding heart, which had taken over and strangled everything else, as, I was learning, bleeding heart will.

There had been a day when I could not stand the garden any longer. Knowing next to nothing about gardening, I had gotten on my knees and ripped up massive handfuls of bleeding heart. The marshy soil easily yielded the intrusive plant. I took the saw that we had gotten at Herrington's and started sawing at the base of the ugly sapling by the door, which also came down with little trouble. I piled up the refuse of the horrible garden into a wheelbarrow and dumped it on the heap of weeds that we had started to pile up beside the garage.

I went out and asked questions at North Mountain Nursery up on Route 22. Tony Parino, or "T.P.," the owner, a transplant with a Bronx accent and an easygoing manner whose gentle nature now led him to keep a Shetland pony in the back to amuse children, sent me home with bright flats of plants that he promised I could not kill if I tried. He and Mrs. Parino became our planting mentors. Sophia and I, and the kids when they were willing, planted crimson nasturtiums, lantana whose blossoms ranged from pink to orange to yellow, and dusty miller with its gray-green leaves. We put into the dark wet earth many pots of the invincible impatiens: cherry-pink, scarlet, and magenta. It was not a subtle garden; our main goal was its survival.

The strip of garden was not large enough for the flowers we wanted to plant, so we expanded the area that we could cultivate by digging up the turf with shovels and using our hands—I had not yet figured out the right tool for this—to pick out the stones. The garden would emerge eventually, but not the way we had imagined it, and not at all easily.

Within a week, the strong sun had shriveled the poppies. I ripped them up and tried again with more lantana, which seemed to be thriving. The previous fall I had put in tulip and hyacinth bulbs, but deer had eaten every one; when it became clear that there would be no blooms from them, I went for new bulbs and brought home with them a book about remedies to ward off deer.

The following week, we had a heavy rain, and water from

the unguttered roof eaves soaked the nasturtiums and threatened to drown them, so we dug channels between them to drain them off until we could get new gutters hung. Two dispirited crab apple trees had been planted against the garage, and a bare space remained where the eye expected a third. I tied the crooked limbs back against the garage wall with a nail and plastic string. The trees looked a bit more cheerful, their shape against the garage wall more intentional, as in the French espalier method. But when the two trees looked happier, the bare space looked even more obvious.

As in a draft, every task undertaken in the garden led to more beauty and order; but, as in a draft as well, each completed task also led directly to more work.

LEONARD had come up to admire the garden, and to show me how to hang brackets for curtains.

Leonard is tall, as I mentioned, and seems thinner every year. He stood a chair at each of the still-bare windows downstairs and climbed up to show me where brackets should go, while I watched nervously. Brackets behave differently on different walls, he explained. The dining chair he stood on was a bit unstable. Or was it Leonard's sense of balance? But my father's pride meant that I could say nothing as he reached out to the wall with the cordless drill in slightly trembling hands. I bit my lip.

He explained that before you drill, you have to find the studs in the wall. After you locate the stud, you have to drive the screw in carefully, so you don't make the hole too big, lest the bracket hang loose. He showed me the difference between a regular screwdriver—flat-edged—and a Phillips-head, and demonstrated how to tighten the screw once it has been driven in.

One bracket I tried to position did fall out. I repositioned it. It fell out again. I had inadvertently made the hole too big in the easily yielding drywall. I felt an inordinate frustration that the mistake was final: you can't delete or rephrase a hole in drywall. "Oh, for heaven's sake," I said. "Let's give up. This is not going to happen. I can't learn to do this."

"Carefully, carefully," said my father. "You have to keep trying. You can't expect to get it the first or second or third time. You have to tolerate frustration, honey. Eventually you'll get it."

I tried again, much more cautiously this time. I focused on the screwdriver and on pushing my weight carefully against it. Caution does not come naturally to me. My mind resisted the care I was taking even as my hands tried to learn. But I calibrated the way I leaned in to the screwdriver, very slowly, so that at last I drove the screw into the drywall neither too deeply nor too weakly. I did it again with the upper edge of the bracket. This time the bracket stayed up. I pressed it with my hand: it was solid.

I hung the white cotton curtains, and they stayed up, too. Between us, we hung brackets on all six narrow windows downstairs. When we were done and the curtains were shielding us from the darkness outside, I felt I had come by something honestly.

When I went upstairs to bed, I thought, Damn it, my dad has always talked about discipline, and he is right. The daughter in me who resisted acknowledging a father's truism wished—petulantly, almost—that I could say that my father was wrong; but the evidence by now was against me.

I thought about how my dad used to call my attention to an off syllable—a syllable!—in a sonnet I had written when I was a teenager. "Honey, this is an off rhyme—meaning it is not a full rhyme with its mate. You can use an off rhyme if you mean to use an off rhyme, and it will work, but if you put one in because you feel lazy—because you don't feel like reworking the poem to include a true rhyme—well, the poem suffers; the reader can tell." The off rhymes that come from laziness had worked their dolorous effects in my own life experience: whenever I'd had a dream but yielded to sloth in relation to it—whether it was putting off stuffing envelopes for a fund-raiser for the teaching institute, or avoiding going back into the stacks to deepen an assertion I had made, or being sloppy with my obligations as a friend or partner, hoping I would get a pass—the poem in question, whatever it was, spiraled downward. Whenever I gave in to my own temptation and hoped that no one would notice my oversight, somehow the whole enterprise deteriorated.

I thought of Rhonda. When I was in her wedding party, she had asked me to wear a dressy maroon floor-length gown of any style. On her wedding day, I was in a rush; I had not had time—no, I had not made time—to go shopping. What I put together at the last minute—a maroon leotard and a rayon skirt—looked from a distance like a proper bridesmaid's outfit, though it really wasn't dressy enough. Without having meant to, I had allowed a careless off rhyme into the poem of her celebration. My dress was a symptom of a carelessness I had brought to our friendship. I had been skipping the discipline called for by friendship. It was trivial, of course, as off rhymes are; but it also was not. Rhonda, of course, let it pass. But the fracture in our intimacy had its metaphor.

In his discussion of discipline, my father was identifying a kind of natural law about the structure underneath any life undertaking: carelessness with one small part can mysteriously weaken the whole, even where the weak part does not show.

In contrast, I had to admit, whenever I was heartbroken or

oppressed by what lay ahead, and I had acceded to my father's discussions about discipline ("Work cures everything . . ."), the undertaking took on an integrity greater than my own personal effort; it was as if, when you did your own part with discipline, help—inspiration, support—would mysteriously come.

"You have to keep trying. You'll get it."

Leonard had always said that continued effort was more important than inspiration. "There are millions of talented people who 'want to write,'" he said. "The main difference between them and the real writers is not talent; it is that the real writers sit down every day and get words down on paper."

I remembered how, when I was a child, after I had told him I wanted to learn about them, he taught the standard forms of traditional poetry. Like a carpenter showing a child how to build a birdhouse, he taught me the basic shapes one could work with; a quatrain (ABAB), a sonnet (ABAB CDCD EFEF GG, for instance), a ballad (ABAB CDCD). He explained the beats of the words: iamb (duh-DUH), trochee (DUH-duh), spondee (duh-duh, equal inflection), anapest (duh-duh-DUH, like the Lone Ranger's theme song), and dactyl (DUH-duh-duh). He showed me what blank verse was—he had to, after all—but it was as if he were teaching me about junk food: if it is not very good, he said, it is bad.

"What sound would a horse's hooves make?" he would ask.

"Ummm . . . anapest?" I would wonder, hearing the beat in my mind's ear (duh-duh-DUH, duh-duh-DUH).

"I think that makes sense. What is this, honey: 'That TIME of YEAR thou MAY'ST in ME behold . . .'"

"Iambic . . . pentameter?"

"Yep. Which some people believe is the natural beat of the English language." It was an amazing concept to me: that language had a natural heartbeat, a natural measure of breath. It felt like walking into a world of huge, friendly, but also awe-inspiring words, and looking around at them.

"This is a *ballade,*" he used to say, and he would show me a poem by François Villon.

> *I die of thirst while at the fountainside*
> *Hot as fire, my teeth are chattering*
> *In my own country, far off I abide*
> *Near the blaze I burn, still shivering . . .*

"Can you die of thirst at a fountainside, literally?"

"No . . ."

"So why do you think he is saying he is dying of thirst?"

"Umm, love?" I asked, embarrassed.

"Sure; but you see that, line by line, Villon gives us contradictory images: being in love, he implies, is joyful *and* painful."

I was eleven. It was Jerusalem, 1973. The Yom Kippur War had begun shortly after we arrived in Israel—my father, my brother, Aaron, and me—for a sabbatical year abroad. Our mother was finishing some graduate school exams and was due to join us in a few weeks.

On Yom Kippur, the loudest siren I had ever heard sounded throughout the city. My father was in the Golan Heights, reporting as a freelancer for the *San Francisco Chronicle*. He had asked Diana Shye, a family friend, to look after us. At the sound of sirens, we all ran into the street. A neighbor ran out and dragged us all downstairs to the air-raid shelter. My brother and I sat, excited and scared, in the dark basement, with all the neighbors of the apartment building seated against its wall. The dark air smelled of Jerusalem stone. One of the neighbors had a radio. Another had a flashlight; we were forbidden to touch the precious flashlight. It was a long, long time before we heard the all-clear siren.

"*Kan Kol Yisrael Mi'Yerushalayim . . .*" the war bulletins on the radio began after that, every day, on the hour. "*Shalom Rav,*" said the announcer. "Great peace to you. The time is nine, and here is the news . . ." The latest news of the war would come on.

It was exciting for us children, and dreadful at the same time. At school we taped the windows so any explosions would not send glass shards into the classrooms. With our teachers, we loaded sandbags against the walls. You would hear of explosions right after they had happened, always just elsewhere, but close enough. "*Ptzatza b'Machaneh Yehuda,*" came the word from radios on verandas to the street-level corner groceries where, at lunchtime, we bought Noga candy bars and Egozi chocolate: a bomb in Judah Camp, the site of the open market. "*Ptzatza B'Rehov Yaffa,*" came the word—a bomb in the pizzeria on Jaffa Street where, on Saturday nights after the Sabbath ended, we went with boys on what were almost, but not yet, dates. Don't go to the Old City, we were suddenly told—that alluring quarter where we all had recently gone in laughing groups, to buy hot sesame rolls to dip in the spice mixture *za'atar,* which the Palestinian shopkeeper would hand you twisted in a piece of Arabic-language newspaper. Don't drive south on the main highway; the Egyptian army is moving closer.

Few foreigners were allowed into Israel after the war began. My mom finally managed to arrive by throwing a full-scale Jewish-mother fit at the El Al ticketing gate, saying her babies needed her; fortunately, the Jewish airline staff understood that particular kind of scene and permitted her on the flight.

Suddenly, the air was full of martial pop songs. "Send me underwear and T-shirts . . . here we are already like animals . . . we fight like lions, morale is really high . . ."

I would come home from school and drop my book bag and read, in the formal, shadowy living room of our flat. I was thirsty for English and tired from the days of exultant tension, the nationalism that was like a drug, and the danger in the air that only heightened the high of the nationalism.

My dad would take a break from his own work and join me for a glass of chocolate milk. I would show him my latest poems —often written in the dreaded free verse, which was of course fashionable at the time.

"Naomi," he would say gently, "don't paint abstractly until you can draw the figure. You can break the form successfully once you have mastered it. Structure has to be the foundation—then you can play with it or depart from it altogether. But you have to know your craft.

"Try this, honey: try to say the same thing, but in a villanelle." He read a quote from a textbook, which explained that a villanelle was nineteen lines consisting of five tercets and a quatrain. It uses just two rhymes. The first and third lines repeat in alternating tercets. "Look at this," he said, showing me an Empson villanelle. "'The waste remains, the waste remains and kills . . .' Look how it is structured, what the echoes do; does it make you feel Empson's desperation? Emotions can be more powerful when they are closely confined by a strict form."

"I think I see what you mean."

"Try the form. See what happens: you might surprise yourself! ABA . . ."

I tried it, and I did surprise myself. It was much harder, but the difficulty made me think harder.

"This is the Voice of Israel from Jerusalem. *Shalom Rav . . .*" intoned the war bulletin from the radio in the kitchen. I looked one more time at the Villon. " 'I die of thirst here at the fountainside,' " I whispered. I tried to follow his music in my head, while at the same time trying to listen to something inside of myself. I took my colored pencils out of my book bag, and a piece of lined paper, and scored the end-rhyme letters down the right-hand side, and began.

"BE DISCIPLINED," Leonard said again, looking up from his class notes. "Do you want to know how to become a writer? It is not romantic." Then he glared from under his white brows and almost harshly said, as much about life, it seemed, as about writing, "There is no revising a blank page. Keep going."

We were on the sunporch again. Dad's black coffee was steaming. A family of birds was building a nest in the shrubs outside the porch, dipping and swooping amid the leaves. The children were napping. More gently, my dad recalled how "when you trek"—he and my mom had gone trekking in Nepal the year before—"before the first day of the trek is done, one discovers the going on of going on. It rains, you go on. It snows, you go on. You walk up a field of rhododendrons bearing snow and pass through it and go on. Half the slats are missing on the hanging bridge you cross over a gorge, and you go on. You can't turn back, because that, too, would be going on. So: even when you do not feel like it—especially then—GO ON.

"Writer's block," he said, "comes about when you let yourself yield to two false notions about your task. The first is that writing is a profound occupation, important as a means of expressing the self, some truth about life, or about the universe. This is all nonsense.

"The second false notion is that writing must at every moment be perfect. No one objects to perfection eventually, but the idea of it does nothing to help you get started.

"It would help the blocked writer—or the blocked any-one—if he—or she," he added dolefully, acknowledging the argument about usage that we had carried on for most of the 1970s, "thought of the writing task as scribbling or typing. It is in the act of moving the pen across the paper, or of typing the next line, that one creates in oneself a readiness to breach the wall of silence.

"It should comfort us to know that first drafts are usually terrible—and infinitely revisable. No one needs to know how terrible your false starts were. But there is no revising a blank page.

"Hence, if all else fails, type anything at all," he said. "I often start with 'Now is the time for all good men to come to the aid of their party'—the typing exercise which I was taught in the eighth grade by Miss Godding.

"The Lubavitcher Hasidim stop Jews in the street and urge them to lay *tfillin*—to wind around their arms and tie onto their foreheads the phylacteries that Jewish males use in order to pray. They tell the secular Jew, or the Jew who has not done it in years, 'Never mind, you don't have to believe in it—just do it.' And in the act of doing it, some Jewish men have rediscovered their faith."

"Why does it work?" I asked. "It sounds almost like there is some element of invocation there."

"It's practical: old people, when they have forgotten a word, repeat another word like it until the brain sifts through the debris and brings them what they want. If you continue to put down words, the words start a process of association to more words until finally you reach the running brooks of your own imagination—or, in the case of the *tfillin,* your own faith."

My father filled up his cup again with black coffee. "A writer's worst enemy," he said, "is a blank page."

"Who said that?" I asked.

"I did. Just now!" He giggled. "The creative mind is endlessly churning images, ideas, characters, plot possibilities, but the writer cannot sit around and wait for them to push their way into his or her consciousness, though it does sometimes happen. I don't want my students to think there is no such thing as inspiration—but only that inspiration is not what you base your work on.

"The professional writer settles for a more pragmatic relationship with the imagination. You have to consult it daily. Consulting it daily ensures you against missing wonderful stuff, which you will certainly miss if you wait only for inspiration."

"A homely example that a student gave me: she said that using discipline and not waiting for inspiration feels like someone who owns a bucket with which she hopes to catch rainwater. If she went out with the bucket only when she knew it was actually raining, she would certainly get some water sometimes. But if she goes out daily no matter what the weather she can catch the rain that falls unexpectedly.

"The curious truth," he said with a little smile, and brought the cup to his lips, "is that the writer who goes out with the bucket daily seems to provoke the rain."

What is another reason to go out with the bucket daily—or, as the writer Annie Lamott puts it, to take your creative task step by step, or "bird by bird"? Because otherwise you can get overwhelmed. When you are overwhelmed, you can't begin, let alone get through the middle or arrive at the end.

Another graduate of our leadership program, Alison, came to visit the house later that June. I had offered graduates of our program an open house for a long weekend, if they needed to get away from the city. Part of our program's mission is to give young women of promise some quiet space in the country so they can work or get perspective on their lives. Alison had responded eagerly. Her interests were product development and marketing—not a world I knew much about. I wondered what I might be able to offer her as a teacher.

When I picked Alison up at the train station, she seemed slightly depressed; as she put it to me later, this time was, for her, "rock bottom." Under the dimming of sadness, you could see the lush lips, slanted eyes, and sculpted nose of a classical Greek-American beauty. But bad luck seemed to be pursuing her: by the time I found her, I had received several calls on my cell phone—she had missed the first train, caught the second; I had miscommunicated the schedules. She sounded frail and nervous, like a child worried about getting lost.

When I got her in the car, I was aware of a good heart and a sensitive nature, but I could feel that her scaffolding was shaky; her inward pain was making her less than fully alert to her outer world. Again, I felt out of my depth; I wondered how I could possibly help her to do what I had already begun to think of as Lesson One—to relax enough to get a sense of what she needed.

After she was settled at home, she brought her concerns with her onto the screened porch. I listened while I began to unpack stones from a new pallet that had been delivered from Herrington's: irregular pieces of gray slate that I hoped to lay down to make a patio. I was glad to be working, because I did not feel confident in what to say.

Alison and her boyfriend had split up; she showed me his photo. Her mother was urging her to get a better job. Her current boss was oppressive. She was doing only menial tasks and was frustrated because she had good ideas.

I asked her to tell me about one of them. I hoped to get her mind on what was possible and off of the many obstacles she was facing.

At my first prompting, Alison, who had seemed so unhappy, unfolded a gorgeous first draft. She described unhesitatingly a business she wished to start, which would assemble and market baskets of handmade personal-care products—prayer and meditation books, healing visualization tapes, aromatherapy and bright fabrics—to sell in hospital gift shops.

As she sketched out the broad plan, she got increasingly excited. A dimmer switch turned up her light. Her big brown eyes sparkled; as she spoke, the energy in her ideas seemed to give vitality to her body; she hoisted herself out of the deep papasan chair.

"Let me help!" she insisted. "I can do it; I'm stronger than I look."

She *was* stronger than she looked, and I was stronger than I thought. First we had to clear the turf in the area that the stones would pave. We figured out that if we dug the edges of our shovels into the peat, and cut the grass down to the sod, we could roll it back like a carpet. After the shovels raised the turf, we knelt in the mud in our sweatpants and pushed at its underside. Our hands were filled with soft warm mud, stones, and worms as we heaved up and rolled the emerald and brown layers of grassy earth and laid bare the wet dirt underneath. We hauled the turf to the compost pile in a wheelbarrow. It took many trips; by this time, we were dirty and sweating.

Then we worked side by side to hoist each of the heavy flagstones, some of them two feet wide, into place in what was becoming a primitive pattern. We discovered how you could fit the jagged edge of one flagstone into the recess created by the edge of another. Slowly the entire semicircular area, about ten feet at its widest point, was filled in. The sun had begun to set. We had been working for about four hours, with a break or two for water.

Finally, we hauled a wheelbarrow filled with sand to the site. We dumped the load of sand and swept it into the cracks of the stones, setting them. Our hands were sore.

Joey tried to heave a stone that was dangerously big for him. When I stopped him, he said crankily, "It's a girls' club," and went off to dig with his toy bulldozer in the garden dirt.

Beside the fact that I appreciated her help, I was pleased to watch Alison get into the rhythm of lifting and dragging the stones. The harder she worked, the better Alison seemed to feel. By the time the flagstones crept from the outer rim of the patio halfway to the edge of the house, she was flushed and enthusiastic and really alive.

As Alison labored, I took a rest. I thought about how I could help or teach her. This was a tough one. She needed to begin and keep going.

She had a great idea, but it was evident she had not been supported enough in listening to her imagination and trusting her plan. The dream of what she wanted to do was overwhelming, because it was still fantasy.

Alison was in good company, I knew. I thought about all the young people I had met who were similarly gifted but blocked somehow, stuck at a crossroads. No matter how talented they were, they often felt overwhelmed by the size of the task ahead and unable to take the first step in the direction of their heart's passionate desire.

Two days into Alison's visit, I called my father. I described my lack of confidence in my role as her teacher.

"It's all the same kind of task," he said. For her, a poem is a basket in a hospital gift shop.

"It's just like telling a writing student to think of the first image. Tell her to think of the first thing she would put into her first basket. Make her tell you what it is. Don't let her stop till she has imaginatively filled up a whole basket."

Leonard insisted that the best thing a creatively blocked student could do was get to work. It was best for all of the student: for her mood, her health, and for that old-fashioned notion that Leonard ties so closely to creative work—her character. Without rigorous discipline, he believes, any creative gifts a student has will tarnish. An artist—meaning everyone—needs a strong work ethic the way an athlete needs a strong body.

My confidence bolstered, I took Alison for a hike along the river in Taconic State Park. In the depth of the forest, there is a path on which you can walk from New York to Massachusetts; my children like straddling the borderline. There is a small gabled wooden church in the heart of the parkland, and a nineteenth-century stone quarry that has been filled with water for swimming. Victorian and Edwardian tourists used to come here to admire the view from the high stone steps facing Bash Bish Falls. Alison and I sat on a wooden bridge overlooking the Roeliff Jansen Kill river. I asked Alison to think about what her work could look like. I suggested that she start by imagining, and do that by taking just one step at a time. She listened and was quieter than she had been yet.

The next day we resumed our labors on the patio. The work was changing us. We spent most of the day with streaks of mud down the sides of our T-shirts and across our faces, and with hands caked with grit. Alison had pinned up her hair with a chopstick, and the tendrils stuck to her neck, which was being reddened by the sun. Every inch of sod we turned made us feel more capable. We admired the stretch of cleared dirt the way we might have admired a pair of shoes in the city. The vestigial princess in each of us had shut up and gone elsewhere. We were becoming the kind of women who knew how to lay down a flagstone patio with their hands.

When the sun was too warm for working, Alison and I went into the shade of the sunporch. I brought out iced tea in jelly glasses and sat next to her. In the afternoons, Rosa would be up on the branch of a tree or hammering slats into one of the treehouse pallets. Joey would be crashing his trucks together on the cool floor of the sunporch.

"So what are you thinking now about your business?" I asked her.

"I am thinking I can do it."

"Great!" I answered, surprised and pleased. "How will you get started on writing your business plan?"

"My uncle could help me with that. He has a small business . . . he imports canned foods . . . he would know how to do that."

"Wonderful, Alison, how lucky!" I said. "Would you like to use the phone to call him? Maybe he could e-mail an example of his business plan. You could get started here."

"But if I start writing a business plan," she said, "and I get a job, I won't be able to finish the business plan . . ."

"Then you could begin to work on it at night and on weekends," I suggested. "And if it takes off, you could eventually quit your job. Either way, no loss . . . Why don't you start with choosing just two or three hospital gift shops to carry your first prototypes? You could assemble the prototypes yourself from home."

"But if it takes off," she said, "I'll need to be able to refill the orders quickly so I don't make the retailers angry. And I wouldn't be able to keep up with the demand if I did it out of my apartment! I would need somewhere to manufacture and store the baskets . . . and a distributor. And what if there's already a competitor in my market?"

"Well, that's easy to check."

She wasn't listening, because she had gone back for a moment into the anxiety cloud. The many possible futures she was seeing were making it hard for her to think about next steps. The prospect of success seemed as unnerving to her as the prospect of failure.

"But, if they do sell, how will I replace the orders in time without a distributor or staff? And if they don't sell, can I even approach the outlets again with another version of the prototype?"

I wondered what I could say to Alison that might help her to be calmer, to listen internally, to use her imagination and get started with one simple thing.

"Just start typing. Just make a first draft. You can worry about revisions later. Alison," I called urgently. She glanced at me. "Tell me just one thing—the first thing you would get to make just one of these baskets."

"Well, I would need the basket! There is this wonderful place in Chinatown, a wholesaler, with beautiful bamboo baskets—he sells them to restaurants for dim sum."

"Okay! And tell me what would be one hospital gift shop you know of—just one—where you would like to see your basket sold?"

"Oh, I know the answer to that . . . St. Vincent's, on Eleventh Street. There are old people who go there for long-term care, and people go in for chemotherapy, but there is nothing in the gift shop to make them feel better in a hospital room—just candy and some paperbacks and magazines and cards and puzzles. I would love to have them set aside a little space on a shelf on the wall there. I know just the one— between the cash register and the refrigerated display case that carries cold drinks and flowers. *Bad* flowers. Carnations," she said.

"Okay!" I said. "Now: What is one thing you would put in that one basket in that one gift shop?"

"Oh . . ." She sighed. "I would have some beautiful sphagnum moss. On the moss . . . maybe some little bundles of dried lavender to make the hospital linens smell good. And a prayer book . . . with a really cool batik cover, not dowdy . . . maybe with prayers from many different traditions, all of them about healing and health, so you can choose your own meditation . . . And a tape for visualization, because all the research says that helps people recover, but who knows how to do that, ordinarily? . . . And a silver frame you can put a photo of people you love in—you could put that on your tray while you eat . . . The basket could have a red and yellow tablecloth, and matching napkins—those hand-blocked linen ones from India, to cover those awful plastic tables they use for meals—that would make you feel better while you eat that bland food . . . And lotions, with aromatherapy, in colored glass bottles. When you were done with the lotions, you could put flowers in the bottles so the light comes through the colored glass and warms the room . . ."

Joey had sat up from his trucks. He was listening, rapt, to her description of the baskets, as if hearing a wonderful bed-time story.

Alison's eyes had gotten that gentle, dreamy look. She looked truly beautiful and strong. Her Mediterranean features had relaxed. She had listened inwardly, used her imagination, and gotten started with the first step. She saw her vision; we saw it. Alison was now doing her work, making her signature on the earth. You can feel it when that happens. She was in the zone, and she was no longer afraid, because the creative act drives out fear.

I imagined that she was seeing the tray, then she added the hand-blocked red linen napkin. Then she was adding a cobalt—no, magenta? no, cobalt—glass jar to the red and yellow floral linen layer on the sphagnum moss in the bamboo basket. As she spoke, you could just about see how this one gracious thing could change the entire feeling in a sterile steel-and-gray-white hospital room.

"'I placed a jar in Tennessee / And round it was, upon a hill," my dad often says about such moments, quoting Wallace Stevens's poem. "When a human hand makes one creative gesture, the entire wilderness organizes itself around a jar," my father explains. "The jar creates the design. Listen:

> *I placed a jar in Tennessee,*
> *And round it was, upon a hill.*
> *It made the slovenly wilderness*
> *Surround that hill.*

The wilderness rose up to it,
And sprawled around, no longer wild.
The jar was round upon the ground
And tall and of a port in air.

It took dominion everywhere.
The jar was gray and bare.
It did not give of bird or bush,
Like nothing else in Tennessee.

"The jar, you see, is the beginning of the creative act," Leonard had said, "but once you take that first step, it orders everything around it; the 'slovenly wilderness.' That is why it is so important just to begin, even with a single thing."

"But how would I find the tapes?" Alison snapped out of the place she had been. She was scared again. I wanted to hug her. "And is there a copyright problem with that sort of thing? I mean, other people have made baskets . . . If I get Caswell-Massey, for instance, do I need a licensing agreement with Caswell-Massey? There is no way I can find all this out and still keep a day job—"

"Alison!" I almost shouted, before remembering I was supposed to stop doing that. "Don't worry about that now!" I said more softly. "The basket is full! You are almost there. You can worry about licensing later. *What color is the soap?*"

"The soap," she said, as if I were asking the most obvious question in the world, "is yellow too."

"Beautiful. And what is holding all this together? How do you tie it up?"

"Rice paper. I know where to get it cheap. That store, Pearl River, the same place I would get the baskets. It's in Soho."

I went to get the New York City telephone book and the telephone reciever. I held them both out. Alison sat up straight.

"This is all you need to do right now, honey," I said. ("Put out the bucket . . . it brings the rain.") "Just call Pearl River, okay? And ask to buy one of those baskets."

Alison took the phone book and the receiver, found the name "Pearl River," and started dialing.

LEONARD believes that artistic discipline has been lost. With the arrival of the Beats in the 1950s, he feels, the balance of rigor and feeling fell apart into loose expressiveness. He objects to permissiveness for its own sake. He sees the self-expression and hippie movements of the 1960s, and the drug culture and entitlement of the 1970s, as perversions of the goal of finding transcendence in the real world.

Bohemians have always tended to value self-expression over discipline, and they have always partied. The Bohemians of the later 1940s and early '50s used language—and then drugs, and sex, and wine—to fan the creative flames. By the time the hippies came around, forget it; drugs had become a shortcut to transcendence that was bad for the work at hand.

Every generation of artists has had its role models for the undisciplined life and its own drugs and sexual excesses. Montmartre had artists' models and absinthe and gonorrhea; the Village in the 1920s, as Ross Wetzsteon describes it in *Republic of Dreams: Greenwich Village: The American Bohemia, 1910–1960,* had rotgut and reefer and back-alley abortions. Edna St. Vincent Millay made a cult figure for the decade out of the intoxicated, sexually liberated poetess, though she would die in 1950 of alcohol-related diseases after a night spent drinking Alsatian wine. As she famously wrote:

> *My candle burns at both ends*
> *It will not last the night*
> *But, ah, my foes, and oh, my friends*
> *It gives a lovely light!*

My father did not approve of the artist burning her candle at both ends if it meant eventually burning out.

But in the late 1940s, Bohemia was finding its own new role models for living the undisciplined transcendent life: Henry Miller and then Dylan Thomas had set the stage. Miller's *Tropic of Cancer* and *Tropic of Capricorn*—with their liberated language and their scenes of personal excess—was being smuggled from Paris through U.S. customs; and Dylan Thomas, the hard-drinking, womanizing Welsh poet, undertook in 1950 the first of two famous American college lecture tours that introduced my father's generation to a vivid illustration of the wild life the poet-libertine was supposed to live. It was the poet-celebrity's antics, rather than his restrained verse structure, that caught the attention of the wider public. Thomas's outrageous actions on those tours became part of an influential model for the out-of-bounds creative life: "I want to rip something away and show [audiences] what they have never seen," he wrote. Defending his flouting of all rules—stealing his host's clothing, appearing onstage incoherent from drink—he insisted that "there is no necessity for the artist to do anything. There is no necessity. He is a law unto himself . . ."

These role models for personal liberation—or libertin-ism—introduced themselves appealingly to the children of hardworking immigrants. The wreckage would come later.

At first, though, this generation's Bohemia seemed idyllic.

My father went back to California—to Anderson Creek, near Big Sur, which at that time was almost unpopulated—with Patricia. For a few months, the young couple lived with a group of writers and poets in abandoned army huts—prisoners' shacks, in fact—set on the cliffs that dropped into the Pacific on the stretch of Highway 1 south of Big Sur.

In this creative Eden there was no electricity or running water, but the young people worked all day, and when their work was done, they hiked the bare cliffs or went up the road to visit Henry Miller, who, as my dad recalls it, was living with Lepska, his young wife, as the guest of an anthropologist who had land two miles north up on Partington Ridge. Leonard re-members with amusement that there was a hot spring on the cliffside south of Anderson Creek, which was later turned into Esalen, the human-potential mecca. In those days, though, it, too was deserted; the young people would bathe nude in its restorative water. Miller, by this time a world-famous hedonist, forbade his beautiful blond wife from taking off her clothes with the rest of the bathers. (Years later, at the home of Ken-neth Rexroth, my father was seated next to the middle-aged sexual memoirist Anaïs Nin, who flirted with him. Of the fa-mous sexual liberation icons, Miller and Nin, Leonard re-marked dryly, "Anyone who believes in those people has never to have met them.")

After five months in the army huts, Leonard and Patricia returned to Berkeley to study. My father's first book of poetry, issued by Bern Porter Press in 1948, was titled *Hamadryad*

Hunted. His family paid no attention to it whatsoever. Neither did reviewers. "It dropped into the deep well of unconscious cerebration," said my father, laughing.

"What's a hamadryad?" I asked.

"A tree nymph," said my dad.

"Oh," I said. "Of course."

The California that this Jewish boy from Cleveland came to experience was still almost as pure as a frontier, since there was little development down by the Berkeley salt flats. The sun slanted over Telegraph Avenue straight from the East Bay. The light in those days, unfiltered by the shadows of tall buildings, was blue-white off the water, like nowhere else in the world. Smells of tar and coal smoke came in from Oakland, which was still an important shipping harbor, since San Francisco Bay was still a shipping lane then rather than a tourist spectacle. The scent of salt water came in on the clear air. Across the Bay, in the city, the soft, small hills called Twin Peaks were not yet ringed with the access road now cut into the landscape, nor shadowed by a massive radio tower as they would be when I was growing up beneath them. Coit Tower, built in the shape of a fireman's nozzle, was still a high point on the San Francisco vista. The city was white-towered still; no gray-black monoliths had been built on the Embarcadero facing the water.

Steinbeck's Monterey was still a town with working herring canneries. Boats came in with piles of fish in their holds. Leonard made extra money there during the summer, dumping messes of herring down a chute.

Leonard's circle of friends lived in the old prewar apartments, though new bungalows had sprung up to house the war workers who had flooded in from the Midwest and the South. The older houses still had their bay windows and complicated gingerbread trim, unfashionable by then. They were affordable for the students and the poets.

The artistic young women of Berkeley tried hard to distinguish themselves from ordinary college girls. College women in general then, my father remembers, wore navy suits and platform shoes with ankle straps; but the young poetesses wore tube dresses, a piece of fabric wrapped around the body and sewn closed. They would stand at parties in these shifts, which they belted with a length of bicycle chain or a man's necktie; only occasionally did the girls wear a conventional belt. Flower-print summer dresses were fashionable among more traditional students, but the avant-garde girl shunned flower prints. Nice girls wore saddle shoes; the avant-garde girl wore thong sandals, even in winter. The women in these circles also wore bright red pedal pushers, or long straight skirts with cinched waists, and white short-sleeved blouses. The conventional girls wore their hair shoulder-length or shorter, in curled bobs that they pinned up at night in the dorms. But if a girl was avant-garde, she would wear her hair long and loose. More conventional girls wore pearls and hats and gloves when they went to the city to shop. The poetesses and girl painters wore men's shirts and paint-spattered jeans. All the girls then wore girdles.

Just as the style for young women in that circle was to wear unusual belts, they did their best to wear strange jewelry: hand-strung beads and big objects that hung on leather thongs as necklaces or bracelets. Men wore chinos or their wartime khakis with flannel shirts. Everyone smoked Chesterfields, Old Golds, Lucky Strikes, and Camels. Cigarettes were mostly unfiltered then.

On weekends, the group drank whiskey. As time passed, more and more alcohol—and later, drugs—seemed necessary to maintain a sense of heightened aliveness. "Drinking made your friends more amiable, more convivial," Leonard reminisced. "Also, eventually, more angry and more repulsive. That was the pattern; in fact, the alcohol generation had that as their design. Everyone adored drinking excessively: everyone could unwind and do appalling things. Men and women both drank too much, and this excused their pawing each other. It was de rigueur to drink too much on Saturday night. There was a lot of lying . . . they would vomit in each other's wastebaskets . . . haven't you been to a New York party?"

"Not one like that," I said regretfully.

"The typical thing was to dance with someone else's wife. They never did much, but they always thought they were about to. And they had the perfect excuse that everyone else accepted for the terrible things they did, as long as they did them when they were drunk."

Indeed, in the biographies of the writers and even the critics of that time, it seems that most everyone was drinking to the point of alcoholism, and seeking extremes of consciousness to the point of mental illness. Adultery, it seemed, was everywhere. The late 1940s and early '50s may have been a straight-arrow era in the mainstream, but at the margins, things were out of control. Whiskey and gin were central; food was peripheral.

By 1948 my father had been admitted to the graduate program at Berkeley. When his English literature M.A. was complete, he sailed with Patricia on a French Line ship, the *Liberté*, to Le Havre, like so many provincial young Americans postwar. From Le Havre to Paris, they took the train and ended up in Cagnes-sur-Mer, a village on the Mediterranean coast. The young couple was still broke, but the dollar went a long way, and the French countryside was beautiful. "It was a wonderful time for Americans," recalled Leonard. "It was a heyday of the book *Europe on Five Dollars a Day*. That should convey it: we stayed in places where you had to get your drinking water from the bathtub. You had to pay for meals that you had no idea what they contained except that they smelled of garlic—something bobbing up and down that posed as meat. We would buy sausage and bread and raw, raw wine and eat and drink in our rooms." In those rooms, you were always forbidden to cook; the Americans carried alcohol burners from place to place, and they always cooked. "In those days, Cagnes-sur-Mer was the lesbian capital of the world. Very artsy-craftsy." The village was situated on a hill, with a main street too steep for cars to climb. The villagers climbed by "horse ladder"—stairs that a horse with a cart could manage to ascend. The expatriates—Dutch, German, British, and American—were all writers and poets and painters.

The idyll did not last. Throughout the 1950s, drug use and alcoholism became almost normative in Bohemia, in the U.S. as well as in Europe: Allen Ginsberg and Gregory Corso were using hashish in Morocco, and William Burroughs was a heroin addict. Neal Cassady had already gotten hooked on poppers, the amphetamine inhalants that could be purchased over the counter, and alcohol. He would be arrested for marijuana possession. "These kids wanted to experience things in a transcendental way—but transcendent moments are not easy to come by. Not pretty; but it was part of the time," said Leonard.

This generation's search for intoxication was catching up with it: Delmore Schwartz was drinking heavily and using amphetamines and barbiturates. In New York, Alfred Kazin and Justin Kaplan and Anatole Broyard were hanging out in cold-water flats in Greenwich Village, drinking straight whiskey and gin. Robert Lowell had swerved his automobile into a tree, disfiguring the face of his then-wife, Jean Stafford. Stafford's biographer, Ann Hulbert, believed Lowell had been driving while drunk. Patricia Highsmith, the mystery writer, was making huge pitchers of martinis at her house in New Hope, Pennsylvania; according to contemporary accounts, she would have a "painting drink" in her hand when she was painting, a "gardening drink," when she was gardening, and a "walking-around drink" when she was walking around, in the course of one afternoon. "But Pat always drank a lot. That was her way," wrote her former lover, Marijane Meaker. To fuel his vivid perceptions of the "dharma bums," Kerouac was drinking entire fifths of whiskey, kept in the corner of the attic room in which he slept, in the Cassadys' Los Gatos house.

Bohemia was retreating further into the margins as the mainstream of the country became more and more conformist. Throughout the 1950s, the mainstream and the counterculture developed their opposition to one another: the Beats emerged and "revered those who were different . . . drugs were also important. They were viewed as the keys to the spiritual world," as David Halberstam summarizes the movement in his history, *The Fifties*. Benzedrine and marijuana were the intoxicants of choice. The "alienation" of those leading conformist lives would be explored in such books as *The Organization Man* and, later, *The Lonely Crowd*. Beat culture made a counterargument to "straight" culture on October 13, 1955, when Allen Ginsberg first read *Howl* at the Six Gallery in San Francisco.

By the mid-1950s, Bohemia was darkening. "The parties in New York continued . . . in some cases out of control . . ." writes Ann Birstein in her memoir, *What I Saw at the Fair*. Burroughs had accidentally shot and killed his common-law wife in Mexico while playing a drunken William Tell game. Eventually, Robert Lowell would be hospitalized at the Austen Riggs Center. "I missed Dick Carroll," wrote Marijane Meaker of her agent, "who'd smoked a pack of Camels every night after work, downing scotches in the Algonquin's Blue Bar until cancer gathered him . . ."

"The waste remains, the waste remains and kills," as Leonard often quotes Empson. Transcendence, apparently, could be reached, but it came with a heavy price: destructiveness and self-destruction. My father drank, too, and mildly experimented with drugs. He says that the only reason he did not become an alcoholic was that he never became famous.

By 1958, the Beats had become well known; after Jack Kerouac was featured on the cover of *Life* magazine as "King of the Beats," my father's and his friends' postwar way of life turned into a cliché. Hundreds of girls and boys in college towns and provincial cities across the country tried to emulate the "Beat style." A typical Beat girl had long black hair, black-lined eyes, "and sat like this," said my dad, gazing into space. She would be in a café, "looking meditative, wiped out, wise, with a cold wisdom. Her hand would be at her temple while she was reading Sartre." As David Amram reported in *Offbeat*, the true Beats lamented: "The Kettle of Fish, the San Remo, the Cedar Tavern . . . all are different."

Weekend hipsters in goatees and black turtlenecks and berets flocked to the Italian cafés in Greenwich Village and listened to jazz at the Village Vanguard. My father and his friends—and Kerouac and Ginsberg by that time, too—watched the trend unfold with horror. Kerouac saw himself as a transcendentalist—"a crazed solitary mystic on the lost American continent."

Among the poets and writers, older now, whom my father knew, the divorces were mounting, and the drying-out trips were more frequent. You could see the wreckage of those who gave their all to the service of "the hard gemlike flame."

"It went awry," said my father. "The postwar poets I admired said that emotion, too, was a legitimate mode of thought. But the Beats made it a law that emotion would be the *only* mode of thought. They put feeling first and thought second. That led to disaster. I thought that was a pity, and I still do.

"The liberation of feeling and the discipline of form need each other. They need to be in balance."

THEY WERE not in balance when my father's first marriage started to come apart in 1955. Patricia, now pregnant, left Leonard in the University of Iowa, where he was enrolled in the Ph.D. program in creative writing. The teachers there were the cream of the midcentury poets and New Critics; Robert Lowell, John Berryman, Karl Shapiro, and Allen Tate visited to lecture. Patricia left for San Francisco to have their baby, my half sister, Sarah, in a place where her parents could look after her. Leonard's reputable WASPy in-laws had always felt that as a poet, he was an insufficient provider. Leonard objected to Patricia going home to have their baby, but he was overruled.

"Couples never argue about what they are really arguing about," he explained. "Whatever was being discussed, the message I got from her, too, was that I was an insufficient provider. What my in-laws had was a fly-by-night poet who lived hand-to-mouth. We had nine hundred dollars for the entire year in Europe . . . it must have bothered Patricia, though she had signed on as a poet's wife. The poverty unconsciously affected her."

When the couple had gone to France, Patricia's middle-class sister had bought her a beaver coat; it would be cold in Europe, and the implication was that Leonard would not be able to supply the bare necessities.

Leonard did not remember feeling insulted, "but unconscious elements make people act," he said. "I won't say I was offended—but I was abandoned. I was left in Iowa City, unable to see the baby. Her unconscious message to me was 'I can't count on you.' My message to myself was 'Her message to me is that she can't count on me.' I always made do, but I didn't earn a full-time living till I was thirty-five."

Alone in Iowa City, which Leonard recalls as a Babylon of extramarital activity among the graduate students and faculty, he began an affair with Selma, the wife of an economics professor. Selma was about thirty, with long black hair worn loose. She wore long flowing dresses. She was what others would call voluptuous, a woman of some size. "Blue eyes," Leonard recalled, "which are always very attractive in a black-haired woman." She smoked; Patricia smoked. What Leonard did not know as he became infatuated with Selma was that she, "a bored housewife," was having various affairs simultaneously.

"We had become close couples together," he recalled. Then Patricia disappeared to her parents' home; Selma's husband went to a conference; and Selma got sick with the flu. "I tended her . . . tending somebody does something very important to oneself. In the course of that, we became lovers.

"That began a terrible time for everybody. I felt just enough guilt to believe that the only justification for the affair was that I was in love with her. I kept getting letters from her once we moved out of Iowa City . . . she was coming, we would be together. I told Patricia what I had done; the minute I told her, I realized I was not in love with Selma and sent her a Dear John letter. But Patricia left me fairly soon after this."

"Didn't you guys have things like couples counseling back then?" I asked.

"The sense of reality was narrower in those years," he said. After Leonard confessed his affair, Patricia went back to Iowa— to be with Selma's husband; the two of them married soon after.

The greatest part of the trauma for Leonard was that Patricia left with Sarah, his then-two-year-old daughter. Sarah is now a teacher of languages and a writer in Baltimore, Maryland, a very tall, very elegant woman with her mother's straight chestnut hair and a fine profile; physically, a birch tree among the hardy scrub of the other siblings.

"When I came for a visit, I took her out for ice cream. All she wanted to talk about was this little boy in preschool who was mean to her. But then when I had to leave to catch my plane, she ran after me. I had to carry her back to her house. That was one of the heartbreaks of my life.

"The rule in the years then was that the mother, always, had the right to take the child."

Leonard, now divorced, was living in San Francisco once more and womanizing intensively—"All you needed was to be tall and a poet," he recalled. He went to Yaddo, the Saratoga Springs colony for writers, musicians, and artists, in 1956.

Yaddo consisted of a main house, where the residents slept, and individual stone studios. Maples and oaks were everywhere. "Everybody had their own bottle in their rooms," said Leonard.

Delmore Schwartz was there at the time; he was then very famous, considered one of America's greatest poets. The painter Maxwell Gordon was a guest then, too, as well as a famous Shelley scholar who used to play badminton and get so furious if she lost that she would break her badminton stick. In the evenings, people would listen to one another's poetry or look at one another's paintings in the studios.

This was also the visit during which Delmore Schwartz accused Leonard of seducing his then-wife, Elizabeth Pollett, an intense beauty who was also a writer. "But I had no interest in his wife," Leonard protested.

"Her stone hut was fifteen yards from mine. The staff would bring us lunch; it was summer. I took my lunch bucket out to my nearest tree; she sat by her nearest tree. We looked across and saw each other, and one of us said, 'Why don't we eat lunch together?' She was pleasant, plump, fair-haired. I had no inclination toward her—it was just lunch."

On the second or third day of that lunch arrangement, Delmore Schwartz walked by. He nodded angrily. "The look in his eyes was ferocious. I saw it but did not know why it was there."

Schwartz returned to New York. "When I was still at Yaddo, I got a phone call. It was Delmore. He said, 'Leonard, I think I've got a publisher for your poetry. Can you come down here and bring your manuscript to New York?' I was euphoric.

"Having no money for a train or bus, I hitchhiked to New York, and stayed in the Earle Hotel, which was at that time a fleabag hotel near Washington Square Park. In the morning, I was wakened by the desk clerk—a pale, scuzzy-looking guy, like a pusher or a pimp. These people at the front desk of the Earle Hotel had seen everything. 'Mr. Wolf,' he rang up to my room.

"'Yes.'

"'Yes, it's Delmore Schwartz at the front desk. He says he's coming up to kill you.'

"I said, 'Send him up.'

"I leaped into my clothes; I thought there must be some confusion. Delmore knocked: 'You son of a bitch, you've been fucking my wife.'"

"'Have you had breakfast?' I said. We went out to eat. Then Schwartz followed me around all day, threatening me with murder. The day was divided into intervals: the times when he was reminded by something interior that he meant to kill me, and other times when he would forget and lapse into chat about poetry, Yaddo, or gossip about people we knew. Then he would remember again and rant: 'I know what you're doing, you son of a bitch! You are trying to distract me: I came here to kill you.'"

"In between the threats, we had breakfast, lunch, and dinner together. At lunch, I offered him wine: 'You son of a bitch,' he shouted, 'you know what wine does to me!' His paranoid system meant that if I offered him wine, I was preparing to do something ugly to him.

"I never felt in immediate danger. I had worked in a mental institution; I was used to nuts. We parted on good terms. I never saw him again.

"The heartbreak was that he was far past his prime as a poet—far past what he had done in 'In Dreams Begin Responsibilities,' which was considered one of the greatest short stories of the age. It was terrible to see what alcohol had done to that fine, fine, disciplined mind."

In 1965, Langston Hughes had written critically of those who were "glorifying drugs and irresponsibility" and recalled his listeners to the Whitman tradition of transcendentalism. As Kerouac had remarked to his friend David Amram, "We were born to share the holy light. The spirit takes over and does the writing."

In spite of the holy light, the brilliant Delmore Schwartz died in 1966 of alcoholism—and no one claimed his body from the morgue for two days. By 1969, Kerouac too was dead of alcoholism. I hoped it was really possible to teach my students that they could be illuminated by the glory of the world—without burning out.

LESSON EIGHT

Pay Attention to the Details

You never know when the trivial will
become the consequential.

I T WAS THE END of July. There was a haze of heat on the grass
outside, and the river was loud with the sound of frogs.
Leonard had brought some instant sugar-free iced-tea mix, a
product that, when you prepared it using cold water, exploded
into a gritty mound of brown foam. I skimmed off the foam,
poured it into a glass, and brought it out to the sunporch.

Today Leonard looked as if he had just come back from
trolling for marlin with Hemingway off the coast of Cuba. He
was wearing a Philippine guayabera shirt and a fisherman's cap
with little loops for bait hooks.

Through the screens, we could see Mr. Christian's latest
work: he had laid a line of slim sapling logs across the stream
that divided the lawn from the forest, creating a makeshift
bridge. This bridge supported the treads of his bulldozer so it
would not sink into the mud of the stream. In the forest, I had
seen that he had transported a load of used lumber to the base

of the tree in which I wanted to install the treehouse—the tree
where we had nailed the wooden steps and from which we had
hung our crooked swing. He was about to construct a brace to
support the two pallets we had completed, which I thought
would form two small rooms for the treehouse. The brace
would be an armature for the treehouse and its details.

"Plot is the armature, the support," said my dad, looking at
his notes, "and detail is what you load onto the armature. The
eighth lesson is that in your life you must PAY ATTENTION
TO THE DETAILS. God lives, they say, in the details.

"My students resist writing a sentence such as 'He walked
across the room.' They don't consider it lyric or literary
enough. But I am asking students for the patience to write sentences such as the following: 'He stood and started toward the
east wall, hoping that he would not trip on the shoelace that,
he noticed, was untied, and remembering that his grandfather
had always been a stickler for neatly tied shoelaces.'"

My father went on with the next item from his lesson plan:
"I want them to describe a place where people are in motion—
like Grand Central Station or a street corner. I take them somewhere busy to look. Why should we observe people in Grand
Central? If they are going to spend the rest of their lives writing, they will need to decide if a given scene is one in which
there is motion or no motion; they must decide if they will
focus on the person dropping trash in a can, or the person racing to catch a train. They will have to see the overall picture,
which arises from a thousand details about which they have
made decisions. I direct them to Salinger's novella, *Franny and
Zooey:* Salinger has a nearly one-page description of the con-
tents of a medicine chest.

"What is the point of that?" I asked.

"It tells you whose house it is."

"Whose house is it?"

"Either Franny's or Zooey's! Honey, I read it nearly fifty years ago. I am not talking about detail for its own sake but significant detail. You have to become responsible for the way the world looks."

"The fictional world?"

"No, the real world. And the way real people act. This means paying close attention. Always, always, everywhere. The development of peripheral vision is a critical skill that every writer needs. The imperative is to eavesdrop, to develop an acute attentiveness to spoken speech. Without the detail, the work lacks texture and clarity. Aristotle said, 'We are holding the mirror up to nature.'

"There was a very famous dialogue between the young Isaac Babel and Maxim Gorky." He looked at my slightly out-of-focus expression and started to laugh. "Gorky is probably the most famous Russian novelist of the twentieth century. And the dialogue went like this:

"Gorky: 'Ah! So you want to be a writer, eh?'

"Babel: 'Oh yes! Yes! I want to express the relationship between man and the universe!'

"Gorky: 'Uh . . . that flower over there. What's its name?'

"Babel: 'I don't know. But I am trying to explain to you—it's the relationship of man to the universe—'

"Gorky: 'And that other flower: what's its name?'

"Babel: 'How should I know? You're not getting the point! It's man's—'

"Gorky: 'And you say you want to be a writer?'

"Babel: 'Yes, yes, a great writer!'

"Gorky: 'Not until you know the names of the flowers.'

"You have to pay attention to the external flowers as well as the internal ones," said Leonard.

"I send the students out again to look at a tree. This time I want to know about leaves, twigs, and branches and bark and roots. Do you know the term *chosisme?* It means a focus on the thing itself.

"Things have their own selves. You have to notice. Look: noticing is a big part of staying in love with someone for forty years. I always bring home Chanel No. 5 from my travels for your mother. I did that when we had no money. Now, you could ask: Why spend money on fine perfume for your wife every single time you leave, after so many years? She is not going anywhere.

"But a gesturing detail is an important part of a relationship. Not noticing, not gesturing enough, to your husband or wife, is more natural, in our divorce culture, than is paying enough attention. But that does not mean it's smart.

"There is a story about a monk who lived in China; he spent his lifetime carving a stone cicada. It was a beautiful cicada. The very last thing he did was to carve a perfect ruby tongue in its mouth. Of course, no one would ever see the ruby tongue. But the monk would know it was there. As a monk who was praying with his work, and as an artist, he knew that only when that unseen detail was finished would the stone cicada be complete."

On my father's seventy-ninth birthday, he decided to issue an edition of all the poems he'd written in his lifetime. At his age, he wanted all his poems to be assembled for his grandchildren—and did not want to wait to find a publisher. He decided to publish the manuscript himself; his friend, Lauren Horwitz, designed a lovely etching for the cover and carefully chose the typeface, paper quality, and binding. He sold three copies on Amazon to strangers and gave most of the rest away to friends. Some boxes of the books remain stacked in his crowded study.

Only a handful of people possess the volume or have ever heard of it, but it is a perfect book, complete in itself, and Leonard is pleased with every detail of its creation. The book is titled *The Stone Cicada*.

SOPHIA had asked if she could come up for a weekend with a friend. I was delighted.

Sophia had moved out of her big apartment uptown. She was legally separated from Malcolm. He was resisting the separation, and clinging to her, seeking to bring her back with promises and with guilt. She was torn, but she had slowly started dating again, even as she slowly withdrew from her marriage. A new man, Paul, came to visit us with her.

Paul was someone about whom I had mixed feelings from the start. He got off the train and looked so alluring—self-consciously so—that you just wanted to throw your arms around him or walk away. It was almost uncomfortable to interact socially with someone so intent on seducing. He had deep brown bedroom eyes; he was about six foot three—Sophia really found tall ones. He wore a self-conscious little goatee and his shiny brown hair fell in Byronic locks. "Sorry to have come empty-handed." He smiled coyly, like a little boy who just knows he will be forgiven. "I left the flowers on the train."

"No problem!" I assured him, opening the car door. He slid into the back, next to Sophia.

You left the flowers on the *train?* I wondered.

On the drive up to the house, he was all over Sophia in the

backseat. I was happy for her, but it made me a bit uncomfortable, especially when I needed to glance in my rearview mirror.

I had given the couple the keys to the car, so they could go for a drive together after they had freshened up. In their hurry to be alone, which I certainly understood, they excused themselves and went upstairs. An hour went by; I realized I could not expect the keys back anytime soon. A second hour went by; I went out to the sunporch to give them privacy. A third hour went by; Joey began to whimper for apple juice, which I had planned to get by driving to the store. But I was too embarrassed to bother them; clearly a big passion was under way. I gave Joey milk, to his frustration, and made him some macaroni for dinner. The sun began to set.

I more than understood and more than forgave Sophia's sense-driven delirium; the man was so very attractive, and her love life had been so meager for so long. I expected nothing at all from her and just wanted her to be happy. But him—I did start to feel that his having forgotten his hostess's keys in the transports of his desire was a bit tacky, especially with a baby in the house.

Rosa was reading. "When are Sophia and Paul coming down?" she asked.

"They're napping," I fibbed. "Let's go out and play."

"Paul didn't really pay much attention to us when he came in," she remarked—not grudging, just observing.

"I know, honey; some people aren't around kids very much and don't know how to make them feel comfortable," I said. But I had noticed the same thing.

As I went outside to put a fresh flat of pink and purple impatiens and a single planting each of parsley, lemon verbena, and Italian basil into the dust below the kitchen window, I thought about why I was growing more and more irritable, and more and more sure that Paul was not the one for Sophia. It had to do, I realized, with a rather old-fashioned script I had about what details you make sure to offer your hostess when you are seriously—or even respectfully—courting her best friend. You bring the damn house gift, I thought. You sit for a decent interval making small talk with the people in the house, even those you don't want to sleep with. You try to show with these seemingly trivial details that you are not just there to bed the best friend. You demonstrate that you are a mensch. *Then* you go to bed. On those kinds of small interactions, I thought, civilization is based—or at least successful family life and courtships.

They emerged after nightfall. Paul was horribly, charmingly sorry about the keys. After I had come back from having driven to the country store for Joey's juice, Paul hung around the kitchen with Sophia, his flannel shirt slightly unbuttoned, languorously draped over the top of the dishwasher. Sophia and I cleared the kids' dinner dishes, washed the dishes, dried the dishes, and stacked them. Joey wandered in and tried to show Paul his truck; Paul glanced at it and ruffled his hair and told pithy anecdotes about his work as a dot-com consultant.

"Truck!" yelled Joey.

"Nice!" remarked Paul, glancing Joey's way, but not getting down on his level to look. "I mean, you would not believe the kind of excess there was in San Francisco in 1999 . . . you name it . . ."

When we all went on a walk the next day, Paul charmed Sophia on the one hand and, on the other, charmed me. I was less charmed when I stopped to pick up groceries and he made calls on his cell phone, not noticing that we needed help loading the car. When we drove him to the train, he gave heartfelt kisses all around and waved gaily. Sophia and I went back to the cottage to strip the beds.

"He is unbelievably sexy," sighed Sophia as she helped me put all the linens and towels from the weekend into a big pile for the wash. "Unbelievable."

"Clearly," I said.

"We are so terribly embarrassed about the keys, by the way," she said.

"No problem," I said.

"He is incredibly sexy. But somehow I don't think he's the one."

"Glad you said it, not me," I said grumpily, stuffing the wet towels into the washing machine.

THE NEXT weekend my father came up. Sophia came up again too. She had ended it with Paul; he had another woman who was "not my girlfriend" but "someone I care about . . . it is kind of undefined . . ."

"Jerk," I said.

Sophia felt all right about the end of the brief affair; it had been blissful for her physically, and a much needed way to help her sever her tie to Malcolm. But the details Paul revealed about his character were all too clear. Sophia needed to find someone serious.

The river was rushing, at its height, and the pool where I told the children that Fala and Lala lived was deep. You could hear frogs sometimes, at night, murmuring.

"How did you know he was wrong for me?" Sophia asked.

"Oh," I replied, not wanting to hurt her feelings, "it was just some details."

Sophia had been in an emotional daze; she could notice very little. I thought about lesson eight; for Paul to insist on helping us dry the dishes while he was talking, he would have had to be a completely different person.

Which details were more telling: Paul's physical strength and height, his seductive eyes, or his not getting down at Joey's level to look at his truck? I knew what I thought, but I was not blinded by having slept with him. Sophia did not need her discernment right away; she was still in rebound territory. But she would need to be able to notice things pretty soon.

MUCH LATER, I received an e-mail from Eva: her latest short story. It was a love story in which a young woman interacts with a young man who has an addiction. It was cerebral, with sharp interactions between the characters, delicately drawn; but the characters seemed to emerge and fade into fog.

I called my dad and read a few of the key scenes to him. I had unwittingly become more comfortable doing so when I had a challenge with a student.

By now, I had to acknowledge that I was teaching much of the time. But it was as if I had resisted acknowledging that I would end up, essentially, in the family business. That summer, though, I was letting my guard down and realizing how good it felt to informally apprentice to a master teacher—even if he was my dad—for my students' sake.

He called back after having thought about the passages. "Lovely moments of interaction, but I don't feel I know the lead character well enough to care about her. What color is her hair? What does she eat for breakfast? A Pop-Tart? Leftover spaghetti? A smoothie that she makes with protein powder in a blender? Each breakfast says something different about this young woman. What kind of furniture is in her apartment? Is it almost empty? Does she have her parents' upholstered couch? Her own stuff from IKEA? What is she listening to on the radio as she gets ready for work? What's she wearing? Where does she come from? What do her parents do? Does she have a pet? If so, what kind? What does she say to her best friend when she hangs up the phone?" I passed on to Eva my father's advice.

Two days later, Eva showed me the first two pages of a sparkling first novel. The main character practically jumped off the page. You could see her, taste what she tasted, feel the summer's heat in her living room. I wanted the third page desperately, though the third page and those after it didn't exist yet. Because Eva had imagined fully the details of her characters before she had started typing, it took only two pages for her to reveal them, completely alive.

"Show, don't tell; of course you have heard that before. The details of a character or a setting," said my father over the phone, "will tell the reader much of what he or she needs to know."

THE IMPORTANCE of showing the details was a lesson I recall my dad having taught me early. When I was eleven, I wrote a poem set in some desert vastness, hosting some exotic activity, that was guilty of the phrase "tamarind-laced wine." (And this, God help me, was after I had barely, regretfully, discarded "tamarisk.") We were in the cool darkened living room of the apartment we were subletting for the year. The sunlight outside was pure white, creating that Jerusalem dazzle that feels spiritual, a blaze that probably contributes to the manic love people have for the place. The sun heated the pine trees and the heavy clouds of honeysuckle that grew over the golden sandstone. Those hot, sweet keroseney smells wafting into a stone room will always suggest Jerusalem to me, and that year of the war, and my own emerging consciousness.

My dad carefully looked over the grubby, torn-out notebook page I gave him, handling it as if it were vellum. The interlocution from Leonard was gentle, but quite serious.

"Have you ever tasted a tamarind?" he asked.

There was a long silence on my part.

"What did you think it might taste like?" he asked. "Can you imagine what color such a wine might be?" (He tactfully omitted to remind me that I had scarcely ever even tasted Passover Manischewitz).

In response to my father's questions, I started to guess. The tamarind-laced wine had seemed so terrific to me, I had wanted it to be real. On a moment's further reflection, though, I admitted to myself that it *hadn't* seemed quite real. I could almost taste it; I wanted some. That was the problem, though: I could *almost* taste it. But I couldn't quite get *exactly* what it would taste like: bitter, sweet, sticky?

"Kill your little darlings," Leonard was always saying, quoting Marianne Moore, about editing phrases that you might be attached to but which do not work. Truly, that wine was one of my little darlings. I had liked the way the words sounded, especially the grown-up "laced." The wine had seemed *better* than real and, more attractive yet, *easier* than real as a phrase with which I had hoped to make a quick literary impression. I didn't want to kill it off. I sensed already that real would be harder.

"Is it . . . a kind of amber?" I asked. "Very sweet, kind of dusty?"

"If you can really imagine it all the way—what it looks like, how it tastes, who would have made it, from what, the glass it is served in—use it. If not, leave it out," he insisted. "The reader can tell if you're guessing.

"Better still, write what you know," he said almost sternly, and gave me back my sheet of paper.

Oddly, I did not feel at all crushed by this rejection of my first effort. I felt invigorated. It was energizing to my confidence to be chided for cutting corners with my imagination, the way my father might call my attention to a half-done job if I had left spoons in the drawer when I was supposed to set the table. It made me feel grown up. It was intriguing that an adult believed I had a body of knowledge at all.

On the other hand, I thought, I was an eleven-year-old kid. "Write what you know" was an irksome instruction. After all, what *did* I know?

I knew my way to school. Down the street, by the trash cans that were chained to an iron balcony I passed every day, was a tree. It was April; the tree was blooming. I had never seen a fruit tree in bloom before.

The following day, I stopped on my way to school and looked at it again. Really looked.

Suddenly, an ordinary almond tree reconfigured itself into a cloud, its minute blossoms into a haze, the haze into matter for a poem; suddenly, I did not need desert wastes and camels.

This led me to write from the point of view of an eleven-year-old child looking for the first time at an almond tree in bloom.

It was my first real poem.

In Leonard's view, being alert to the details of the world—which is hard work—is the key to maintaining a state of transcendental awareness, because the ordinary details, what poet Richard Wilbur calls "The Things of This World," are innately sublime. If you are bored, there is something wrong with you, Leonard feels. If you are focusing on what is mundane or depressing, you have blinders on. He often quotes Gerard Manley Hopkins's sonnet about the transcendental nature of ordinary reality, to describe the way the everyday world blazes if you see it for what it really is.

The world is charged with the grandeur of God.
It will flame out, like shining from shook foil;
It gathers to a greatness, like the ooze of oil
Crushed. Why do men then now not reck his rod?
Generations have trod, have trod, have trod;
And all is seared with trade; bleared, smeared with toil;
And wears man's smudge and shares man's smell: the soil
Is bare now, nor can foot feel, being shod.

And for all this, nature is never spent;
There lives the dearest freshness deep down things;
And though the last lights off the black West went
Oh, morning, at the brown brink eastward, springs—
Because the Holy Ghost over the bent
World broods with warm breast and with ah! bright wings.

"Listen, honey: Hopkins is talking about a perfectly ordinary day," my dad said a few weeks after I had written about the almond tree. "People are not communing with nature barefoot; they are wearing their daily shoes, like you wearing your galoshes to school when it rains. They are caught up in their work, their ordinary problems—'man's smudge' . . . his 'smell.' They are looking at a bleak man-made landscape—this was

England in the nineteenth century—coalpits and factories and grim working-class housing. But there you are, and you look down and you see something: 'gather to . . . greatness like the ooze of oil / crushed.' Hopkins is probably referring to the pressing of olive oil, but look"—at this my dad had me put on my galoshes. He opened the door and took me out to the street. Rain had fallen earlier, and the asphalt was slick. "Do you see something that has 'gathered to a greatness'?"

I looked down at where he was looking, an empty space between two parked cars. I saw the curb; black tar. Oil spots. Wow! Then I saw what he saw—an "ooze of oil" floating on a pool of rainwater—ordinary gasoline. It was a veil of liquid rainbow just on the sidewalk, shimmering with every conceivable color.

"Hopkins is saying that ordinary things, your trip to your job or to your school, the details of the world, and our human feelings are implicitly full of glory. This glory is often hidden, waiting for us to do our work of noticing it rightly.

"It is up to you, to anyone human, to be willing to notice 'the dearest freshness deep down things' on a perfectly ordinary, even apparently awful there's-nothing-good-for-lunch kind of day."

Dad's noticing does bring unexpected slicks of rainbow into his own life. In the 1960s, when my father was teaching at San Francisco State, which remained his home base for the rest of his formal teaching life, he was becoming terribly concerned that his students had started turning to drugs as the quick, easy route to these transcendental moments. The commercial success of the Beats in the 1950s had created a trend for creative young people to emulate: get lost in your ecstasy, drop acid, smoke reefer (then "pot," then "weed," then "doobies")— burn your bridges, churn out the verse or novel in a stream of consciousness. Leonard was appalled; he saw the counterculture's glorification of chemically charged transcendence as a distortion of the disciplined path of the mystic or true artist.

As the new decade turned and unfolded, he watched his students' unrest rock the campus. By 1966, the students were rebelling against all authority, including the university president, John Summerskill. The students protested so violently that police battled them and the campus was shut down.

My father felt that reaching the students was urgent, but that it was poetry, not drug culture on the one hand or repression on the other, that would save them. He met with Summerskill and promised that if he got funds to start a center for the hippies, he could renew young people's faith in teachers. He thought he could get them higher on verse than they could be on drugs.

Leonard did raise funds to open Happening House, a Victorian building in the heart of the Haight-Ashbury where, by this time, the hippies were flocking. They were beating bongo drums in the park and shooting up in doorways.

His bet failed. The young people found the quick high easier and more gratifying than pursuing the details and discipline of the poet's high. One day in 1967, a group of yippies decided to mock authority—including my father's—by staging a nude ballet at Happening House. The police arrived and asked who was in charge; my father arrived next, having known nothing about the spectacle, and he told them that he was. He was promptly arrested for contributing to the delinquency of minors.

Some months later, after a three-week trial, he was acquitted, and Happening House folded. The 1960s led their rampage through the lives of his students, wrecking some of them. Worst of all, Leonard felt, the bond between teachers and students had been severed.

Thoreau's route to transcendence—apprehending the brilliant world—is harder work than getting high on chemicals. It is harder work than tuning in to other intense experiences—whether it is consumerism or overwork or sex addiction—that took the place of drug culture in the 1970s and '80s. Thoreau is clear:

> *The same sun which ripens my beans illumines at once a system of earths like ours . . . This was not the light in which I hoed them. The stars are the apexes of what wonderful triangles! What distant and differing beings in the various mansions of the universe are contemplating the same one at the same moment! Nature and human life are as various as our several constitutions . . . Could a greater miracle exist than for us to look through each other's eyes for an instant?*

Thoreau, like Blake and Whitman, is, according to Leonard, pointing out the real "trip." If you notice that the sun by which you "hoe your beans" (make your commute, do your laundry) is the same sun that orchestrates a cosmos, you are living a transcendent life. If you are open to the possibility that in any one moment—in the backyard with your kids, in the mall with a friend, in the office with a coworker—you can use the miracle of your imagination to open up worlds within worlds, then you are living a creative life, in touch with "the dearest freshness deep down things."

A lifetime of noticing the details of transcendence in the daily world has borne out its promise in my father's life. The traffic roars outside my parents' apartment, and people shout at one another in a chaotic New York street below, where cheap shoes are sold. Leonard looks out his window, though, on a scene of Whitmanesque surprises.

Inside, my dad has collected treasures: he has a Chinese peddler's scale that was used to weigh out rice, "or opium," he muses. "Of course, we have any number of fossils." He has a Bennett miniature folding typewriter from 1912; he has a grandfather clock retrieved from a Dumpster—"that doesn't function, you understand," he explained—which is stopped at three-thirty; he has a mortar and pestle from Hebron; and he has his own framed photographs of the inside of a Spanish cart, a blue rowboat on grass, the stone wall of a cemetery, a Turkish bath—in Turkey, and equally carefully framed drawings by his grandchildren.

An entire corner of the apartment has been taken over by green plants. A corn plant, a scary Amazonian thing that reaches to the ceiling and overshadows the TV—"It promises to eat the house," he remarked—edges about a foot farther into the living space every year. An assortment of ming aurelias are also creeping slowly toward the center of the room, giving the whole interior the feeling of a jungle. My father has scattered children's marbles around the fronds of a wandering Jew.

On top of a table that my father made out of an 1850 sewing machine base and a plank of Honduras mahogany—"no varnish"—is another set of treasures. A burled piece of wood has two red eyes glued into it: it is a dragon. The white porcelain top of a cereal jar, with two eyes and a Modigliani mouth drawn on it in black marker, becomes a modernist mask. A tiny brass turtle shakes out another tiny brass turtle, and inside that is a tiny brass chicken. The branch of an olive tree has been carved into a boat. A miniature gilded furniture set has been created out of the twisted tops of champagne bottles. A tarnished brass samovar sits in a niche. "It's a Persian samovar . . . just not functional. Someone punctured a hole in it."

"Why do you have a samovar with a hole in it?" I asked.

"We were in Isfahan—it was in the bazaar—and it is a real work of art. There is a sequential narrative carved alongside it, a fairy tale."

"What about?"

"I don't know," said my father happily.

Leonard has assembled a wrought-iron bench that he found in a Dumpster, and arranged papier-mâché dolls from Mexico on the bench, each one with different-colored hair and a different-colored dress painted on her. Each of the dolls is painted with a name.

At first he got one, but he thought she looked lonely. He got two more. Then he decided he liked the look of them, convened in the living room as if chatting at a village well, and he collected half a dozen.

Then, with the help of his friend Bob Schrank, the handsome eighty-three-year-old ex–Communist labor organizer, Leonard made a little toy cart, called an Irish mail cart, from pine wood. The toy moves like a railroad pump-handle cart.

Then Leonard sat one of the dolls on top of the cart, and set the cart on top of a wooden trunk.

"Uh . . . why is the doll sitting on top of the cart?" I foolishly asked him recently.

"Because it looks wonderful," he said. "It's improbable. The world is full of improbable things, all most exciting to encounter.

"Your mother and I were in a restaurant in one of those driving rains: not just cats and dogs but rhinoceroses. A man rode by on a unicycle; in one hand he held an umbrella, and in the other he held a delivery of pizza aloft in the driving rain. Lovely. The improbable is a lovely possibility for all of us."

"Why?" I asked again.

"Because it *wakes you up*," he said, looking at me with forbearance, as if I had asked, "Why set the alarm on an alarm clock?"

"And it gives you a wonderful sense of the creativity of the natural world. You know, of course, about the crocodile bird."

"Uh . . . no . . ."

"Crocodiles are infested with little bugs that make them itch. Nature has contrived a bird called the crocodile bird, which lives in a symbiotic relationship with the crocodile. It follows the crocodile, perching on its back and eating the bugs. That's one of those improbable things."

"Why is it improbable?"

"Because you don't usually think about the crocodile and the bird as being in a collaboration!"

Leonard's inner life is so vivid that he is often somewhat out of touch with the expectations of modern life. When we are waiting in a mall parking lot for Dad to find a store, my brother and I will place bets on how many times he will pass back and forth, searching, in front of the three-foot-high neon OPEN sign by the wide-open electronic door. Once, we counted four times before my dad eventually just wandered off around the corner of the building, like a shepherd following a stray, and our mom made us stop.

To Leonard, noticing the details that matter doesn't entail getting bogged down by the details that do not matter so much. In fact, it can have the opposite effect. Leonard's decision to remain keyed to the Thoreauvian glory of the daily sun can take a toll on his awareness of the beans. Leonard has lost his wallet so many times that he finally found a way to chain it to his belt loops. The only downside is that sometimes he forgets to detach his wallet when the trousers go through the wash. He has the cleanest cash in Manhattan.

Having secured his wallet, he would misplace his keys so

often that, finally, he ordered an electronic key ring gadget, which emits a series of beeps when you clap your hands, to attach to his keys. It is so sensitive that it goes off whenever anyone raises his voice. We had to start talking in murmurs to avoid making it beep. So he detached his keys from the beeping gadget, but it had become like a pet by then; he could not bear to throw it out. Now, from underneath piles of pillows or catalogs, it yelps whenever the conversation heats up. Leonard still loses his keys, but he can always find his key ring.

When I raise this point—the downside of living "among triangles of stars"—he refuses to yield. "Noticing details does not mean that you make no choices. There's a hierarchy of what's important in things to notice," he said a bit testily. The M8 bus honked, and from under a pile of pillows, Dad's key ring yipped.

"Sometimes you tune out on lesser details," he explained, "like where is your key, or wallet, so you can save energy for the more important details that relate to your creative work—for the flamingos in the backyard. I think the discovery of a flamingo in your backyard is of a higher order of excitement than 'Where the hell's my wallet?'"

"But Dad," I pointed out, "what if you *aren't* doing creative work? And what if there *aren't* any flamingos in your backyard?"

"Oh, Naomi," he said, and sighed. "If you are living your life as you should be, you are *always* doing creative work. And," he said, "there are *always* flamingos."

Your Only Wage Will Be Joy

Your personal greatness is utterly irrelevant in the process of writing. The next word alone is what is relevant.

"IN THE NINTH session I teach," my father said, "I say that they must begin to distrust everybody, including myself, who tells them that their work is good or bad. Listen to people's reactions, but don't accept it as truth. THE WORK IS ENOUGH.

"When my students feel the work is authentic, their relationship to it is the most precious thing they can have. Careerist concerns are wholly beside the point. The students must never be deceived into thinking that they are great or that they are failures. They must do their best, if they can, to look at their work as if it were not their own; to find ways of improving it that have to do with the work itself.

"That's the dynamic I want them to live with: their creative work, whatever it is, is a living process. The imperative is to keep doing it in the face of its never being perfect. Or having a wide audience.

"Or, possibly, any audience at all."

My father has written twenty books. Some have done well; others were ignored. Critics liked some and detested others. Sometimes it was hard for him to find a publisher. His method is to focus on the creation, ignore the reception, and get on to the next page. He has no regrets and he keeps working.

"My novel, *The Glass Mountain,* took thirty years to find a publisher. Did it get better in the interim? Of course not. My sense was that it was always important, and I kept sending it out."

"If no one had taken it?' I asked.

"It still would have been my best work, in my judgment, and important for that reason alone. My students should leave me with a sense that there is something that they want to make, and when they have made it and are convinced they have made it right, they have to stick with that knowledge, no matter what the world says.

"My life tells me that I have to—as they say—'stand on this line all summer.'" He laughed.

"What does that mean?" I asked.

"It's a Civil War phrase: some Civil War general said, 'I will fight on this line all summer,' because he knew he was right. It means that I have to defend this point forever.

"You have to have a very strong sense of self—it is different from egocentrism. Egocentrism says, 'It's great, it's great.' I say: pay attention, pay attention, pay attention—do the work itself, if you have to do it."

I thought with regret about how often I had called him in distress about a hostile interaction, or high from accelerations, or low from setbacks, based on the outer world's opinions. He had always told me that these considerations were completely irrelevant. When I was in the midst of those feelings, I had felt like an addict listening to Nancy Reagan saying, "Just say no." But now I thought about my students, and how intimidated and seduced they were by the commercial aspects of their dreams. How I longed to give them the distance that I now saw as a lifeboat.

"You have to be drawn to your vision, whatever it is, passionately, or you are in the wrong line of work. And you have to be loyal to your vision, if it is an authentic vision, even if it costs you something. I buy the concept of fire in the belly—you do it because you have to, independent of publication and critics.

"In that sense I am a Romantic. I do it because I have to.

"Then you have to complete it, and step aside from it, and be confident that you've done it.

"And then it may be a great work! Flaubert says at the end of one of his letters to de Stael, 'I think I've got something there.'"

"And if it isn't?"

"Tough. Your only imperative is to do it.

"And then mail it."

IN EARLY AUGUST the house seemed happy. The flagstone half-moon patio that Alison and I had put in alongside the kitchen had settled in; moss was growing up between the edges of the stones. I had bought a glass table with a green umbrella and four outdoor chairs to put in the center of the patio. The furniture had been on end-of-season sale at the Sears down Route 22 in Amenia. Joey loved driving his dump trucks under the table, where he would line them up: it was his garage. "Back 'em up!" he would say in a growly voice, completely absorbed with life in his garage.

I had painted the formerly murky-purplish front door a glossy red. John Werner, a local contractor, had come by to open up the ceiling in the kitchen. The old, stained drywall was piled in the garage now, and the awkward fan, which had threatened to decapitate anyone over six feet tall, had been taken down. The diagonal roofing in the kitchen was a revelation: it was old, dark, rough-edged, and humble. Again I wondered who had built the scrappy little house.

Teresa had come back to Boston Corners Road with Clara; they had a few more days to visit with us. Teresa's eyes looked brighter; she told me about a lunch meeting she'd had with a writer from another publication—male, single—whom she'd liked.

"Yes? And?" I nudged her.

"Oh, bugger off," she said. "That's it. We had a nice lunch. It's work."

I stopped pushing for the time being. David was still working hard to keep up with news events: bombardment; the opening of a prison base in Guantanamo; the suspension of certain civil liberties; the formation of the Afghan *loya jirga* and new government; the escalation of suicide bombings in Palestine and Israel; the daily deaths of the U.S. troops.

Ordinarily I too would have been engaged in these events—thinking or writing about them. But stronger every day was my sense that we had gone desperately astray by leading with the mind and not the heart. I did not want to live in my head anymore; what I wanted to think about was the heart's wisdom that I had neglected, the human connections with my husband, my father and mother, the children, our friends, my students, the earth itself. I was realizing that my father had been right: for me to teach Eva what her potential voice could be like, or to help Rosa build her treehouse according to her authentic image of it, was more crucial for the world, in a way, than my signing yet another petition, or concluding another public argument. Not that there was no value to politics; but I was finding out in my own daily struggles—to be a good wife and mother, to be a decent teacher—that if politics was not based on the heart's wisdom, it was arid.

Teresa faced pressures of her own back in London, so the girls and the mothers were glad to enjoy this respite, and to resume our project, while Joey dug in the sand.

The girls had been working hard on the treehouse pallets, hammering in more slats. When they were finished, we had two floors for two rooms. The pallets also had four frames, one on each side, rising up to make walls if we wanted to put plywood over them. The girls put down their hammers at length; they were hot and sweaty from their labor.

"Can I slide, Mom?" asked Rosa.

"Go for it," I said.

The treehouse carpenters dropped their tools, ran across the lawn, and slid into the ooze that lined the river as if they were sliding into third base. As they went down, they screamed with laughter. Rosa's sweatpants had been white; now they were brown. Clara's navy-blue cotton shorts were caked with mud, too. The girls' bare feet were encased in boots made from chunks of mud.

The whole edge of the lawn was churned up into a mud sea streaked with green turf. The girls thrashed and howled. Joey was jumping up and down in the red paint by the porch. I was thinking about laundry and the fact that my dad always advocated for bliss taking priority over laundry.

If you never forget how to do that, my dad believes—how to

find the joy of the creative act—then, no matter how old you become, you can always be happy. But it takes a willingness sometimes to let go and fall in the mud.

That weekend, Eva was coming to visit and was bringing her good friend Madeleine. When Eva got off the train, she looked as robust as ever. She had tried to shake up her good looks by dyeing the tips of her jet-black hair magenta and wearing black T-shirts and ripped cutoffs. She now had a butterfly tattoo on her left shoulder. Madeleine seemed more matter-of-fact: Lebanese-American by birth, she had been growing up fast, having insisted to her traditional family that she had to come to the city to try her hand as a writer, rather than settle down in Detroit in an early marriage to a suitable boy from a good Muslim family. Madeleine was tall and strong; that day, she wore simple cotton jeans and a navy T-shirt. She had eggshell skin and sleek black hair that she wore in a braid down her back. She was low-key and confident. Madeleine was shelving files for a science archive so that she could work on her screenplay. Eva by then was working two part-time jobs so that she could get on with her novel. She was turning out something spectacular and fresh. But her article about her friend had not yet been accepted, and she was discouraged. Her delight at starting her novel had yielded—temporarily, I hoped—to concern. Both young women arrived uncertain about the future.

Their uncertainties were well-founded, it turned out, given their training. Both young women had been taught in creative writing programs. Both felt that their teachers were bitter about the marketplace and cynical about their lives in general. The classes had focused aggressively on professional technique, but no one had taught them that creative work should, above all, make them happy.

As Eva and Madeleine explained the problem, their work gave them tremendous joy, but they felt their teachers had conveyed to them that the joy alone could not be trusted. Both had arrived at the point of wondering if a life spent trying to do their creative work was feasible. They told me about their lives: both had parents who were divorced; Eva's single mom took every kind of job to raise her child. Madeleine's father, a banker, had left her mother for a tennis instructor. They had no shortage of material.

But in spite of Eva's two fantastic pages, and a screenplay Madeleine was writing, they were still, understandably, scared. When I asked them why they felt this way, it became evident that, as my dad would put it, their teachers had confused the career of the writer with the life of the writer.

My father had always made the distinction between the two. "Didn't your teachers ever tell you your work can be a source of joy no matter what?" I asked them as we sat on the grass. "That your success in the world is irrelevant to the creation of the thing you need to create?"

"No," Eva said. "They talk about the career. About how impossible it is to make a living. Or about how no one wants novels or poetry. Or how, if you publish nonfiction first, you will be seen as having lost your 'edge' as a fiction writer. Or they talk about how to cultivate contacts with editors."

"But . . . they don't say anything to you about the happiness of doing your work no matter what comes of it?"

The two young women stared at me as if they could not believe I was saying what I was saying.

I took a deep breath and repeated to them the essence of the notes I had taken from my father's discussion of joy. They listened and yet seemed afraid to believe in what I was describing. They were so scared about not making it, about being obscure; they had been taught that commercial success gave essential meaning to creative work. But they were thinking.

I CALLED MY DAD in the city again to ask him for what were, I was coming to accept, my teaching notes: what should I say to Eva, especially, who was still so frightened of failure that she was scared to devote herself completely to her work, in spite of her terrific growth spurt. Madeleine was a bit more confident because her screenplay had attracted commercial interest. I knew that Eva, as a novelist, gifted though she was, might never have the kind of commercial success that I could envision for Madeleine. But it would be tragic if Eva never completely devoted herself to her stunning new novel; how could I assure her that she *could* base her life on her creative work?

"You are always telling people to follow their vision whether it brings them worldly success or not. How do you justify that?" I asked my dad.

"By pointing out that the worst thing is to come to the moment of death and discover that you've wasted your life."

"But if someone—Eva, say—takes your advice and spends her life writing what she needs to write and never finds a huge audience, will she not feel she's wasted her life?" I asked.

"No, because she did what she was meant to do. That's Blake. That's Emily Dickinson."

"Dickinson didn't like it," I objected. "Her obscurity."

"She may not have liked it," he agreed. "But she kept writing."

"Isn't that faith in doing one's work contradicted by how

many great works of art don't sell?" I was trying to prepare for
Eva's questions that I knew would come the next day.

"That's beside the point. The great works of art still work.
They just don't have an audience. John Donne disappeared
from English literature from the beginning of the eighteenth
century to the beginning of the twentieth. T. S. Eliot, around
1910, wrote an essay and resurrected him, and he is still with
us—the work was still there and still living."

"Even if no one's reading it?"

"Of course! The work lives; the work is alive. The fact that
no one's reading it doesn't mean anything."

"But Dad, that's a very old-fashioned view of the canon. I
mean, feminists would take issue with that. There were great
women writers who were never discovered—" I started to argue.

"But they were always great," he said.

"It's almost as if you believe in another dimension," I said.

"I believe in the vitality of the work itself. Just because it is
imprisoned by a couple of centuries of ignorance doesn't keep
it from living."

"Who puts that there? That sense of mission or destiny?" I
asked.

"I really know the answer to that. And this really takes us
into the realm of the immaterial," Leonard said gleefully. "The
nineteenth-century view—Blake's view and Thoreau's—is that
the universe has a soul. All things are an endless manifestation
of the soul of that creation. Since you are part of that, your imperative is to work with it.

"Then there is the mystic's view. The Jewish mystics say that
God withdrew into Himself, to create space for that light which
is a manifestation of Himself. And the vessels of creation burst,
and that light is now in the universe. The imperative for us is to

heal the universe by gathering up the light—so if you gather up your light, you are doing God's work."

"By writing poetry, you are doing God's work? I thought you didn't believe in God," I argued. How was this going to help Eva and Madeleine? I was standing by the window, looking out at the trees, and my head was spinning.

My father replied, "The God I don't believe in and I get along very well."

I rolled my eyes but smiled, too. "Why is this light you are talking about unique to each person?"

"Because each person is unique," he said. "Eva is unique; Madeleine is unique; they have to write to realize their own unique light. Other people have to do other things."

"How can I make that case to them, Dad? That is so . . . mystical! They have bills! It won't pay their rent!"

"Yes. But if you say this to them, their inner selves—hearts, if you like—will know it's true, and will recognize that for them to live in a way that leaves no room for their gifts will be a terrible waste, no matter how 'successful' they become. Being true to the inner light is absolute. By the way, you know that something is true in the illumination of that inner light because your own soul recognizes it. So don't worry about how to explain this to them—their minds may resist, but their souls will know what you're talking about."

I felt a kind of cracking in some defense inside me; we had stepped out of my comfort zone—the critic's arena—into the realm of teacherliness, if you like, where possibility calls to possibility on some level that is not easily explained.

Over breakfast the following day, I took a deep breath, realized that I might sound ridiculous to these two smart young women, and reported back to them Leonard's answers of the night before. I felt vulnerable as I did so, my critic's armor pierced. They listened quietly, and both looked thoughtful.

It was a misty, humid day, so we wanted to do something indoors. I took Eva and Madeleine to Johnson's Barn, a used furniture store located on the main road of Millerton. Furniture was much cheaper in the country than it was in the city, and the young women wanted to see if they could find something to bring home in the back of their rented car.

The barn housed displays of every kind of old household item, passed down through the generations and then sold off: Victorian shaving mirrors with black roses stenciled on the wood above the tarnished glass, which was almost bare of mercury, left over from when this area was rough and farmers were trying to hack the dairy pastures out of old oak forests. We walked down aisles of white-iron filigree lawn sets and broken spindle beds resting against the walls.

We walked through bouquets of floor lamps: bridge lamps from the 1920s, with art deco incisions like the top of the Chrysler Building; rooms of mahogany lamps from the 1940s, with colonial revival brasswork; 1960s cocktail floor lamps, with a shelf for your martini built in around the pole. At the edge of the barn floor, the young women moved into an area where tables were displayed.

Both went into a kind of trance. They moved slowly through displays of tables of all kinds: farmhouse tables with slices in the wood from chopping knives; enamel-topped folding kitchen tables from the Depression; Danish modern tables with blond wood veneers; block tables for a gourmet kitchen; card tables for late nights playing poker with friends; hall tables for mail and credit-card bills; and coquettish bedroom side tables to hold bouquets from a boyfriend or fiancé. There were a hundred fantasies—symbols of someone's heart's desires—embodied in the various tables in that barn. I wondered what the young women would want to look at. What would they decide about what made them really happy?

I wandered around by myself, then drifted back down one aisle lined with chairs. At the end of it, Madeleine was touching a piece of furniture gently. Her expression was wistful. I came closer to see, then backed away; what she was doing was so private. She was running her hands along the surface of a rough old pine table, the perfect size for a screenwriter or playwright to spread out her pages.

I turned the corner down the next aisle. Eva was there, standing with her arms crossed over her chest. She was looking so intently at something that her dark brows were knitted. It was a low pine desk cut into an angle so it could fit into the corner of a tiny apartment, with a shelf built on top, and a row of pigeonholes, and a hole for an inkwell. Her eyes had gone ebony black; she had that look.

I watched her take a deep breath and step forward. She touched the inkwell with her finger. I believe she was thinking only about what she wanted to write next.

On her face was a look of joy.

LESSON TEN

Mistakes Are Part of the Draft

You're either making mistakes, or you're dead.

A T THE END of August, my father looked over his notes in the dining room. He had brought up, in case the weather turned, his Greek fisherman's sweater, which smelled a bit like sheep—something Homeric—and a Greek sailor's peaked cap. He had paired his Greek sailor look with what must have been Greek boating boots: green rubber on the outside, tire treads down below. When he doffed his hat, his white hair stuck up and out in several directions. The sun beat down relentlessly on the grass and made the lantana blaze.

Today Leonard was drinking a glass of bright-green liquid that looked like carburetor fluid. It was from a bottle of liqueur that he had picked up in France on his last visit; he and Julius had gone on vacation there. "Absinthe," he said proudly. "Or something very like it—real absinthe can't be made anymore . . . people kept going insane . . . this was Rimbaud's drink."

Earlier, Leonard had handed me a plastic bag filled with

realistic-looking songbirds in several colors, complete with bright beady eyes, real dyed feathers, and wires where their feet would be. By twisting the wires, you could place these imitation songbirds wherever you thought you needed an imitation songbird: say, by your computer, or on a curtain rod or paper towel holder or light fixture. My parents' apartment had a flock of them. Dad ordered these things from catalogs.

Recently he had taken to drying food in the oven. He had experimented in my childhood—unsuccessfully, I thought—with dried vegetables; mercifully, he had moved on to fruit. Today he offered me a thick brown thing that looked like a section of inner tube. It was homemade fruit leather. I wrenched off a piece with both hands and started chewing dutifully.

Leonard cleared his throat and quoted from Robert Frost's "The Oven Bird":

There is a singer everyone has heard,
Loud, a mid-summer and a mid-wood bird,
Who makes the solid tree trunks sound again.
He says that leaves are old and that for flowers
Mid-summer is to spring as one to ten.
He says the early petal-fall is past
When pear and cherry bloom went down in showers
On sunny days a moment overcast;
And comes that other fall we name the fall.
He says the highway dust is over all.
The bird would cease and be as other birds
But that he knows in singing not to sing.
The question that he frames in all but words
Is what to make of a diminished thing.

"You will always make mistakes when you are writing," Leonard said. "Or living. The key is to know 'what to make of a diminished thing.'" My father believes that "The Oven Bird" is about making use of imperfection, making do with what you are given. "Life often gives us 'diminished things,'" he says. "We need to make them glorious."

WE HAD BOUGHT two Adirondack chairs. Sophia had helped me to put them together; the screws held, and the bolts were tight. Now I sanded one of the chairs and primed it coarsely with white primer. It was a hot, moist day; dragonflies entangled themselves in our hair. Where the children had trampled it, the grass smelled like a dairy. Earlier in the day, Rosa had seen a box turtle slowly crossing the drive. Elsewhere, there was war and heartbreak, and yet it was one of those days when you felt that everything can somehow be all right.

I had a pint of carmine-red Rust-Oleum paint, and two black bristle paintbrushes. Joey swept the red across one arm of an Adirondack chair over and over again, and he dripped huge red spatters onto the grass. The big brush and its arcs of red paint were hard for his small hand to manage.

"I'm dripping," he said. "Sorry, Mom."

"Joey," I said, "an artist has to drip sometimes."

"An artist has to drip," he repeated happily, every time the paint ran down his wrist and onto the grass, where it would leave a chaotic, trampled, brown-and-red expressionist scene on a corner of the lawn. The smatter of paint would remain on the grass for the rest of the summer and into the fall, long after Joey's painted chairs had been put away.

"Beautiful," said my father to Joey of the painted grass,

which was spectacular; he ignored the finished chairs, which were well covered in paint, but uninteresting.

False starts are sometimes what lead you to the beginning of the real work, my father feels. There is such an important place in anyone's life for false starts, he believes, for dead ends from which you reverse and for imperfections; human error. He believes in accepting that there will be first and second and third drafts. If you are stuck or going the wrong way, it's okay. Just stop and revise.

"That's what Wite-Out is for," he said in the red dining room. "Or was, before you had all these computers. But don't be scared of your mistakes. They are important.

"One of the most beautiful found poems in the English language is the series of street signs that say:

STOP.
GO BACK.
YOU ARE GOING
THE WRONG WAY.

"There is no shame in realizing you are going the wrong way. The only thing to worry about is being afraid to go anywhere.

"Perfection is the enemy of the good," he said. "Waiting for perfection can stop you in your tracks."

MY FATHER is a very imperfect man. He made at least one gigantic mistake; monumental, some might say unforgivable. He fathered a child in 1950, and knew about his son, and never told us about our half brother.

All my life I thought I had one brother, Aaron, who is two years older, and is now teaching earth sciences in Corvallis, Oregon, and one half sister, Sarah. But one evening in 1998, I picked up the telephone.

"Honey, are you sitting down? I have to tell you something."

"What is it, Dad?" I asked. Of course, when a conversation starts that way, you expect the worst. I thought he was going to tell me he had an inoperable disease.

"I don't know exactly how to say this, honey. You have a brother I never told you about."

"A brother?"

"Yes. His name is Julius. I am sorry, this must be such a shock for you."

"From before or during your marriage to Mom?"

"Before, honey."

I started to laugh. This was it? I was so relieved he wasn't dying that a new brother seemed relatively easy to get my brain around—at least at that moment.

My mother's experience of learning about Julius was even more surreal. As she described it later: "Your father was walking around looking even more preoccupied than usual. You know how he gets—the eyebrows. Finally, I asked him, 'Darling, what is it?'

"He said: 'I can't tell you. It's not my health.'

"I said, 'If you don't tell me, I'll worry!'

"He said, 'I can't tell you.'

"I said, 'You have a child!' What else was it likely to be, for heaven's sake?

"He looked at me in amazement: 'How did you know?'

"I know it's harder for you guys that Dad didn't tell us about Julius as you were growing up. He was afraid I wouldn't be able to handle it, or that I would leave. He tried to tell me several times, and tried to find Julius several times, but did not follow through. I see why, though it is still hard to accept: I was a young, dumb bride, and he knew I was having serious trouble being a stepmother to one child already."

Eventually, the whole story came out. One night in 1957, my father was at Yaddo. A knock came at his door; it was a shy, thirty-seven-year-old novelist. Their brief tryst resulted in a pregnancy. Julius grew up with his mother, in a rural Maryland town. He was adopted by his stepfather at ten, when his mother married.

My father stayed out of their lives. But for reasons I still cannot fathom, he never told his new family about the little boy he had fathered, the half brother we could have known, even after Julius had grown up.

When Julius was thirty-eight, a dark-haired, handsome, bearded man with golden-brown eyes and a strong nose, he saw a photograph of our family in a magazine, in an article about a book of mine. In the black-and-white photo, my father was thirty-eight. We were all seated around a linen-covered table on an ocean liner. In the photo, my father has dark eyes, a prominent nose, and a black beard. He looks exactly like Julius, who had known Leonard's name but had no image of him nor any way to find him. At that moment, he knew he was looking at his biological father.

Still, he did not reach out to us; he thought that Leonard must not want to hear from him. Two more years passed; by this time, Julius had become deeply religious. One day he was sitting in a doctor's waiting area and idly picked up a copy of *Glamour* magazine, which he never reads. In it was an article I had written about the racism of well-meaning white people. The subject happened to be his: he was spearheading a drive to teach white, upper-middle-class, well-meaning physicians who worked with inner-city populations how to recognize their own unconscious racism, to be more effective healers. At that point he decided the universe was suggesting that he get in touch; he wrote his father a letter. The day that Leonard actually reached Julius was the date of his now-deceased adoptive father's birthday, February 8.

The two men first saw each other under the clock at Penn Station in February 1996. Julius says he did not know what to expect; he reached out to shake Leonard's hand. My father—his father—embraced his son as if he would never let him go.

I, too, when I met Julius, felt that a piece of a puzzle I always sensed but never understood was finally in place: I, too, felt we had missed him, without knowing it, all those years. How strange is biology; Julius and I share the same dream imagery; he and my father make the same terrible puns; he and my other brother wear the same obscure brand of trousers and choose the same unflattering shade of green for their shirts. He gestures like our family; his inflection is my father's inflection. They finish each other's sentences.

They have spent the last few years trying to make up for all the time they lost: traveling together, cooking together, and telling stories. Julius is wonderful. And, like Leonard, he is far from perfect, a trait he shares with my brother Aaron and with me.

I asked Julius if he is angry that our dad was not around for his growing up. "I wouldn't have been the person I am now if things hadn't happened as they had," he explained kindly to me. "I got a lot out of the circumstances I had. I don't feel that the way things played out was a mistake; I got to have my life, and now I get to have a relationship with Leonard and you guys."

My brother, Aaron, and I are angrier—we feel our father made a huge mistake in not letting us know earlier about Julius, so we could be with him when we were growing up; so we would not have to revise our view of our father to include something pretty hard to absorb and less than admirable. But we realized that there was no point in expecting our father to be perfect; much of what we cherished from him was his assurance that we were not expected to be perfect, either. It was left to Aaron and me to rethink our untempered admiration for our father—to conclude that "what to make of a diminished thing" is better and truer, in a way, than to pretend that nothing changes or disappoints. We slowly accepted that what we got from Dad's mistake was not only a new brother, but also another kind of gift: a more nuanced understanding that Dad is flawed and human, and in some ways inexplicable—just like us.

THE SUMMER was now palpably diminishing: the intense purple irises and orange tiger lilies of July turned into the fading bulrushes and saffron-colored marigolds of August. Yellow-petalled black-eyed Susans had overtaken part of the garden. The wildflower carpet that we had rolled out earlier in the summer had failed to grow; we had not watered it regularly enough. Other efforts we had made in the garden had failed too: the raspberry canes we had put in had refused to thrive; they remained disconsolate and berryless in their too-shady plot by the garage. One of the two small decorative evergreens I had planted on either side of the front door had turned a sickly pale yellow and would have to be dug out and composted. The garden on which we had worked so hard was flawed. Several of the slats that the girls had hammered into the treehouse pallets were now askew; I would have to rehammer them in straight when no one under eight was looking. Mistakes were everywhere.

But the decaying lilies and failed wildflowers were just as much a part of the richness of the garden as were the basil, parsley, and lantana that had successfully taken root. The wrong nail-holes left in the slats of the pallets were now part of the story of the treehouse.

After I reset the crooked slats, Rosa and Clara—who luckily noticed no difference—spent several days sanding and priming the pallets. They splashed their paint into murky lines to make crude stripes from the colors they had chosen. When the lines converged, they waved their paintbrushes in the air, redipped the bristles, and painted over. They could not wait until David Christian was ready to hoist up the pallets and make them into our treehouse in the woods.

Teresa was sleeping and eating well. A ruddy Irish flush had come back into her face, and her freckles were emerging. In the mornings since we began taking the children to the quarry in the nearby state park to swim, her arms and legs had gone from London-pale to a light nut-brown.

On Saturday we went shopping in Millerton. After we did our main tasks—buying water shoes for the girls, a package of white socks from the general store, groceries from the supermarket, toothpaste from the pharmacy—I demanded that we do something for Teresa. In a little store on a corner, I made her try on a chestnut-brown wraparound cotton dress, styled like a kimono.

"Oh come on," she said. "That's not me."

"How do you know till you've tried it on?" I nagged. "Just try it. You can mock me later."

She sighed theatrically and went into the dressing room. She took off her purple-and-white striped T-shirt. She put on the wraparound dress and let me thread the sash through the eyelet holes around the waist. As she drew it closed, I tugged it straight.

A pair of black high heels was in the dressing room. "Yes!" I said, putting them in front of her bare feet.

"No," she barked.

"Yes! Come on," I said. "You have to see how the whole thing will look when you go out."

"If by some chance I ever do, it won't be with some twit who likes Barbie shoes."

"Just take a *look,*" I said.

"Oh *fine,*" she growled.

There was no way to deny it: she was indeed glamorous. The sash around her waist drew the eye. The V of the neckline was flattering. The brown of the dress made her bronze hair gleam.

"Oh, please," she said.

"Oh, please, yourself," I said. "You have to get this."

"Okay, if it makes you happy," she laughed.

She paid and we left. We took a long walk along the rail trail, under the trees, and talked about her life. She spoke of long days, hard work, late nights, and her steady focus throughout on her daughter: on Clara's schoolwork, her social life, and her sports. "Okay," I said, knowing that Teresa understood that we were seldom linear in our conversations, "you will need a new bra to go with that dress. You should get La Perla—underwire."

"I do not want La Perla underwire," she protested.

"Well," I said, "I'm not going to nag you."

*　　*　　*

I THOUGHT of the obstacle that is perfection when I was talking to Teresa. She was burdened by an expectation of perfection in herself. My nudging did not help, because it is hard to pass this sensibility by if you are the conscientious sort of person Teresa is. But if the mistake is not a failure at all, but an important—in fact, crucial—part of the draft, then maybe even conscientious people can move forward more easily.

TERESA TEASED ME like her old self—mocking my interest in "fakey country things," as she put it—as we made our coffee the following morning. The girls were watching the cartoon *Kim Possible*. Joey was hiding things under seat cushions, his new hobby: keys, small cars, jelly beans if he could get away with it. His big discovery was that you could slide a filched credit card into a VCR slot, thus efficiently disabling both at once. I made a mental note to check under the living room couch cushions and in the VCR slot when he wasn't looking.

Teresa took her coffee out to the sunporch, and I saw she was going through a pile of catalogs—mostly furniture catalogs, but some fashion catalogs too.

"It's not fakey country," I yelled at her back. "At least not very fakey."

"DON'T YOU regret what you did, what you wrote?" I am often asked. I have made plenty of excruciating mistakes. But because of my father's faith in the teaching power of mistakes, I can't say I regret them. They were the best I could do at the time.

I wished I could pass on that feeling to my students. They are so often paralyzed with the wish to be perfect; their mistakes haunt them and define them and too often take them over. When I forget my father's lesson about this, I fall into the same spiral of burning self-recrimination: Why did I write that, say that, do that? How can I tolerate seeing my own failures of effort, judgment, execution?

My father was fascinated by the imperfections—and worse—in the human capability. Leonard began to ask himself, after the chaos of the 1960s and '70s, about the nature of human transgression. He spent the 1980s intrigued with the very darkest parts of human nature; he interviewed criminals in prison and developed a specialty of studying and writing about horror fiction and films. He annotated editions of *Dracula* and *Frankenstein*, trying to see what the authors were conveying with these terrifying allegories. He was sure the vampire legend came out of the human wish, a moral temptation, to deny death; in the case of Frankenstein, he saw the creature as representing what was unacknowledged in the interactions of abusive families. He wrote fiction about Shabbatai Tsvi, the corrupt seventeenth-century Turkish Jew who was believed by his followers to be the Messiah and who preyed upon the longing of his people for a savior. He wrote about the historical monster Bluebeard. Later, Leonard wrote about the Dreyfus affair, in which the top tier of the French military elite colluded in sentencing an innocent man to exile. He kept insisting on looking straight into the darkness of the human soul. "How could we understand Dante's *Paradiso*," he asks, "without the *Inferno?*"

We were, of course, aghast: Why should this life-affirming man be so curious about the dark side of human possibility? My grandmother could barely bring herself to ask him about his work; I essentially threw up my hands—until I had a conversation with him to try to understand his interest better.

"Honey, my father had twelve brothers and sisters. Six of them died in the ovens. How can you pretend to be a humanist unless you are willing to look at everything the human soul is capable of? Milton knew that you had to sketch out Hell as well as Heaven to give the reader a true moral compass, to really engage his free will. We are capable of anything, and if we are not aware of that—it is very dangerous."

Though I resisted this position, I also slowly came to understand—especially as I began taking my duties as a teacher more seriously—how important it was to look at what we really were: flawed, tempted, weak, and possibly cruel, as well as noble and capable of the highest good. That is the humanist position. My students who refused to look at their own capacity for mistakes or destructiveness could not walk the path that would lead them to their creative work. Their denial of their imperfection, their potential for darkness as well as for light, would, paradoxically, block the light they had to work with.

The same, of course, was true for me.

FROM LEONARD'S point of view, so long as you are doing what you are meant to do on this earth, mistakes and revisions are necessary. How can you have regret? If you are living within your vision, all missteps, mistakes, even disasters, are crucial parts of the various drafts that make up your life, your love, your work; they are your practice. All failure leads to the final shape of the truly lived life.

That night Sophia arrived with her new man, Alan. Alan was someone I had been hearing about for a few weeks. I only hoped he was as good as he sounded. Sophia had been telling me—so often I had begun to worry—how wonderful he was:

kind, thoughtful, loving, idealistic, expressive, handsome. I was ready to receive him with huge skepticism.

To my amazement, and the children's delight, he was everything she had said, and more; he was a mensch. Sturdy and strong, smiling and with a level gaze, he came in, his hand gentle on Sophia's back as they walked through the door. He brought coloring books for the kids and a bottle of wine for us. He sat on the sunporch for a very long time, talking to us and letting us check him out; understanding without words the tribal necessity of going through this process, of courting our friend in a proper way. When my husband arrived later that night, Alan stood side by side with him, as men do, talking about work, then helped David set up the volleyball net.

All the adults played ball with the kids. Joey rode on his daddy's shoulders. Alan made the girls feel like superstars every time they lobbed the ball over the net; they were smitten.

The thing is, Alan didn't look like or sound like Sophia's "perfect" old ideal of what her true mate would be. Alan was a warm, straightforward, down-to-earth guy who had grown up in the suburbs; he wore T-shirts and chinos and sneakers. He was not tortured, elegant, or European. He was not Malcolm or any semblance of Malcolm.

Alan stayed that night with Sophia; they asked if they could sleep on the porch in sleeping bags. They wanted to see the stars. The next day, David, Alan, Sophia, Teresa, and Clara set the table for dinner. Alan offered to go to the store for milk and juice—we had run out, and the children were thirsty. Later, he grilled the hamburgers for lunch. Sophia looked on and beamed. From time to time, Alan would look up at her, and I could see that he was truly seeing her, in her joyfulness and kindness and loveliness, and he would smile slowly, with amazement and acknowledgment. She was an enchanting being in her own right.

I rinsed silverware and put away the leftover food in the kitchen, and eavesdropped, smiling. Joey and Clara were swinging on the play set and David was reading in the living room. Sophia was drinking tea with Teresa and Alan on the sunporch. Teresa's voice was animated. She was laughing and making everyone laugh. There was nothing inappropriate or disrespectful to Sophia in her enthusiasm, but Teresa was responding to Alan's presence a bit, livening up in conversation with an attractive man.

I cut up some peaches for dessert, feeling pleased. Innocently, respectfully, but definitely: our girl Teresa was turning on the charm.

By EARLY AUGUST, some of the people who had passed through Leonard's world were living revised—if still perfectly imperfect—versions of their previous lives. Sophia and Alan were now deeply in love. They were always together, and when they were together, they were talking. He brought her home to Cleveland; she loved his family, and they loved her. She was getting poorer and poorer, and happier and happier. When I see her now, she is wearing soft Indian-cotton skirts and simple brown leather sandals.

"What a pretty skirt!" I exclaimed recently.

"Five dollars, H&M," she said. The expensive blowouts, the manicures and tailored suits, are entirely part of the past now. "Can't afford them," she remarked serenely. She has left her high-paying job and barely scrapes by coaching people in how to set up their own nonprofits, but her business is growing. She is a little more rounded; her freckles show. The enormous diamond ring is gone from her right hand; she sent it back to her ex-husband's family, against his wishes, in a small black velvet-lined box. She dances when she walks.

I told Sophia she and Alan should get married on the grass by the river at the little house. She slapped my knee and laughed. "Don't jinx it!"

"A nice young man," said my father happily.

MADELEINE was in Toronto, producing her first screenplay in a low-budget experimental production.

Eva was not as successful—outwardly. She was struggling financially, but she was actually not struggling spiritually. She was committed fully to her writing, no matter what would become of it.

I saw her at a training program we run at Woodhull. She looked less frail, less like a tiny, pretty pugilist; more substantial, somehow, though very tired. We were standing on the porch of the farmhouse where the retreats are held. Dusk was falling, and from where we stood, we could see the Taconic Range before us and, if we turned to the left, the foothills of the Berkshires. There were dark circles under Eva's eyes; she had spent the day indoors, in a class about how you can manage your money even if you don't have much to live on.

She was writing nights. She was sending things out. She believed—most of the time—that she could support herself and live a creative life. Her goal was to arrange her life to give her all to her writing, whatever the challenges.

"I got a job working for a website that connects volunteers with organizations that need help. I work three full days a week, and the rest of the time I can work on the novel. It pays the bills. I don't have medical insurance—I'm trying to figure that one out, got some leads in class—but I got a secondhand laptop that works beautifully."

"Where are you working?"

"I took my kitchen table and placed it perpendicular to the window. Who needs a kitchen table? I make food on the counter and eat on the coffee table."

"All *right*." I smiled. "Who needs a kitchen table, indeed?"

"I'm halfway into the second chapter. I have to say, it is a hell of a second chapter."

"How are you feeling?" I asked.

"Tired. Scared," she said, giving me her nervous, slightly evasive pixie smile. Then the grown woman in her, the writer who knows how good she is and what she has to do, came into her face, like a hologram. "And happy. Really happy," that woman replied.

"Good," I said.

AT THE END of August, I had to give a talk at a local YMHA. Afterward, I was chatting with a group of people who had attended the discussion. A quiet, confident, self-possessed young woman, whose hair was smooth, whose posture was tall, and whose shoulders were straight, passed by and placed something on the chair beside me.

I did not recognize her at first glance, she was so changed. And when I realized who she was, I was amazed. I had been so afraid that she might not get started on her true path. But Alison, who had been tentative at our house, was standing tall as a dancer. The sweatpants and T-shirt had been replaced with a becoming rose-colored sweater that wrapped and tied at the side. She wore a tailored black skirt and professional-looking pumps. Her whole being was radiant. Her eyes were bright.

She looked every inch the young entrepreneur. Most of all, she looked in focus; actually, like herself. The Alison who had been there but in hiding, not yet emerged, when she had stayed with us, was out and blazing.

I had to keep chatting with people who wanted to talk, but when I glanced over at what it was that Alison had put on the chair, my eyes welled up. She had done it. Even as I tried to carry on polite conversation, I could not stop crying. "Excuse me," I finally said to the person I had been talking to, and went over to pick up what Alison had brought.

It was beautiful: a Chinese box made of curved bamboo. Inside was a blue-and-white-enameled porcelain Chinese teacup with a lid to keep the tea hot; a box of ginseng tea; a prototype of herbal body lotion with the words "Your name here" on the label; a prototype of herbal shampoo; and an aromatherapy candle. The objects lay on an elegant piece of green rice paper. Also tucked into the tissue was a small calligraphed card explaining that a portion of the profits from the basket would go to four charities: the March of Dimes, UNICEF, the Susan G. Komen Breast Cancer Foundation, and the American Heart Association.

Then Alison handed me another card. This one was a business card. It, too, was elegant. It showed a calligraphy rose, and Alison's name and contact information were on the upper right-hand side. Under her name was "President, Baskets of Bliss: Healing Gifts with a Conscience."

I hugged Alison so hard I am sure I scared her. While I was crying with pride, she was laughing.

"Okay," she said. "Don't get too excited. I haven't quit my

day job. And my boss is still driving me nuts. But I have my résumé out for other work. And in the meantime, as you can see,
I did get started."

Had I changed, too, maybe in ways that weren't so obvious?
When I went back to the city, I looked at everything I was doing
and dropped all the commitments that were neither essential
for my work nor for my loved ones. I bought a Crock-Pot and
tried to cook a stew. I bought an ivy plant for the window ledge
and watered it. With the hour here or there I now had—having
dropped so many non-vital activities—I could sometimes be
home early enough to play cars with Joey before his dinner and
bath. Most of all, when my husband or children would try to
tell me something I wanted to resist, I would take a deep
breath, will myself to relax, and try to listen. Embarrassed as I
was about it, I started to pray. A little at first, hesitantly, as if I
was disturbing a stranger on a train. Soon it was no longer a
stranger to whom I spoke.

BY SUMMER'S END, my family was back in the city. Teresa and
Clara were back home in London. I got an e-mail from Teresa.
She was working hard. She'd stopped smoking. She had
started taking dance classes.

There was no one special in her life. She had no expectations that there would be. But she was giving Clara some space
of her own, and had made a beautiful new bedroom for herself
out of the unused loft space in the attic. It was white with white
accents and skylights, and it had a deep bathtub in a renovated
bathroom beside it. A private, grown-up retreat. It sounded, I
thought, romantic.

Teresa was wearing her nut-brown kimono from time to

time, for special occasions. She said that she got a lot of compliments when she did so.

Two weeks later, in mid-September, Teresa's latest e-mail, after the usual news report, closed with: "Much, much more important: you will be pleased to know that I went out and bought *two* new underwire bras the other day. They were so expensive that I had to stick my fingers in my ears and say 'Lalala' when the sales assistant told me the total: 46 pounds!

"So you see, I do listen to you. Sometimes.

"More later . . . love, Teresa."

LESSON ELEVEN

Frame Your Work

The Chinese artists have something they call "the doctrine of the final inch." When one of them nears the completion of a project—with, say, only an inch to go—he stops; goes away; meditates; prays; then comes back and approaches the final inch as if beginning the project anew.

SUMMER was ending. Here and there, the leaves of the forest were turning red-brown. My father emerged from the kitchen in the house in Boston Corners. He wore a T-shirt with a vampire bat on it and painter's pants, because he had been helping Joey paint clowns on paper. He waved a bologna sandwich. "White bread!" he exclaimed. "One thing old age has taught me: white bread! It's so *good!*

"Look at this," he said. "Fascinating." He was holding up a tin-and-plastic item ordered from a catalog. "You need one!" It was a spatula that opened up to become tongs. You could scoop up a pancake and toss some lettuce without changing utensils, if you needed to; if you lived in Leonard's world of infinite possibilities, in which pancakes and salad could reasonably be part of the same meal.

As if merely going on to the next discovery, he said gleefully, "I just ordered my burial plot!

"You'll love it. I looked all over for just the right place.
This plot has a lovely view of Manhattan from Queens. But
best of all, there is a hot-dog stand down at the foot of the
cemetery hill, run by a nice Turkish man. When you and your
brothers and sister and your mother come to visit, you can all
have a hot dog. In fact, I think we should have a party there
before I actually die, so we can all enjoy the view together—and
the hot dogs—at least once."

"Dad, I hate it when you talk like that," I said irritably. "It's
macabre."

"It's not macabre. Haven't you heard the Middle English?
He that ne sterven can / Ne liven can."

"What does that mean?" I said, shuffling through a stack of
catalogs from Macy's and from my dad's woodworking suppli-
ers, trying to distract myself and change the subject.

"'He who does not know how to die / Does not know how
to live.'

"Honey, don't pretend it's not going to happen. That's
what's wrong with the world now: everyone is pretending we
live forever. Death is—I won't say beautiful, but necessary. It's
the frame.

"In the next-to-last class I teach," my father went on, taking
out his notes, "I draw a rectangle. What does a rectangle or
frame teach my students? I get them to understand that the
frame includes but also excludes. You have to know when your
work is done. You have to know when and how to frame it, and
then how to let it go.

"The frame is not just about content, but about what you
put in. Every aspect of what you do within a frame affects every

other aspect. An interesting difference between, say, *War and Peace* and *The Red Badge of Courage* is the frame. The books are both about war, but Crane's scope has to be smaller. That imposes restraints on Crane. He can't give himself the scope to expand character, explore motivation; while Tolstoy has time and insight to spare.

"The frame emphasizes that you are making a thing that has dimensions, finite, instead of a formless utterance of the soul.

"Read Robert Browning's 'Childe Rolande to the Dark Tower Came.' At the end of the poem, the narrator stands before the Dark Tower—which of course is his own death—and hears:

> . . . *Names in my ears*
> *Of all the lost adventurers my peers—*
> *How such a one was strong, and such was bold,*
> *And such was fortunate, yet each of old*
> *Lost, lost!* . . .

> *There they stood, ranged along the hillsides, met*
> *To view the last of me, a living frame*
> *For one more picture! in a sheet of flame*
> *I saw them and I knew them all. And yet*
> *Dauntless the slug-horn to my lips I set,*
> *And blew. "Childe Rolande to the Dark Tower came."*

"That is our goal," he said, setting his white-bread sandwich in two neat triangles on a plate. "That is a well-shaped life. To be 'a living frame / For one more picture.'

"There is no frame in nature. The landscape is endless. The frame is a human invention. Frames make it possible for us to endure reality. They give it to us in experienceable units. Otherwise, we would die of awe.

"You need to really look at the end, and not turn away from it or pretend it will not happen, to understand the full story. In our culture, we pretend the ones we love will never die. Then so many people are distraught when someone they love dies, because they never had the conversations they should have had and now it's too late. That doesn't have to happen; if you keep 'the frame' in mind at all times, if you face the fact that everyone you love will go someday—then those are the conversations you will be having with them every day.

"*We* begin and end." He laughed. "That is why reading saves us. Reading gives you more lives. Reading is the nearest we can come to immortality."

Later on, we went out to put some of the last touches on the pallets and to sand the steps that went up the side of the tree. He took sandpaper and showed me how to sand the splinters off. His right hand trembled as he did so. I had always resisted the evidence of my father's aging by reassuring myself that he had always been forgetful: the moments when he stared into space were nothing new. But the by now frequent tremor in his hand was the first sign of my father's mortality that I could not simply explain away.

Julius had explained that first sign of age to me some weeks earlier. He had called it a tremor—the Latin term from which "tremble" derives. "It can be caused," he had said in that deliberately casual, low-key way thoughtful people have of giving alarming news, "by caffeine overconsumption, or stress, or age."

"What on earth are you talking about?" I had wanted to say.

My dad had finished the sanding and was showing Rosa and me how to replace the sandpaper in its metal holder. His hands were now sure. Julius had said that the tremors of age vanish temporarily when there is an effort of intention.

I remembered a teacher I'd had in college, who taught Homer. He was a brilliant man cursed with a serious stammer. In his ordinary lecturing, his brain would sometimes lock, and his tongue would trip and trip agonizingly over a word.

One day he showed us how Homer himself would have spoken his poetry to his royal listeners. His eyes were bright; he clearly had looked forward to this day all term.

The professor took in his hand a wooden staff almost as tall as he was; he strode into the center of the classroom, and he spoke. The shy, long-limbed New England scholar transformed himself into a witness in a linen robe, describing armies pouring over a plain. Though we could not understand a word of the archaic Greek he was declaiming, we also did somehow understand. We could see the horses. We could hear their hoofbeats. In line after line, the speaker's cadence was as sure as an ocean and his articulation was perfect. We were watching a miracle take place.

When he was done and there was silence among us, he slowly, reluctantly let the vision go. He laid aside his radiant cloak and shrugged on his old, frayed identity; he resumed his mortality and his stammer.

There are miracles in art, I thought, watching my father's now-steady hands with the sandpaper holder.

We set aside six additional brackets and the lumber to join the second pallet to the first, as Mr. Christian had suggested; we had plywood sheets that we were saving to go on the outside of the frame, and we planned to cut a door with a jigsaw. Then we would have the floor and sides of the treehouse and its four walls and its roof finished.

We stepped back and looked at that small bottom half of a house shape, such an ancient human thing to make. A shape anyone anywhere would understand.

Leonard believes that the making of whatever beautiful thing you are supposed to make—*poesis*, the Greek root of the word "poetry," means "creating" or "making"—can stand against age; against infirmity. He says, anyway, that he believes the thing made can also stand against death.

WHEN WE thought we were done with the treehouse base and sides, and thought we had only to ask Dave Christian to hoist the pallets up into our tree, and secure them, we had a taste of "the doctrine of the final inch." Dave had an insight that made us, almost at the end, begin again.

My father and his friend Bob Schrank, two men who had been so physically powerful in their earlier years, had planned all summer to hoist the heavy, solid-wood door I had found in the garage to form the base for the pallets. The weekend for that activity kept being delayed; Bob Schrank was not feeling well. It took an effort, I think, for my father to let me know that he thought I should ask Mr. Christian if he would be willing to hoist the pallets up onto the tree and nail them down on a base.

When he spoke, I had a physical memory of my young father lifting me effortlessly and throwing me, again and again, into the air. I remembered concluding that he could lift anything, forever. It took an effort for me to hear his suggestion and agree to it.

But when I asked Mr. Christian to go ahead and lift the finished pallets into the tree where the stepladder was waiting, he made a request: just to go out and look before we committed ourselves to the shape we had decided upon.

I went out to the meadow to take a look; the ladder on our tree was still standing sturdily. The meadow was still clear. But Mr. Christian had identified, about fifteen feet away from our tree, a triangle where three tall trees stood together. As with one of those puzzles in which you are asked to see a grid between unrelated points, I had never noticed it before. David Christian had spiked three long boards horizontally into the three trees about ten feet up from the ground, connecting the triangle. And he had laid a dozen shorter boards down flat over the triangle, hammering them to create a sturdy platform. He had brought our finished pallets into the woods but had not put them on the lower tree where we had envisioned them, where our ladder stood. Rather, he had set the pallets out to serve as the ground floor, deck areas, and lower walls of the two-story treehouse he had created, as if out of thin air.

Damn, I thought, impressed. We were wrong. *I was wrong;* there, I said it. He was right.

I wanted to be annoyed, but I was now firmly seated, psychologically, in the student's chair, and admiring what David Christian had done. With a few simple gestures, he had created a proper, safe treehouse with a solid, sturdy three-point base— much safer than what we had envisioned, which would have involved balancing two very heavy rectangles unsteadily on one long branch. His rightness did not exclude what we had created with such pleasure in our own first draft; he had used our finished, painted pallets to create the lower level of the structure, and he was fifty nails away from having perfected an upper level. Our original tree, if we only put up a board against

the perpendicular branch, could still be part of the structure—
as a reader's nook, accessible from the main treehouse by the
rope ladder Rosa had wanted, or the pulley she had envisioned.

I smiled. I was so wrong! Wow, was I ever wrong. So it went;
this was better. The draft had been useful. Rosa and Clara's
hammering had been useful. Opening our hearts to David
Christian had been useful. All our wrong turns had been useful, and all of our imagining. The treehouse, as Dad would put
it, was more important than its byline. Its need to come into
being transcended all of us.

I went back into the house and got my drill. I could not do
what David Christian could, but I had really concentrated over
the past summer, and there were a few things I had learned. I
took a metal drawer handle that we had bought at Herrington's, and I screwed it into the side of the original tree, so
Rosa's reading nook—her treehouse auxiliary—would have a
handhold. When the handle went in straight and firm, I felt ex-
hilarated. I took a handful of nails and picked up the wire shelf
that we had salvaged from the original kitchen, and I nailed it
carefully, with good strong blows, to the side of the tree so Rosa
could have a place for her sodas and her books. I climbed up to
the bough with a bracket and a board, and I drilled the holes
for a level seat for her to read in. I looked over at the beautiful
structure fifteen feet away, so much more impressive, and
thought the two structures were not in opposition to each
other—they were in conversation. What my dad had taught me
over the summer left me looking at the two structures without a
pang; that was Dave's unique creative signature, and this was
our more modest one, and they were connected, since the
world has room for them all.

A week later, I went up to the house in Boston Corners to

prepare it for fall. Chrysanthemums were appearing on the roadside stands, and were ranged in rust- and tomato-colored rows at the Agway in town. I entered the little house and walked the rooms, and my footsteps echoed. The afternoon light fell in the rose room, the yellow room, the blue room, and in the lilac room in which Sophia had wept for so long.

It was so quiet with no Joey banging his truck on the floor, no Rosa hammering outside, no David spiking a ball over a net, no father settling into a chair with a sudden declamation from Wordsworth. We had come to the part I had feared so much: the end of one story that I wanted never to end. My father had no more notes to give me from his lesson plan.

From the upstairs window, I saw sunlight pick out the red of the Adirondack chair, and the halo of paint that Joey had left scattered on the grass. Light fell in a haze on the sunporch, which looked empty now, since I'd had to bring in the cushions from the wicker couch and chairs where so many conversations had taken place. Sunlight lit up the hollow in the red-berry bush outside the screen where we had found an empty bird's nest, which now sat on my daughter's bookcase in the city. Sunlight illuminated the finished treehouse, the main area in the triangle of trees and the reading bench in the lower tree; the platform had been painted by the two girls, and adorned with their reflectors and wind chimes and the yellow plastic rope and pulley.

The light was shining through the window full into my eyes. As they started to tear, I felt overwhelmed with love.

I saw them all: there was my father, his long legs stretched out in the Adirondack chair, an angler's hat on his head; there was Joey digging in the dirt by the parsley plants, and David grabbing Joey to throw him in the air. There were Rosa and

Clara screaming as they slid in their white shirts and sweatpants in the mud by the little river. There was Teresa in the chair on the sunporch, drinking a beer and not smoking and saying something hilarious without breaking into a grin; and there was Sophia lying on the concrete floor in a sleeping bag next to Alan in his own sleeping bag, their hair in tangles and their faces at rest.

I had wanted it all to stay that way forever. I wanted Joey to be a soft-skinned little boy forever, and Rosa and Clara to be screaming, sliding eight-year-olds forever, for David and Alan to be men in their prime knocking a volleyball over a net to the little girls forever, and I wanted my father to be there, reading Zola in the Adirondack chair, answering my questions, forever. I wanted to hold on—to the light, to the garden in its fullness before the snows came, to the people I loved, so they would never grow up or leave me or die.

I went back down into the strip of garden. The lamb's ear and nasturtiums I had planted had faded into wilted threads. I lifted out the torn tangle of the root-balls and threw them onto the compost heap by the garage; I was learning. The yellow-and-red lantana had finished spreading and was turning brown. The parsley by the kitchen window was a heavy ruffle of brown-tipped green. The basil was sodden and turning purple from the rains that had recently begun, presaging autumn. I pulled up the only two still-healthy stalks of the basil, wrapped them in paper towels, and laid them in the backseat of my car. The rich dirt clung to the roots. I would take the leaves off and steep them in oil, and maybe we would taste the flavor of that summer throughout the winter to come.

But was there anything I could really do to keep the cold and darkness at bay?

*   *   *

WHEN IT WAS completely finished, the treehouse was a world
of its own. David Christian had outdone himself: the platform
had been completed among the three sturdy trees; a crossbar
had been nailed above it, with a plywood sheet coming down at
an angle on each side, making a roof; a white ladder had been
recycled from somewhere and poked up from the base of the
treehouse through a triangular opening in the platform. And
at the base was our own proud contribution: the pallets, which
now formed the floor of the lower level. David Christian had
nailed recycled wood from the pallets to the base of the platform, creating a lower room; and he had taken the good solid
wooden door that I had found in the garage, laid it out in front
of the pallets, fixed it firmly, and covered it with more plywood: it was the front porch.

The extra miracles were there for the finding; he had left
them for the children to discover, like an Easter egg hunt. In
the corner of the ground-floor room was a small, real nest—
with colored plastic eggs in it. As you approached the treehouse from the path through the woods, you came upon a
mailbox; at the base of the mailbox sat a green plastic frog. And
at the corner of the front porch Mr. Christian had carefully left
intact—and groomed—a red-berry bush with scarlet fruit that
had been hidden under the thorns.

If you climbed up to the platform, you could see over the
tops of the trees as if you were flying. If you climbed down, well,
in the shadows and sun between the opened-out boughs, you
had your own private wonderland.

"There are always flamingos," I heard in my mind. I looked
around in the sun-dappled shade, and half expected one to

peer out from behind a birch tree. David Christian—and the girls—had done it; they had made a complexly logical miniature world. And my dad and I, I was proud to see, had built a good floor for their dreams.

Every single thing there had its own magical task: you needed the nest because you had the eggs. You needed the boat of the treehouse because you had the waves of the trees.

And you had no doubt at all that you needed the mailbox and its guardian frog, because something was going to be delivered for sure, and when it came, it would be marvelous.

IT WAS NOW the very end of the season. The asters were dry sticks in the ground. I pulled them out and threw them onto the compost heap. Scarlet geraniums and rusty orange marigolds alone had survived. The leaves were starting to turn on the mountain, over which fog had begun to drift. The sky was overcast.

The things around me had started to change and decay: Joey's little wooden chair, worn by the summer sun, was peeling and turning gray. Some garden trowels I accidentally had left out in the rain had begun to corrode. Paint was beginning to curl away from the windows on the exterior of the house, and also from the garage, which I had spray-painted a brash crimson only that summer.

I went for a walk down Boston Corners Road; sadness was like a companion. Everything my eyes settled upon seemed to change and fall away, and I thought with skepticism about my father's certainty that creative work really lets those you love live forever.

I paced up the paved road, past the hamlet with its half-dozen small cottages and manufactured homes all arrayed at the foot of the mountain. The cottages had, perhaps, been built for the Irish settlers who, in the early part of the last century, had come to make new lives working on the now-defunct railroad. At the end of the road was an old white house that still bore the sign THE HOMESTEAD INN. It had been the local bar for many years. I smiled at this rakish corner of the world, where a mile-long stretch of country road had required its own tavern. The inn was now a private home, but the owner had kept the sign up out of affection for the memory of the tavern.

At the old inn, I turned left to walk up a gravel road that mounted to a higher plateau running parallel to the valley floor. From here, you could see something chilling: the quarter-mile that stretched up from The Homestead Inn had been leveled flat by a tractor. The trees that had fallen under the tractor's jaws were stacked up as timber at the base of the gravel path. Our neighbor who lived in the white house was apparently chopping the great trunks into cordwood; the sprays from his chainsaw lay fresh and pale-gold on the gravel.

Just past that raw, flattened quarter-mile was a second quarter-mile along which half the berm remained standing, about twenty-five feet high, rising from the valley floor; it was intact on the side facing the hamlet, and still thickly, beautifully forested there. But from where I stood, you could see that the teeth of an earth-moving machine had gouged away the entire back of the berm in an effort to level it, too. The once-bare teethmarks in the earth were now seeding over with grass and saplings.

A yellow tractor was rusting at just the place where the gouges came to an end.

I knew exactly what I was seeing, and it made my scalp tighten.

Two years earlier, I had been exploring the land where I now stood, to get a sense of what lay around the house. I had come upon a handsome, sixtyish man sitting in a bright yellow tractor, busily leveling the berm that ran behind our house— and behind the entire hamlet.

I greeted him, and he stopped what he was doing long enough to chat. We liked each other immediately; he was, I found out, a retired inventor. I will call him Frank. He lived alone in a farmhouse on the side of the mountain.

Sophia and I eventually paid him a visit, and he proudly showed us the expensive, state-of-the-art laboratory he had built in a converted barn to house his current projects. He had, years ago, invented something important that protected fiber optics; in spite of his self-presentation as a simple country man in a plaid shirt, he had become a multimillionaire.

He had used his money and his vision—and the power both gave him—to create a massive estate, a fiefdom of sorts, above Boston Corners. He had been born poor, he explained, not far from here, so after he made his fortune, he had wanted to come home and make his mark locally. He confided to us that he had bought the flank of the Taconic range where he and his brothers had once hiked as kids; he offered to let me and Sophia hike it, and I felt sorry for him because he seemed to have no one to hike that expensive swath of mountain with him now. His children were scattered, and he seemed very much alone. He had created an entire golf course for himself and his friends out of a spectacular outcropping of land over-looking the valley; I walked it with Sophia one day, stunned at the view. But I never saw Frank or his friends in the clubhouse. I never saw anyone playing there at all.

As time went on, I learned from local gossip that Frank's

dreams of grandeur were generating enormous hostility among his neighbors. The state of New York was trying to buy the berm of the old railroad track—which was on Frank's land—in order to connect two long stretches of rail trail for hiking and bicycling. Frank was in a strong position: they needed that land.

Frank was a multimillionaire for a reason: he was a sharp negotiator. He decided he would pressure the state into offering him something better than money—specifically, Frank wanted a prime piece of state land, with majestic views, across the valley, that he could develop and sell at a massive profit. He gestured to a tract of pine woods on the hillside opposite us; it was a glorious piece of pristine woods.

So Frank was putting the screws on the state government by going out on his tractor, day after day, to slowly and very publicly destroy the mile of berm the state would need to make the rail trail complete. The destruction could not keep the state from wanting the land, since there was no alternative route; rather, it made every day that the bureaucrats failed to meet Frank's terms more costly.

Frank was an artist; but he was sort of a Machiavellian genius too. I could see him as a poor boy imagining the day that he would return to take control of the entire valley and both its mountain flanks. I didn't admire the methods he was using to manifest his fiefdom, but he was surely pursuing a creative vision.

Frank's hardball tactics with the state would have an unfortunate effect on his neighbors: the berm he was destroying ran behind all of our houses. Not only had it provided a backdrop of leafy trees to shelter each home, but it formed a barrier between the melting snows running off the mountain and the houses below. Frank was exposing us all to floodwaters. Day by day,

Frank's project ate away at the beauty and shelter behind a given house, and the house next door could see what was coming. The tension in the community, when Frank's name came up, was palpable. Still, I liked him. I kept seeing the humiliated child behind the isolated, monomaniacal man. I hoped that the friendship we had started to have might soften his determination to destroy the berm; after all, he knew that our house lay almost at the end of his planned path of devastation.

That was how things stood the day that Frank, while seated at the controls of his yellow tractor, its teeth filled with the limbs of trees, suffered a massive heart attack and died.

Now, as I walked, I almost saw him again, sitting in the rusting tractor, winking at Sophia and me. I saw on my right what had so recently been the green of his golf course; it had gone back to weeds and brush already, and a sign identified the land as being up for sale. I saw the strip of hiking trail Frank had bought; it had almost gone back to forest. I looked at the berm that had been spared by his death; it was more thickly forested than ever. I took in the piles of cordwood that Frank had imagined crackling in his own fireplace for winters to come; the logs would heat his tenant's living room this winter instead. Frank and his ruined, slightly demonic masterpiece, now so quickly returning to the elements after their author's death, reminded me of Percy Bysshe Shelley's poem "Ozymandias of Egypt":

> *I met a traveller from an antique land*
> *Who said: Two vast and trunkless legs of stone*
> *Stand in the desert. . . .*
> *"My name is Ozymandias, king of kings:*
> *Look on my works, ye mighty, and despair!"*
> *Nothing beside remains . . .*

As I turned back, wishing Frank peace wherever he was, I thought of my father. He was not right, I speculated: the work doesn't grant any kind of life after death. Frank was younger than my dad; death—mutability—dissolves all into chaos; the destruction is unredeemed. We let our loved ones go into this void—this forgetting—and grass grows over all of their works within a year or two. For a moment, grieving my father's loss while he was still with us—as he asked us to do by looking squarely at "the frame"—I lost all faith in my father's sense of serenity.

I turned back and descended again into the hamlet. There I noticed, as if through Leonard's eyes, many things that I had never seen before. Each house was telling its own story.

The owners of number 107, a timber-harvesting family who lived in a neat modern home, had planted ivy in a dignified half-circle around a flagpole which flew an American flag; a squirrel statue had been placed along the ivy's rim. The neighbors who lived in number 122, a brown-shingled cottage, whom I had never met, had an Italian flag flying over the garage, and Harley-Davidson signs posted all over the front porch. The couple in number 120, a yellow saltbox, had put a "welcome" sign in a bed of hostas, and had draped artificial greenery in loops from the house's eaves, creating a festive effect. The older man who lived in number 118, the small cottage right next to our house, had had someone paint his beautiful wooden garage a peacock blue. A mirrored blue ball sat before the cottage in beds of neat chrysanthemums.

All these neighbors were making their own poetry out of their own sensibilities. Their voices would emerge no matter what. I smiled in spite of myself. Those loves, those selves, those visions, would go into their kids, their work, their neighbors, their communities, their gardens. Maybe it is love, somehow, in the creative gesture that makes the gesture last, I thought. And a completely different line from a completely different poem— Elizabeth Bishop's "Filling Station," describing a potted begonia beside a doily that someone has placed in a dusty gas station—came to mind:

> *Somebody embroidered the doily.*
> *Somebody waters the plant . . .*
> *Somebody loves us all.*

JOEY AND ROSA came back one more time. Joey clamored to go up into the main part of the treehouse, but I lured him back to the house. Rosa climbed up; she tucked herself with her back against the tree, hugged her knees, and looked dreamily into the leaves.

Mr. Christian had seen a fort and a ship, and had helped to build that, because that was his vision. But Rosa, looking at the same structure that she, too, had helped to build, was seeing something else; her own escape into the jungle. "Once the work is out in the world, it is none of your business what your readers make of it," my dad always says.

Rosa's treehouse did not have a fort or a prow; it had, in her imagination, room service and a library. It had a music system and a home theater. It had a kitchen. It had an escape hatch. It had a yellow rope with a pulley to swing from to reach the reading tree, because she was more interested in exploring the jungle than in fighting off attackers or sailing to a new continent. Rosa's treehouse was just what she had imagined.

She was singing something. The whirligig spun in the wind.

The wind chimes sounded. Her book, *Double Fudge,* sat next to her on the floor. She had a box of graham crackers in her lap. Now Rosa stretched out on her back, her knees bent, and, with her hands behind her head, gazed into the blue of the autumn sky.

The treehouse that Rosa had imagined really did have a swimming pool. You just had to go into it by leaping up, not down.

LESSON TWELVE

Sign It and Let It Go

A work of art is never finished—only abandoned. You need to know when to put down your tools.

AT THE BEGINNING of the fall that year, we went on a camping trip to the Cascade Mountains in Oregon. Our family was there with my brother, Aaron, and his children, Yardena and Eitan. When we get together, Aaron and I revert to the bad habits of adolescence; when the kids were asleep in the tent, he would break out a six-pack of hard cider ("How can you drink that?" I asked) and Marlboros, and we would sneak down to a culvert close enough to hear the children, and smoke.

In the morning, I had taken the four children with me on a hike, to give Aaron time to clean the campsite. Two big girls and two little boys struggled up the pathway between old-growth pines.

When we paused to catch our breath beside the path, we found an agate stone on the ground, under the pine needles. We leaned against the trees, then found places to sit on the huge roots that emerged from the rich dirt.

"Look, it's magic," I said to the children, and held the agate up to the light, remembering how my father had shown me the celestial city inside a slice of similar stone; the city that I had disavowed, and then tried to return to.

"No, it's not," said Eitan, a practical little boy.

"Yes, it is. I believe it is, anyway," said Rosa, equally stubborn, to her cousin.

"No, it is not," yelled Eitan.

Rosa gave up the argument, apparently bored with a debate that was by definition subjective. She took from my hands the disposable camera I had bought to record the trip, and she aimed it at the tops of the trees.

Leonard had said that morning that he was going to the VA hospital for tests. For once, incredibly, he was using the voice of a very old man. On the answering machine, it had sounded scratchy, like a recording from another century. Like a memory.

(Why do you want to do that, Pop? I could not stop myself from wondering.)

It would be fine, this hospital visit. And the next one, of course, God willing, will be fine. Then sometime, sooner or later, he will go to the doctor, or get the results of some test, or someone in the doctor's office will call, and everything will not be fine.

And yet that, too, eventually will be okay. If we are living the way Dad wants us to. It will have to be.

"If you can live with 'the frame' in mind and do your creative work, you will face death with sadness, perhaps," said Leonard, "but not despair."

At the end of the final lesson, in the red dining room, when he was talking about the frame, my father said, "At the very end of his life, Goethe says, 'More light! More light!' Alexander the Great, when he was visiting the philosopher Diogenes said, 'Is there something I can do for you?' Diogenes said, 'Get out of my light.' Every person has a destiny or task, and if he or she pursues it, that is his or her light."

"Why do you believe that?" I asked.

"Because I've observed people making things that are so beautiful, working in the most obscure places: children making dolls in the Sahara out of wooden spools. The creative process is everywhere. I would like to feel at the moment of my death that I had honored that light."

"I really wish," I said, "that you would stop talking about the moment of your own death."

"You can wish all you want, honey." My father laughed. "It's not going to change the outcome."

ROSA HAS the treehouse. Even when she can no longer climb in it, when the house is sold someday and her grandpa is gone, when her dad and I are gone, Rosa will have the treehouse in her, I thought, the way that the little house tilting on the hillside in San Francisco, in which people said yes, yes, to children's visions, is in my brother Aaron and in me. This was comfort, but it was not the comfort I wanted. I could practically hear my father's answer to my wish that his story would never end: *Honey, let it go.* A work of art, he always says, is never finished; it is only abandoned. You need the frame. If death did not bracket our lives, we would never create of our lives the art that we are meant to.

You want to hold on to the people you love forever; of course you do. But the way they live in you, the art they make in you, means that it has to be okay that you can't. Because of course you can't.

*　　*　　*

ROSA WAS aiming the camera upward, concentrating. What did she see? I looked up, too. Nothing was there. Then I looked up again. It was one of those moments my father had taught me about. What would I notice?

I could see clearly enough that a child was about to waste perfectly good film by preparing to click a camera at nothing. Or I could choose to notice, as the child was, the frame around the "nothing": after I stared for a few seconds, I understood that the tops of the pine trees came together, because of the perspective, in a ragged circle. Light was streaming through the center of the circle, and some of the shafts reached all the way to the earth.

Nothing or everything? It depended on what you were looking at.

"Grandpa is really going to like this picture," said Rosa. She tilted her head back further and took a photograph of the empty sky.

Acknowledgments

I AM GRATEFUL to David Shipley, and to Rosa and Joseph Shipley, for everything.

Support and insights upon which I drew for this book came from Susan Devenyi, Robin Stern, Wende Jager-Hyman, Jillian Strauss, Chari Anisman, Thomas Jackson, Erica Jong, Karla Jackson-Brewer, Tara Bennett Goleman, Daniel Goleman, and Lyuba Kozelko. I could not have had a more incisive, thoughtful editor than Amanda Murray, nor a more valuable pair of mentors than John Brockman and Katinka Matson. I am lucky to have David Rosenthal's sharp reading and acerbic sense of humor. Annie Orr was both effective and thorough. I owe Russell Weinberger a debt of gratitude for his perceptive remarks. Victoria Meyers and Rachel Nagler added their advocacy to the project, and Aja Shevelew, Eva Young, Tom Pitoniak, and Beth Thomas brought their clear, conscientious eyes to the stages of the manuscript. Roger Scholl encouraged me to write about Leonard. My brother Aaron Wolf shared his memories, as did my patient mother and steadfast reader, Deborah Wolf, and all the friends and students who passed through the Boston Corners house; I am thankful to them all. The preceding pages, of course, are my thank-you note to my dad.

Printed in the United States
By Bookmasters